THE BRITISH ARCHAEOLOGICAL
ASSOCIATION

CONFERENCE TRANSACTIONS
For the year 1987

XIII

MEDIEVAL ARCHAEOLOGY

AND ARCHITECTURE

at Lichfield

Edited by
John Maddison

1993

Previous volumes in the series

I. Medieval Art and Architecture at Worcester Cathedral
II. Medieval Art and Architecture at Ely Cathedral
III. Medieval Art and Architecture at Durham Cathedral
IV. Medieval Art and Architecture at Wells and Glastonbury
V. Medieval Art and Architecture at Canterbury before 1220
VI. Medieval Art and Architecture at Winchester Cathedral
VII. Medieval Art and Architecture at Gloucester and Tewskesbury
VIII. Medieval Art and Architecture at Lincoln Cathedral
IX. Medieval Art and Architecture in the East Riding of Yorkshire
X. Medieval Art, Architecture and Archaeology in London
XI. Medieval Art and Architecture at Exeter Cathedral
XII. Medieval Art, Architecture, and Archaeology at Rouen

Copies of these may be obtained from W. S. Maney and Son Limited, Hudson Road, Leeds LS9 7DL
or from Oxbow Books, Park End Place, Oxford OX1 1HN

ISBN Hardback 0 901286 36 2
Paperback 0 901286 35 4

British Library Cataloguing-in-Publication Data
A catalogue record for this book is available from the British Library

PRINTED IN GREAT BRITAIN BY W. S. MANEY AND SON LIMITED
HUDSON ROAD, LEEDS LS9 7DL

CONTENTS

LIST OF ABBREVIATIONS AND SHORTENED TITLES

in use throughout the volume. See also individual contributions

Archaeol. J.	*Archaeological Journal*
BAA CT	*British Archaeological Association Conference Transactions*
BAR	*British Archaeological Reports*
B/E	N. Pevsner *et al.*, ed., *The Buildings of England* (various dates)
BL	British Library
BM	British Museum
Bull. Mon.	Bulletin Monumental
CA	*Congrès Archéologique de France*
CBA	Council for British Archaeology
Gent. Mag.	*The Gentleman's Magazine*
HBMC	Historic Buildings and Monuments Commission
JBAA	*Journal of the British Archaeological Association*
JRIBA	*Journal of the Royal Institute of British Architects*
JSAH	*Journal of the Society of Architectural Historians*
LJRO	Lichfield Joint Record Office
NMR	National Monuments Record
PRO	Public Record Office
RACAR	*Revue d'art Canadienne/Canadian Art Review*
RCHM	Royal Commission on Historical Monuments
RIBA	Royal Institute of British Architects
SRO	Staffordshire Record Office
TBAS	*Transactions of the Birmingham Archaeological Society*
TNSFC	*Transactions of the North Staffordshire Field Club*
TSSAHS	*Transactions of the South Staffordshire Archaeological and Historical Society*
VCH	*Victoria County History*
WMANS	*West Midlands Archaeological News Sheet*
WSAS	William Salt Archaeological Society

PREFACE

The publication of these Transactions has been much assisted by generous grants from the Dean and Chapter of Lichfield Cathedral, and from the Idlewild Trust, for which the Association is most grateful. The volume has been a long time in preparation and I should like to thank the contributors for their patience. It has, I believe, been rewarded by a collection of papers which will remain an important resource for all those who are interested in the history of Lichfield Cathedral and its diocese. I should also like to thank Linda Fish for seeing this volume through the press with such cheerful professionalism.

JOHN MADDISON
Editor

LICHFIELD CATHEDRAL.
GROUND PLAN.

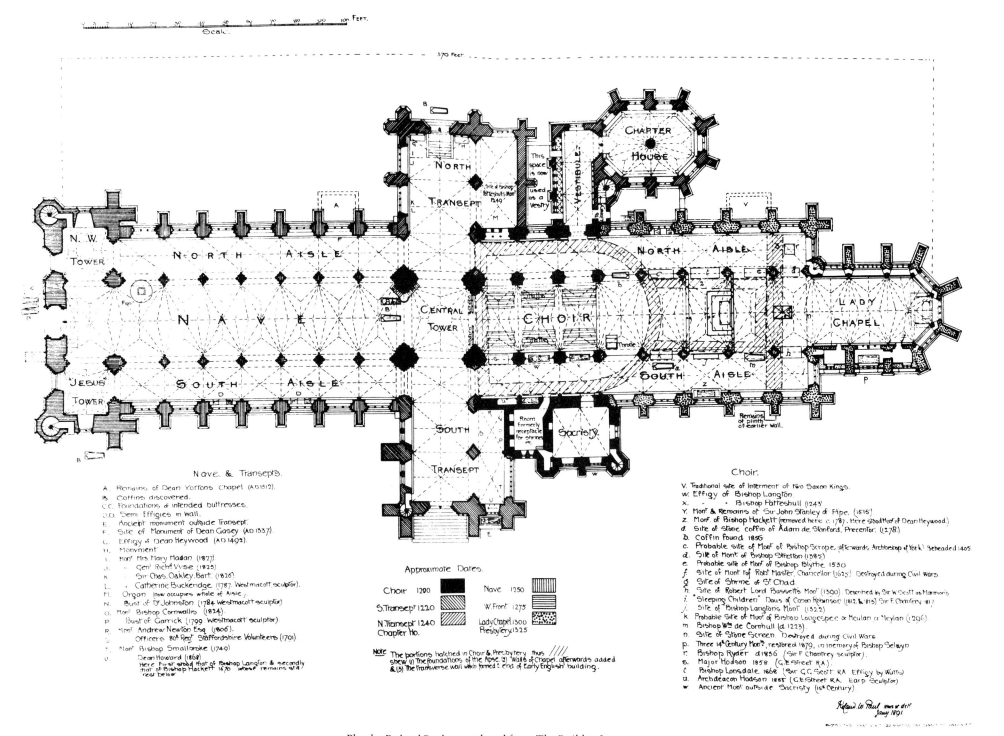

Plan by Roland Paul, reproduced from *The Builder*, January 1891

Lichfield before St Chad

By Jim Gould

INTRODUCTION

The origins of Lichfield lie in the Roman town of *Letocetum*, some two-and-a-half miles south-west of the centre of the present city (Fig. 1). The Old Welsh name for the Roman settlement was *Luitcoyt*,[1] in modern Welsh, *Lwytgoed*, the grey wood, the town probably taking the name of the surrounding area. This district was part of the Midland forest belt; not the dense, oak woodland of Sir Cyril Fox's *Personality of Britain*, but open woodland between scattered settlements, with a preponderance of alder, birch, hazel and elm as witnessed by pollen analyses.[2] The earliest known form of the name 'Lichfield' is *Lyccidfelth*; it occurs in the earliest surviving copy of Bede's *Historia Ecclesiastica* (the Moore MS), and means the cleared land pertaining to *Lwytgoed*. Other Saxon place-names indicate woodland clearances, and in the 11th century the area enclosed by the rivers Tame, Trent and Penk (Fig. 2) became the Norman royal forest of Cannock.[3] Despite the meaning of the name *Lyccidfelth*, very little Roman material has been found at Lichfield — just a few sherds of pottery and three coins,[4] though Bassett has identified some very early enclosures nearby, predating the Roman Ryknield Street.[5] It has been suggested that early *Lyccidfelth* was an area of hamlets, not a compact settlement.

STATUS OF *LETOCETUM*

Ignoring the evidence of a scatter of worked flints, settlement at *Letocetum* began as a series of four successive Roman forts of the 1st and 2nd centuries.[6] During this military phase, which lasted into the second quarter of the 2nd century,[7] a bath-house was built, accompanied by a Romano-Celtic shrine and a very large well or shaft.[8] When the military phase ended, the bath-house continued in use and was extended.[9] *Letocetum*, which appears in the Antonine Itinerary as *Etocetum*, became a posting station, a *mansio* on the Watling Street, three-quarters of a mile west of the crossing with the Ryknield Street. As a posting station, an inn and stabling would be required. The building, the stone foundations of which lie some forty feet east of the bath-house, is now usually referred to as an inn, though this identification relies on the building being near and on the same alignment as the bath-house. The rest of the known Roman settlement is an intermittent straggle for some two miles eastward along the Watling Street.[10] A native-type farm, at present unexcavated but believed to be of the 1st century, lay east of the crossroads, whilst further south was a Romanised farm occupied between the 2nd and 4th centuries.[11] West of the bath-house was the roadside cemetery (Fig. 1). In the 4th century strong defences were built astride the Watling Street at its highest point.[12] These consisted of a wall, nine feet thick, backed by a turf rampart and fronted with three ditches. Nearly six acres were so enclosed. These were not typical town defences. The bath-house and 'inn' lay outside of them, though both buildings continued in use.[13]

It is usually considered that *Letocetum* lay within the Roman administrative tribal area of the *Cornovii*, with its capital at Wroxeter, though Richmond has suggested otherwise.[14] Rivet considered that with the fragmentation that occurred in the 4th century, *Letocetum* may have become a small, late *civitas*.[15] Some support for this comes from the compiler of the Nennius' attempt to name the twenty-eight cities to which Gildas had referred. The last

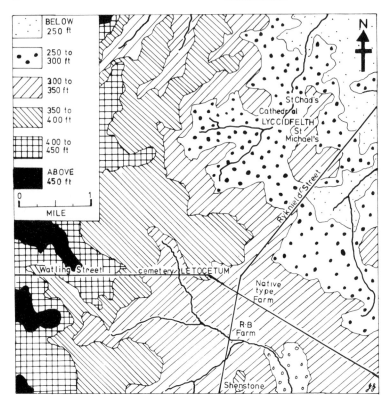

FIG. 1.   Letocetum and Lyccidfelth

entry on the Nennius list reads *Cair Luit Coyt*. Henry Bradley also suggested a *civitas* here when he reconstructed a corrupt Latin text (Harleian MS 3859) using an early Welsh text (Harleian MS 2289) to give the phrase *qui venerunt a civitate quae vocatur Loytcoyt*.[16] Even if *Letocetum* were not a late *civitas*, it must have been some sort of administrative centre — a *vicus* or the centre of a *pagus*. Unfortunately we know very little of Roman local administration in Britain, but if *Letocetum* were a *mansio* with bath-house, inn and stabling, then there must have been some form of local administration, especially if, as has been suggested, *mansiones* became focal points for the collection of the *annona*. A glance at the *Ordnance Survey Map of Roman Britain* shows how thinly inhabited this area was in Roman times. Wroxeter, the tribal capital, lay some thirty-seven modern miles away. Local farmers must have needed a much nearer market to dispose of any surpluses. To the west, the nearest town, Pennocrucium, was fourteen miles distant, to the east *Manduessedum* was sixteen miles away; *Letocetum* appears to have been larger than either of these. Along the Ryknield Street, Littlechester was twenty-five miles northwards, whilst to the south, Alcester was thirty-one miles away (Fig. 2). Hence any area administered from *Letocetum* is likely to have been of several hundred square miles. Much would have been woodland pasture and waste, with farming concentrated on river terraces[17] or close to the roads. It has been said that there was no suitable accommodation at *Letocetum* for high-ranking officials, but much of the land near the bath-house, and almost all the interior of the late defences, have not been excavated. An eastern ditch of the late defences cut through stone foundations where there was much window glass and an iron window grille.[18] There was also the Romanised farm to which reference has already been made. Thus there are several possible sites where an official residence may have been. Taking all factors together, they point to *Letocetum* being a centre of some local importance, small though it may have been in comparison with better known towns.

CHRISTIANITY AT *LETOCETUM*

The status of *Letocetum* is important since, when Christianity became the official religion of the Roman empire, the organisation of that religion then followed the same lines as those of civil authority and was based on towns. When the Romano-Celtic shrine at *Letocetum* was destroyed, at least nine carved or inscribed stones were re-used in the foundations of the 'inn'.[19] The stones were re-used upside-down. One stone, so far not published, was covered with ten large chevrons. This must have formed part of a border or frieze, yet only one such stone has been found. It suggests that originally there may have been many more carved stones than are yet known. Perhaps some were placed in the foundations facing inwards, thus defying discovery. This treatment suggests a deliberate attempt was made to depaganise the stones. Martin Henig has commented on Christian remains in the late Roman period, often replacing Romano-Celtic temples,[20] and the building that succeeded the shrine at Wall should be reconsidered. The 1912 excavators called it a 'villa' but it is now called an 'inn' from its proximity to and alignment with the bath-house, and the failure as yet to find another building which may have been the inn. The bath-house foundations run into a field to the south which has not been available for excavation, where stone foundations and late pottery are known, but have not been properly recorded. The inn may have been there.

The 1912 excavators of the '*mansio*' reported that the floors were of plaster, but in another place said the floors were of concrete. Whatever they were, they must have been removed, for the interim reports of recent excavation make no mention of floors at all and seem to have been primarily concerned with foundations. These were considerable, for the subsoil of this steeply sloping site is of light sand. The stone foundations can be seen to be of more than one period and the different phases need to be firmly established if sense is to be made of this building. It must be later than most of the archaeological strata recently encountered. It is said to have been destroyed in the late Antonine period. This is based on pottery found in the robber trench of a preceding building,[21] but that surely means that it was constructed later than that period and not that it was destroyed then. A similar dating has been suggested from a mortarium found beneath tiles and burnt timber in the colonnade.[22] As there is no mention of a floor beneath these tiles, and as elsewhere the building is said to have had a slate roof, it would seem that the tiles and mortarium relate to an earlier building. With the date of the building in doubt, the Christian depaganisation of the carved stones cannot yet be ruled out. The 1912 excavators found 4th-century coins but did not distinguish between those found at the '*mansio*' and those found at the bath-house.[23] The recent interim reports speak of much painted plaster,[24] some with floral patterns[25] from the '*mansio*' as well as from earlier buildings, and it is hoped that work will be done on this.

One stone recovered by the 1912 excavators[26] and subsequently lost, has recently been refound with other material from *Letocetum* that had been stored following re-organisation of the museum. On this stone is a clear linear cross, perhaps inscribed to further depaganise the stones. The cross has a faint suspicion of a circle enclosing three well-defined, equal arms, whilst the fourth arm continues beyond the possible, but far from certain, circle. The present writer has only been able to see a photograph and not the stone itself. Such crosses are hard to date, but most likely belong to the period between the 6th and 9th centuries,[27] thus speaking of post-Roman rather than late Roman Christianity.

The best evidence for Christianity at *Letocetum* is the small bronze bowl with an embossed chi-rho symbol that was found in 1922 by Francis Jackson of Wroxeter. A photograph and a brief description were published[28] but without stating where it was found, other than it came from a 1922 excavation at *Letocetum*. It is known that during 1921 Jackson worked in the cemetery area,[29] and the 1922 excavations are known to have been there also.[30] When it is added that a note in the Birmingham Museum states it came from a stone-lined grave, then it is almost certain that the bowl came from the cemetery area. The museum note is based on information from the late Miss L. Chitty, then the doyen of Shropshire archaeology, who had met Jackson. She stated that Jackson had no authority to excavate on the land where the bowl was found. Hence it is not surprising that the published note does not give a specific find-spot. I am indebted to D. Symons of the museum for this information and for drawing my attention to a recently published report that the bowl contained one 1st-century and thirty 4th-century coins not mentioned in the original report.[31] Whether viewed as a small coin hoard or as a grave deposit, the bowl must have belonged to a local inhabitant and was not a chance loss.

The story of the cemetery excavations is a sorry one. Cremation urns were first found during ploughing and were destroyed. During 1921 and 1922 brief excavations were conducted on the north side of the Watling Street, but no proper reports were published. The Walsall Historical Association joined the excavations one weekend in November 1924[32] when some thirty urns were found. One member, W. Blay, subsequently described the work.[33] He wrote

our rather irregular digging gave us the impression the interments were two or three yards apart,

a comment which hardly inspires confidence. He continued:

Some bones showed no sign of the application of heat, even the delicate internal grooves of the skull ... were uninjured. The long bones however had been sufficiently heated to allow easy fracture for nothing but fragments of bones were found. On the other hand, short bones, like the vertebrae and the patella were unaltered.

When it is added that all these excavations also found nails, it is obvious that inhumations had been encountered as well as cremations, though in the acid, sandy soil were not recognised as such. Also, a vague note appears in *The Journal of Roman Studies* XIV (1924), 226, that a dozen interments in coffins were found in 1924. Further cremations were found by Hodgkinson in 1926[34] and by Oswald in 1965.[35] All this digging was on the north side of the Watling Street, though there are vague references to the cemetery being on both sides of the road. Jackson's unauthorised work could have been to the south. The very few urns that can be dated from published descriptions (only one has been drawn) belong mainly to the 1st and 2nd centuries, though the inhumations show that the cemetery continued in use long after that. Hodgkinson recorded a ditch seven-and-a-half feet wide, five feet deep, parallel to the Watling Street, and an air photograph by Dr St Joseph (AV87) shows a small roadside enclosure in the cemetery area. Complicating matters is a not-well-authenticated account of finding a stone coffin with bones, about 1840, when the road west of the late defended enclosure, near the Trooper Inn, was lowered.[36]

One vexed question is, when did the settlement of *Letocetum* end? The latest Roman coin came from within the late defended enclosure, was worn and had been minted in 381.[37] Lack of coins and datable pottery make it hard to recognise 5th- and 6th-century deposits, though a 5th-century date has been suggested for one deposit.[38] There is also the evidence of the linear cross previously referred to. A very reduced settlement may have stuttered on until an independent manor of Wall emerged in the 12th century.[39]

HISTORICAL EVIDENCE

One very difficult and not very satisfactory piece of evidence comes from an obscure Welsh poem, one of the elegies for Cynddylan. It is only known from a corrupt 18th-century copy, though it is believed to have been written in the 9th century as a poetic interlude in a prose saga relating events in 7th-century Powys. It records a raid from Powys on *Lwytgoed* when 1,500 cattle and 80 horses with other booty were taken.[40] This was despite 'bishops' and 'book-grasping monks'. Cynddylan, a prince of Powys, had been an ally of Penda, heathen king of Mercia, in the battle against the Northumbrians at Oswestry in 642.[41] If that is taken as Cynddylan's *floruit*, then the raid on *Lwytgoed* is likely to have taken place during the following decade or two, possibly when direct Mercian control was extended at the expense of local rulers. Unless the reference to bishops and monks is a 9th-century anachronism, the elegy points to Christianity at *Lwytgoed* or the surrounding area about the middle of the 7th century.

Fortunately much firmer historical evidence confirms this. It comes from *The Life of Bishop Wilfrid* written by Eddius Stephanus about 709,[42] and from Bede's *Historia Ecclesiastica*[43] written a generation later. Eddius Stephanus was a contemporary of Bishop Wilfrid and probably knew St Chad personally. He described how Wilfrid was friendly with King Wulfhere of Mercia (657–74) and how that king had invited Wilfrid to perform various episcopal duties in Mercia and had given Wilfrid various places where Wilfrid was said to have founded monasteries.[44] Eddius also stated that lands given to Wilfrid by kings were holy places deserted by British clergy in the face of Saxon expansion.[45] Probably Lichfield was such. When St Chad was sent as bishop to Mercia, Wilfrid gave Lichfield to him, considering it to be a suitable place for an episcopal seat. To be suitable implies that there was a church, probably a British church and monastery at Lichfield before the arrival of St Chad in 669, for Wilfrid is not known to have spent any time at Lichfield. The gift was Lichfield (*Onlicitfelda*), not *Letocetum*. It is not clear why this should be. Perhaps the major settlement had moved following the Cynddylan raid; perhaps the decline of *Letocetum* followed the collapse of traffic along the Roman roads. There are many other possibilities. Or perhaps the settlement at *Letocetum* continued and the change was due to that in church organisation which became centred on monasteries and no longer on urban bishoprics in the immediately post-Roman period. If so, *Letocetum* and Lichfield could have resembled the *llys* and *llan* of British communities further west,[46] although the emergence of Tamworth nearby as an important Mercian centre before the end of the 7th century would have changed that.

Bede wrote that when St Chad came to Lichfield, he built himself a more retired place, not far from the church, in which he could read and pray privately with a few of his brothers.[47] It would seem that there was not the privacy at the existing church that St Chad desired, so that although he was at Lichfield for only two-and-a-half years before his death, he built himself an oratory a little distance from the church and its Celtic-type monastery.

Professor H. P. R. Finberg, whose brother-in-law was at one time rector of St Michael's, Lichfield, has suggested from topography and analogy with Bishop John at Hexham, that the pre-669 church, which was dedicated to St Mary, was on the traditional site at Stowe, on the outskirts of the present city. Slater has recently drawn attention to the antiquity of settlement in that area. The medieval church that stands there now is dedicated to St Chad. Finberg also suggested that the oratory was in the huge hilltop graveyard (seven acres) dedicated to St Michael. It is just half a mile from the church at Stowe.[48] The place-name 'Stowe' has religious connotations,[49] whilst the dedication to St Michael was a favourite one for early graveyards. When the parishes were formed, Lichfield was divided between the parish of St Chad and that of St Michael. The latter parish included *Letocetum*. At the end of the Middle Ages, St Michael's graveyard was considered to be very ancient.[50] There may be a parallel here with those early cemeteries such as Cannington,[51] which had their origin in the late Roman or sub-Roman period, especially in western Celtic areas, often on high land. In 1975 a section was cut across the graveyard boundary[52] but there was no evidence at that point to show that the yard had been enclosed with wall, ditch or bank in the pre-Conquest period. Later, excavation within the yard, on the limited site of a new vestry, encountered forty-eight burials, one of which was crouched, and a single sherd of Roman pottery.[53] Unfortunately, bones submitted for carbon fourteen dating were too decayed for a date to be obtained.

LICHFIELD ABOUT 669

Bede states that on St Chad's appointment, King Wulfhere gave him an estate of fifty hides at Barrow (Lincs.)[54] and that St Chad did organise matters there. Yet it was at Lichfield that he had his seat. It is tempting to see Lichfield as a quiet retreat, a sort of wooded Mercian Lindisfarne or Lastingham, to which St Chad could retreat between preaching tours. That concept may well be misleading. Place-name evidence shows that pagan Saxons settled nearby at Wednesbury, Wednesfield and possibly Weeford[55] (Fig. 2), and archaeology has identified an early Saxon site alongside the Trent at Catholme that may have begun in the 6th century.[56] Place-name evidence also points to British survival in this area.[57] As Aldhelm's letter to Geraint makes clear, many 7th-century British Christians had little love for their Germanic oppressors, even after conversion.[58] It is at this time, too, that big changes in civil administration (if that is not too grand a term) took place. By Wulfhere's reign (657–74), Mercia had been united into a viable kingdom which hoped to levy tribute over most of England, as is shown by the Tribal Hidage.[59] Earlier, tribal organisation had seen the setting up of the Tomsaetan to the east of Lichfield, reaching along the Tame and down part of the Trent — from present-day Birmingham to Breedon on the Hill (Fig. 2). To the west were the Pencersaetan, along the river Penk and further south.[60] By the time of the Tribal Hidage, these had been united into a much larger Mercia, for neither tribe was assessed independently. By the end of the 7th century, too, a Mercian royal tun had been established on the Tame at Tomtun, the later Tamworth.[61] That must have superseded *Lwytgoed* as an administrative centre at least when royalty was present. Some of the turmoil which all this must have involved may be depicted in the Cynddylan elegy previously referred to. There one Morfael is said to have been prominent in the raid from Powys on *Lwytgoed*. Morfael is known from genealogies to have been a member of the same ruling family in Powys as Cynddylan[62] and is said to have come from *Lwytgoed*.[63] This makes sense if Powys is regarded as the successor state to that of the Cornovii to which *Lwytgoed* had probably belonged. It looks as if a British (Powysian?) overlord, Morfael, had been displaced from *Lwytgoed*, presumably by expansion of direct Mercian rule, for which the raid by Morfael with his kinsmen Cynddylan was retaliation.

An alternative explanation has been put forward by Jenny Rowland in her definitive *Early Welsh Saga Poetry* (1990). She suggests that there may have been a battle in the Lichfield area in which Cynddylan helped Penda against the Northumbrians. However, the elegy makes mention neither of Mercian nor Northumbrian armies. No historical source refers to such a battle. Cattle and horses (the booty) fit the known later medieval economy of this area and are what a sudden raid along the Watling Street would hope to capture from the locals. Had a Mercian army been present, would the Welsh, even if allies, have been allowed to drive off such booty?

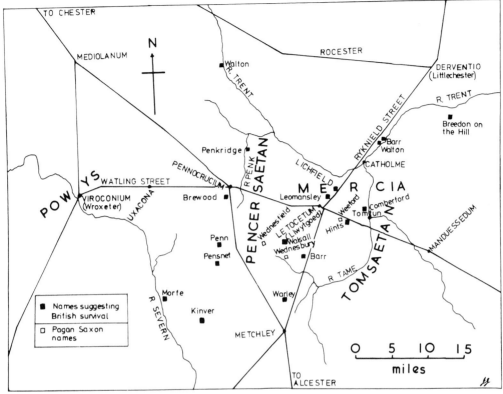

Fig. 2.   British and Saxon, Lichfield

The above is the possible milieu into which St Chad came. His training had been Celtic and his way of life, as described by Bede, was Celtic. This would have helped make him acceptable to the surviving British, and he even appears in one Welsh genealogy.[64] Similarly his appointment by Wulfhere and Archbishop Theodore would have made him acceptable to the dominant Saxons on their conversion. Eddius Stephanus, who had no cause to praise St Chad for he had been Wilfrid's rival at York, paid tribute to St Chad's ability as a teacher.[65] That and his well-known humility must have been great assets. Of his popularity there is no doubt, and when miracles were ascribed to him after death, hopeful pilgrims flocked to his tomb.[66] About 700 his body was translated to a newly built Cathedral, dedicated to St Peter. This was on the site of the present cathedral, where the well-drained, southern slope would be preferable to the low-lying damp site at Stowe. What was on this new site prior to the Cathedral is unknown at present. Eight feet below the floor of the present Cathedral an unusual burial was found in the 18th century. The body lay in a 'strong leaden coffin' with a loose lid banded with strong ribs and iron rings at the side. The lead was said to have been 'very corroded so that it easily broke asunder'. With the bones was a dry friable substance that sparkled by candlelight and was both tasteless and odourless, together with some folds of linen and possibly silver lace.[67] This has been suggested as a possible late Roman plaster burial, when the body, wrapped in linen, was sprinkled with gypsum or sometimes lime, whilst lying in a lead-lined wooden coffin.[68] However, the presence of the iron rings (coffin handles?) shows this was not a Roman burial and the suggestion must be abandoned.

AFTER ST CHAD

Very little is known of Lichfield during the two centuries that followed the death of Bede. Presumably pilgrims still flocked to St Chad's tomb, but there is no contemporary reference to them. We do have a list of the bishops that followed St Chad but no details of their deeds. According to the Anglo-Saxon Chronicle and also Florence of Worcester, the dissolute king, Ceolred (709–16), was buried at Lichfield, though later Mercian kings were buried elsewhere. The 14th-century Lichfield Chronicle[69] contains no local, pre-conquest traditions and almost all references to that period were lifted from the writings of Bede and of William of Malmesbury. Sadly it even mistakes the identity of Lichfield's one archbishop. We do know that the diocese was reduced by the formation of other sees — Worcester, Lincoln, Hereford and, for a time, Dorchester and Leicester — though the diocese remained large. Towards the end of his reign, Offa (757–96), who sought to diminish the authority of Kentish Canterbury, persuaded the Pope to make Lichfield an archbishopric with sway between the Thames and the Humber, and with authority equal to that of Canterbury. Offa may have applied some sort of pressure to achieve this, for a letter from Pope Hadrian to Charlemagne anxiously refers to a false rumour that Offa intended to depose the Pope.[70] However Offa (whose favourite saint appears to have been St Peter) seems to have been on good terms with the Pope once the archbishopric was established.[71] About this time too a letter from Alcuin to Offa[72] refers to the sending of a scholar from the Continent at Offa's request. One wonders if he might have been destined for Lichfield. Dr Kuhn has suggested that a school of illumination was set up there producing such masterpieces as the Golden Gospels of Stockholm,[73] but many scholars remain unconvinced by Kuhn's contention.[74] There are no other details of the archiepiscopate save that it ended three years after Offa's death.

REFERENCES

1. K. Jackson, *Language and History in Early Britain* (1953), 333; A. L. F. Rivet and C. Smith, *Place-Names of Roman Britain* (1979), 387f.
2. H. Godwin and J. H. Dickson, 'Plant Remains in Organic Deposit below Roman Road at Wall', in J. Gould, 'Excavations in Advance of Road Construction at Shenstone and Wall', *TSSAHS* 6 (1966), 17; J. Greig, 'Pollen Spectrum', in F. and N. Ball, 'Rescue Excavations at Wall 1980/81', *TSSAHS* 25 (1985), 16f.; S. Colledge, 'Botanical Material from Saxon Levels at Lichfield Cathedral', in M. O. H. Carver, 'Excavations South of Lichfield Cathedral 1976–7', *TSSAHS* 22 (1982), 47–50.
3. M. Gelling, 'Evidence of Place-Names', *Medieval Settlement*, ed. P. H. Sawyer (1976), 206; J. Gould, 'Food, Foresters, Fines and Felons', *TSSAHS* 7 (1967), 21–39.
4. M. O. H. Carver, 'Archaeology of Early Lichfield', *TSSAHS* 22 (1982), 97.
5. S. Bassett, 'Medieval Lichfield: Topographical Review', *TSSAHS* 22 (1982), 97.
6. F. H. Lyon and J. Gould, 'Section through Defences of Roman Forts at Wall', *TBAS* 79 (1964), 11–23; J. Gould, 'Excavations at Wall 1961–63', *TSSAHS* 5 (1964), 1–50.
7. J. Gould, 'Excavations at Wall', *TSSAHS* 8 (1968), 11.
8. A. Ross, 'Pagan Celtic Shrine at Wall', *TSSAHS* 21 (1980), 3–11; A. Round, 'The Mansio', *TSSAHS* 21 (1980), 1–2. The oft-repeated story of a temple to Minerva and the findings of her statue does not stand investigation.
9. G. Webster, 'The Bath House at Wall', *TBAS* 74 (196), 12–25.
10. J. Gould, 'Excavations at Wall 1961–63', *TSSAHS* 5 (1964), 15.
11. H. R. Hodgkinson and P. Chatwin, 'Roman Site at Shenstone', *TBAS* 63 (1944), 1–32; J. Gould, 'Romano-British Farming near Letocetum', *TSSAHS* 13 (1972), 1–6.
12. J. Gould, 'Excavations at Wall 1961–63', *TSSAHS* 5 (1964), 2–7.

13. The recent excavation of both buildings has been bedevilled by the work of earlier excavators and the wholesale removal of late levels, well illustrated by the photographs that Mott included in the first *Guide* to the excavations. The 1912 excavators recovered 4th-century coins from this site. N. C. Dibben, 'Roman Coins from Wall', *TNSFC* 49 (1915), 147; 50 (1916), 121f.

14. I. A. Richmond, 'The Cornovii', *Culture and Environment*, ed. I. L. L. Foster and L. Alcock (1963), 254.

15. A. L. F. Rivet, 'Some Historical Aspects of the Civitates of Roman Britain', *Civitas Capitals*, ed. J. S. Wacher (1966), 109.

16. W. Bradley, 'Etymology of Lichfield', *Academy* (9 Nov. 1889), 306.

17. C. Smith, 'Valleys of the Tame and Middle Trent', *Iron Age in Britain*, ed. J. Collis (1977), 51–61.

18. E. Greenfield, 'Wall', *WMANS* 7 (1964), 9.

19. A. Round, 'The Mansio', *TSSAHS* 21 (1980), 1.

20. M. Henig, *Religion in Roman Britain* (1984), 127.

21. A. Round, 'The Mansio', *TSSAHS* 21 (1980), 1. For painted concrete floors see C. Lynam, 'Archaeology', *TNSFC* 48 (1914), 111.

22. A. Round, 'Wall', *WMANS* 17 (1974), 55.

23. N. C. Dibben, 'Roman Coins from Wall', *TNSFC* 49 (1915), 147; 50 (1916), 121f.

24. A. Round, 'Wall', *WMANS* 17 (1974), 55; D. R. Wilson, 'Roman Britain 1974', *Britannia* 6 (1975), 247.

25. A. Round, 'Wall', *WMANS* 19 (1976), 39; R. Goodburn, 'Roman Britain 1975', *Britannia* 7 (1976), 328.

26. A. Ross, 'Pagan Celtic Shrine at Wall', *TSSAHS* 21 (1980), 5, no. 2.

27. Nash Williams, *Early Christian Monuments of Wales* (1950), 20. C. Thomas, *Early Christian Archaeology of North Britain* (1971), 106–20.

28. Anonymous, Open Meeting, 23 Jan. 1924, *TBAS* 50 (1927), 50, Pl. xiii.

29. J. H. Beckett, 'Archaeology', *TNSFC* 59 (1925), 186.

30. *Lichfield Mercury*, 24 Nov. 1922, 4.

31. S. S. Frere and R. S. O. Tomlin, *Roman Inscriptions of Britain* 2 (1991), fasc. 2 (1991), 61, no. 2415.64.

32. *Walsall Observer*, 22 and 29 Nov. 1924.

33. W. Blay, *Letocetum* (Walsall 1925), 22–5.

34. H. R. Hodgkinson, 'Excavation in Roman Cemetery at Wall', *TBAS* 52 (1930), 308–11.

35. A. Oswald, 'Observation of Construction of By-pass at Wall', *TSSAHS* 8 (1968), 40.

36. Col. Bagnall, 'Recent Excavations at Etocetum', *TBAS* 4 (1873), 38f.

37. J. Gould, 'Excavations at Wall 1961–63', *TSSAHS* 5 (1964), 19, no. 29.

38. F. and N. Ball, 'Rescue Excavation at Wall', *TSSAHS* 25 (1965), 5.

39. Pipe Roll 13 Henry II.

40. Jenny Rowland, *Early Welsh Saga Poetry* (1990), 174–9.

41. I. Williams, 'Poems of Llywarch Hen', *Proc. of British Academy* 18 (1932), 296.

42. Eddius Stephanus, *Life of Bishop Wilfrid*, ed. B. Colgrave (1927).

43. Bede, *Ecclesiastical History of the English People*, ed. B. Collgrave and R. A. B. Mynors (1969).

44. Eddius Stephanus, ch. 14.

45. Ibid., ch. 17.

46. G. R. J. Jones, 'Historical Geography and our Landed Heritage', *University of Leeds Review* 19 (1976), 53–78.

47. Bede, *EH*, Book 4, ch. 3.

48. H. P. R. Finberg, 'Archangel Michael in Britain', *Millenaire Monastique du Mont Saint-Michel* 3 (1971 Paris), 459f.; T. R. Slater, 'Topography and Planning of Medieval Lichfield', *TSSAHS* 26 (1986), 18–21.

49. M. Gelling, 'Some Meanings of Stōw', *Early Church in Western Britain and Ireland*, ed. S. M. Pearce, *BAR* 102 (1982), 187–96.

50. D. and J. Gould, 'St Michael's Churchyard, Lichfield', *TSSAHS* 16 (1975), 58.

51. P. Rahtz, 'Late Roman Cemeteries and Beyond', *Burial in the Roman World*, ed. R. Reece, CBA Research Report 22 (1977), 55–9.

52. D. and J. Gould, 'St Michael's Churchyard, Lichfield', *TSSAHS* 16 (1975), 55–9.

53. P. R. Wilson, 'Investigations in St Michael's and St Mary's Churches', *TSSAHS* 22 (1982), 70–6.

54. Bede, *EH*, Book 4, ch. 3.

55. M. Gelling, 'Further thoughts on Pagan Place-Names', *Otium et Negotium*, ed. Folke Sangren (Stockholm, 1973), 109–27.

56. S. Losco Bradley and H. Wheeler, 'Anglo-Saxon Settlement in Trent Valley', *Studies in Late Anglo-Saxon Settlement*, ed. M. R. Faul (1984), 103.

57. M. Gelling, *West Midlands in Early Middle Ages* (1992), 60.

58. Aldhelm, *Prose Works*, ed. M. Lapidge and M. Herren (1979), 158 translation.

59. W. Davies and H. Vierk, 'Contexts of Tribal Hidage', *Frühmittelalterliche Studien* 8 (Berlin 1974), 237–40.

60. D. Hooke, *Landscape in Anglo-Saxon Staffordshire* (1983), 12.

61. F. M. Stenton, 'Medeshamstede and Its Colonies', *Historical Essays in Honour of James Tait*, ed. E. Edwards (1933), 315ff.
62. P. C. Bartum, *Early Welsh Genealogical Tracts* (1966), 60, no. 36; 85, no. 25.
63. Ibid., 12, no. 25.
64. Ibid., 64, no. 66.
65. Eddius Stephanus, ch. 14.
66. Bede, *EH*, Book 4, ch. 3.
67. *Gentleman's Magazine* 21 (1751), 398.
68. C. J. S. Green, 'Significance of Plaster Burials', *Burial in the Roman World*, ed. R. Reece, CBA Research Report 22 (1977), 48a.
69. H. Wharton, *Anglia Sacra* (1691), 423–33.
70. A. W. Haddan and W. Stubbs, *Councils and Ecclesiastical Documents* III (1964 reprint), 440.
71. For a full discussion of the establishment of the Lichfield Archbishopric see Nicholas Brooks, *Early History of the Church of Canterbury* (1984), 111–27.
72. D. Whitelock, *English Historical Documents* I (1955), no. 195 translation.
73. S. M. Kuhn, 'From Canterbury to Lichfield', *Speculum* 23 (1948), 591–629; 'Some Early Mercian Manuscripts', *Review of English Studies* NS 8 (1957), 355–74.
74. K. Sisam, 'Canterbury, Lichfield and the Vespasian Psalter', *Review of English Studies* NS 7 (1956), 1–10.

Wolverhampton: The Foundation of the Minster

By Della Hooke

THE FOUNDATION OF THE MINSTER

The date and circumstances of the foundation of the minster at Wolverhampton remain unclear. In 994 it seems that the Lady Wulfrun, a Mercian noblewoman of some standing, founded or re-endowed the minster here and donated extensive estates scattered throughout the southern part of Staffordshire. However, the confirmation charter which records this transaction cannot be accepted as authentic, although it may incorporate a genuine gift.[1] The late Professor Finberg, followed by Hart, felt able to accept the document,[2] but the manuscript only survives in 17th-century transcripts and tales of the discovery of the original invite suspicion, for it was said to have been found in the ruins of a wall *c*. 1560.[3] In a recent study, Simon Keynes has, indeed, had to declare it 'spurious' although based upon an authentic gift. It combines 'elements derived from a papal privilege and from a royal diploma issued in the mid-990s'.[4]

It may further be queried whether Wulfrun was not merely granting lands to a minster which had already been established at Wolverhampton for some time. The wording of her grant may imply this, for the charter speaks of the 'revered' monastery *quod in moderno nunc tempore constructum est* ('which has now in modern times been built'), holding all things *à priscis temporibus* ('from former/ancient times'), but the terminology is far from clear. There are traditions of an older foundation, one claiming that the monastery had been founded by Wulfhere, King of Mercia, in 659 and dedicated to St Mary. In 1548 the founder was thought to have been King Edgar, who was said to have given the land to Wulfgeat, Wulfrun's kinsman.[5]

Finally, doubt even surrounds the identity of Wulfrun herself. In 985 a lady of this name was granted ten *cassati* of land by King Æthelred, nine *cassati* of which lay at *Heantune* ('Hampton'), one *manentia* at *Treselcotum* ('Trescott').[6] The bounds of the estate at 'Hampton' can be traced with reasonable certainty and seem to have encompassed the parish of Wolverhampton together with Upper Penn.[7] If Wulfrun was granted the estate at this date, endowing the minster some nine years later, can she have been the Wulfrun who was captured by Olaf Guthfrithson in 940? Assuming she was the daughter of someone important, and probably rich, when she was kidnapped, it is possible, but she must have been elderly when she endowed the minster, a widow at least approaching her seventies. Indeed, she seems to have been dead when her son Wulfric drew up his will between 1002 and 1004. Her connection with the Mercian court is unknown but another son, Ælfhelm, became ealdorman of Northumbria and she had undoubtedly been an heiress of some standing, if not of royal descent.

Danish attacks were severe in this part of Mercia in the 10th century and it is not unlikely that they might have destroyed monasteries of early foundation. This may also have provided an opportunity to reorganise the ecclesiastical pattern of the minsters and their *parochiae* and, perhaps, the nature of the foundations themselves. It is, however, possible to consider how closely the location of known minsters fitted the administrative territories of early Mercia.

Many early minsters seem to have been founded as ecclesiastical 'central places' within major folk regions, usually at or near royal centres. At Leominster, for instance, in Herefordshire, a minster, possibly of British foundation, was established within the ancient district of Leen, allegedly *c.*660.[8] It stood within a royal manor still held in the immediate pre-Conquest period by Queen Edith and traditionally the centre of King Merewalh of the Magonsæte. Leominster became the ecclesiastical focus of the region but Kingsland, a few miles distant, was retained as a royal estate.[9] In contrast, the minster of Much Wenlock, also established in the later 7th century, was set upon the northern borders of the Magonsætan kingdom, and Merewalh's daughter, Mildburg, became its first abbess. It was granted vast estates both in the vicinity and some considerable distance away.[10]

A not dissimilar pattern can be identified in south-west Staffordshire. Here, it is possible to identify a folk region based upon the Penkridge area, extending southwards across the west of the county.[11] Penkridge was the successor to Roman *Pennocrucium* and may have lain at the heartland of the territory of a group known as the Pencersæte. This folk are referred to in a mid-9th-century charter of Cofton Hackett and Alvechurch in Worcestershire,[12] as this estate lay just beyond the furthest limits of their territory. This apparently reached across the Birmingham Plateau as far as that of another Staffordshire folk, the Tomsæte. The far southern reaches of the Pencersæte, an area of open heathland and light woodland on the Upper Coal Measures and Triassic sandstones of the plateau, seem to have lain in a sort of no man's land in which tribal groups intercommoned before precise boundaries were drawn up. When the bounds of the diocese were finally fixed, they followed the River Stour and ran across the Birmingham Plateau. Within the Pencersæten territory, Penkridge appears to have been the ecclesiastical focus of the northern heartland, with the minster of Wolverhampton forming a southern focus, eventually outstripping its northern counterpart.

There were extensive royal estates in the Wolverhampton region. Many were still in royal hands in 1086, and it is not improbable that an early minster had been founded here upon such a royal estate in the 7th or 8th century. In 1086, the crown still held the surrounding manors of Tettenhall, Willenhall, Bilston, Wednesbury and part of Wolverhampton itself, and Wolverhampton could easily have lain at the focus of this territory. The names of Wednesbury and nearby Wednesfield both contain a reference to the god Woden, and although Gelling[13] has suggested that such names might indicate the survival of paganism in remote areas, one is reminded of the adherence to paganism by the Mercian King Penda, well into the 7th century. Penda was not, however, unwilling to allow Christian missionary activity within his kingdom.

Wolverhampton minster was to become a royal free chapel, a status which frequently reflects religious importance in pre-Conquest times.[14] It was not, however, the only one in the vicinity, for the church at Tettenhall was also to be so designated. Both Tettenhall and Wolverhampton were royal estates and the dual nature of the two foundations in such close proximity may be cause for reflection. Tettenhall did not belong to Wolverhampton and its church seems to have been separately endowed with (if the Domesday text is not misleading) two hides of land.[15] One is reminded of the dual foundations of Gloucester: the old minster founded in the 7th century and the new abbey of St Oswald founded by Æthelflæd in 909, the latter closely associated with the royal palace at Kingsholm. The royal lands of Tettenhall lay to the north and south of the church, those at Wolverhampton well to the east at Stowheath. No archaeologically attested royal palace or hall is known in this area, but one may well await discovery.

THE ESTATES OF WOLVERHAMPTON MINSTER

The estates included in the foundation charter appear in the order in which they are listed in *Domesday Book* and it is possible that this survey forms the most reliable record of the early possessions of Wolverhampton minster,[16] the monks adding to their charter those Old

English boundary clauses that they had in their possession after that date. The boundary clauses are, however, thought to be genuinely pre-Conquest and to represent closely the estates given by Wulfrun to the new minster. As a territory, they show little unity (Fig. 1). The estate most distant from the minster lay at Upper Arley, located in what is now Worcestershire but which in 1086 lay within Staffordshire and within the Lichfield diocese. It had been granted to Wulfrun's kinsman, Wulfgeat, by King Edgar in 963,[17] although in 1086 the clergy claimed that half a hide 'in the other Arley' had been taken from them 'by force'.[18] With its appurtenant swine-pastures, likely to have lain within woodland, the estate was separated from any other Wolverhampton estates by Earl Algar's manor of Kinver, an area which was to become a royal forest. *Eswich* has been identified as Ashwood in Kingswinford and in 1086 it was declared 'waste', having already been taken into the king's forest. Other woodland manors lay far to the north-east, Ogley later lying within one of the 'hays' of Cannock Forest. Again referring to the pasturing of pigs, a swine-fold appears as one of the boundary landmarks of that estate in 994. The estate of Hilton lay nearby. The boundary clause of Pelsall, the other eastern Wolverhampton manor, also seems to refer to marginal land, for it refers to 'the wallowing-place of the hart' and 'the hunter's track'.

Although the king still held Penkridge in 1086, the Wolverhampton clergy apparently administered its church, for no less than nine clerics held one hide there from the king. The charter claims an estate at Kinvaston, listed separately at Domesday, but also includes Rodbaston in its boundary. This probably reflects the nature of the boundary clause that the monks had before them, for in 1086 Rodbaston was held by Richard Forester and had already been a separate estate in the time of King Edward. Nearby, Hatherton lay astride the Watling Street, and Hilton (described as 'the other Hilton') with Featherstone, lay a little further to the south. None of these were rich manors and Hatherton contained considerable quantities of woodland.

Closer to home, the church in 1086 held one hide in Wolverhampton itself, one virgate in Bushbury, one virgate in Trescott, five hides in Wednesfield, and two hides in Willenhall. Of these, the hide at Trescott had formed part of the original gift to Wulfrun, while Wednesfield and Willenhall are included within the endowment charter. The monks shared the area of Willenhall parish with the king and, interestingly, were not able to produce a boundary clause for that estate. They did, however, have one for Bilston, combined with Wednesfield, and Bilston is also included in the endowment charter, although it is uncertain whether the monks had any rightful claims there. This latter region was one of medium prosperity in 1086.[19] 'Hamton', by 1074–85 known as *Wulvrenehamptonia* ('Wulfrun's Hampton [high *tūn*]',[20] was situated at the northernmost end of a spur of land which rises to a height of over 500 feet. The name may describe its position but could alternatively have indicated 'high' status.

The settlement seems to have lain at the focus of numerous routeways, many of which can be reconstructed from the boundary clauses. The ancient Penn Way can be traced running along the boundary between Wednesfield and Bushbury, apparently running from the royal centre of Cannock towards Penn, the upland beyond Wolverhampton. It may be speculated whether the hilltop at Penn had ever been fortified; others have postulated the existence of a defensive rampart upon the Wolverhampton peninsula itself, where a 'Bury Hill' place-name might support such an idea. There is as yet no archaeological evidence for an early fortified site, but Slater[21] suggests that there may have been an Iron Age enclosure set astride the ridgeway which approaches the town from the north, with the minster being sited at its centre at the highest point, an association between early defences and a minster similar to that found at Hanbury in Worcestershire.[22] Such an association would not, however,

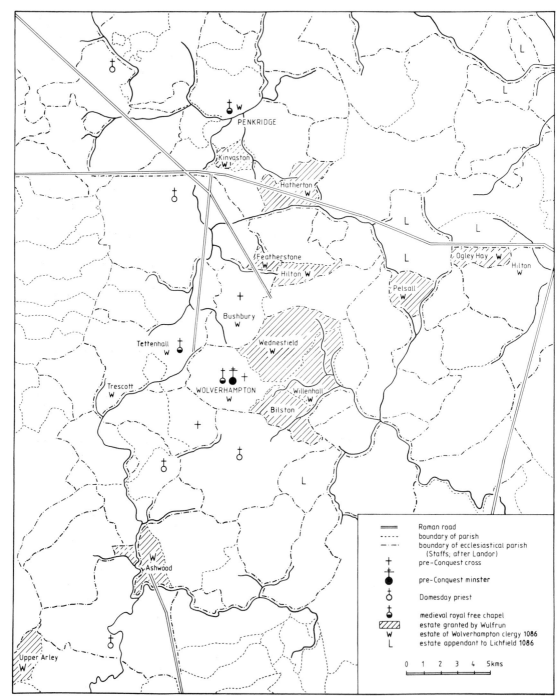

FIG. 1.   The estates of Wolverhampton Minster

necessarily indicate territorial continuity or even continuity of function — merely a convenient location.

Little remains of any early fabric in the church of St Peter at Wolverhampton. The church was greatly restored in the 19th century and only a little 13th-century work survives. Outside, however, stands the Wolverhampton cross, and debate still continues as to whether this should be assigned a 9th- or 10th-century date. This is important if it is remembered that Wulfrun's interest in the estate dates only from 985. Moreover, the boundary clause which accompanies King Æthelred's grant to Wulfrun refers to 'the road which leads from the stone of Byrngyð', one of the roads leading south-south-east from the town. The same road is called *Beorgiþes stanes strete* ('the road of Beorngyð's stone'), in the boundary clause of Bilston.[23] One wonders whether the stone, first recorded in 985, might have been the forerunner of the cross, if not the cross itself, perhaps confirming some earlier ecclesiastical function on the site of the later minster.

ACKNOWLEDGEMENT

I should like to thank Dr Simon Keynes, of Trinity College, Cambridge for his helpful comments on the Wolverhampton charter.

REFERENCES

1. P. H. Sawyer, *Anglo-Saxon Charters, an Annotated List and Bibliography* (London, 1968), S.1380; W. Dugdale, *Monasticon Anglicanum*, ed. B. Bandinel, J. Caley and H. Ellis (1846), VI, 1443–6 (no. 1).

2. C. Hart, *The Early Charters of Northern England and the North Midlands* (Leicester 1975), 97–8; H. P. R. Finberg, *The Early Charters of the West Midlands* (Leicester 1972), 124–5 (f. 331).

3. A. K. B. and R. H. Evans, 'Wolverhampton, St Peter', *VCH Staffordshire*, III (1990), 321, n. 1, citing *Historia Ecclesiae Lichfeldensis, Anon.* (1575) in H. Wharton, *Angliae Sacra* I, 444 seq.

4. S. D. Keynes, 'Studies in Anglo-Saxon Royal Diplomas', 2 vols, unpub. Fellowship thesis, Trinity College, Cambridge, 1976, 595–629; *The Diplomas of King Æthelred 'the Unready' 978–1016* (Cambridge 1980), 252.

5. D. Knowles and R. N. Hadcock, *Medieval Religious Houses, England and Wales* (London 1953, 2nd edn 1971), 444, citing J. Murray, *Staffordshire* (1874), 132.

6. Sawyer, op. cit., S.860; J. M. Kemble, *Codex Diplomaticus Aevi Saxonici* (1839–99), K.650.

7. D. Hooke, *The Landscape of Anglo-Saxon Staffordshire: The Charter Evidence* (Keele 1983), 63–5; D. Hooke, 'Wolverhampton: the town and its monastery', in D. Hooke and T. R. Slater, *Anglo-Saxon Wolverhampton* (Wolverhampton 1986), 19 and Appendix, 46–7.

8. D. A. Whitehead, 'Historical introduction', in R. Shoesmith, *Hereford City Excavations Volume 1, Excavations at Castle Green*, CBA Research Report 36, 3.

9. D. Hooke, *Anglo-Saxon Territorial Organization: The Western Margins of Mercia*, University of Birmingham, Department of Geography Occasional Paper no. 22 (Birmingham 1986), 21–3; 'Early units of government in Herefordshire and Shropshire', *Anglo-Saxon Studies in Archaeology and History*, 5 (Oxford Univ. Comm. for Archaeol. 1992), 47–64.

10. Hooke, ibid., 25–30.

11. Hooke, *Anglo-Saxon Staffordshire*, op. cit., 14–19.

12. Sawyer, op. cit., S.1272; W. de Gray Birch, *Cartularium Saxonicum* (1885–99), B.455 (1).

13. M. Gelling, 'Place-names and Anglo-Saxon paganism', *University of Birmingham Historical Journal*, 7 (1) (1961), 7–25; 'Further thoughts on pagan place-names', *Otium et Negotium: Studies in Onomatology and Library science Presented to Olof von Feilitzen* (Stockholm 1973), 109–28.

14. J. H. Denton, *English Free Chapels 1100–1300, a Constitutional Study* (Manchester 1970).

15. J. Morris (ed.), *Domesday Book, 24, Staffordshire* (Chichester 1976), 7, 5.

16. Keynes, op. cit., 626.

17. Sawyer, op. cit., S.720; Birch, op. cit., B.1100.

18. Morris (ed.), op. cit., 7, 2.
19. P. Wheatley, 'Staffordshire', in H. C. Darby and I. B. Terrett (eds), *The Domesday Geography of Midland England* (Cambridge 1971), 174–94.
20. H. W. C. Davis (ed.), *Regesta Regum Anglo-Normannorum 1066–1154* (Oxford 1913, 1956), 57, 125.
21. T. R. Slater, 'Wolverhampton: central place to medieval borough', in Hooke and Slater, op. cit., 39.
22. D. Hooke, *The Anglo-Saxon Landscape: The Kingdom of the Hwicce* (Manchester 1985), 91–2.
23. The charter boundary clauses are reproduced in Hooke (1983), op. cit.

The Development of the Choir
of Lichfield Cathedral:
Romanesque and Early English

By Warwick Rodwell

The eastern arm of Lichfield Cathedral comprises eight aisled bays terminating in a square end, beyond which projects a polygonal Lady Chapel. The first three bays of the choir, east of the crossing, are Early English in style and have generally been assigned a date in the bracket *c.* 1195–1210. The remaining three bays of the choir and presbytery, together with the two-bay retrochoir and Lady Chapel, were constructed during the second quarter of the 14th century, and were intended to provide a suitable setting for the sumptuous shrine of St Chad. Lateral openings in the third bay of each aisle lead, respectively, into the Chapter House vestibule on the north, and a sacristy on the south (Fig. 1). The sacristy is generally known as the Consistory Court, for which purpose it was used in the 19th century (Pl. IIA.).

Evidence for earlier arrangements of the eastern arm was found when the floors were disrupted during the installation of a new heating system in the middle of the 19th century. In 1856, a trench was driven through the centre of the choir for the construction of a hot-air duct; this led to the discovery of a large central apse and other foundations. Partial records of the discovery were made by interested parties, including John Hamlet, the stonemason.[1] Then, in 1860, during Sir Gilbert Scott's restoration of the choir and presbytery, the eastern arm was subjected to extensive disturbance: the floors were entirely renewed and a more comprehensive heating system installed. Further archaeological discoveries were made.

Robert Willis paid a three-day visit to Lichfield in August 1860, in order to inspect the new discoveries and to make an assessment of the architectural history of the Cathedral. Willis prepared a detailed account of his observations, incorporating information supplied by others, and he set out his posited architectural development of the building in a seminal paper.[2] In essence, Willis was able to demonstrate that the Norman choir was of three bays and that the presbytery terminated in an apse, to which was later added a small rectangular Lady Chapel on a slightly skewed alignment. The entire eastern arm was replaced in *c.* 1200 by a simple rectangular choir and presbytery of seven bays, with a continuous ambulatory. The east end terminated in a set of four identical chapels (Fig. 2). Later, a two-storeyed chapel complex was appended to the south aisle: this is now the Consistory Court, with St Chad's Head Chapel above.

In his article in *The Builder*, Roland Paul basically followed Willis's thesis except in one matter, namely the length of the early Gothic choir. Instead of having seven bays, it was suggested that there were only six originally, to which one more was added some time in the 13th century.[3] A plan showing such an arrangement, prepared by W. St John Hope and J. T. Irvine, was published by Paul, but was not accompanied by a reasoned argument (Fig. 3). In Dr A. R. Dufty's account of the development of the Cathedral Willis's original scheme was followed, with the additional observation that the Norman apsidal presbytery was originally finished by a small eastward-projecting chapel, also of apsidal form.[4] This feature antedated the rectangular Lady Chapel.

Sir Nikolaus Pevsner followed Willis entirely, paying no heed to subsequent views; he suggested that the apsidal presbytery might have been built as late as Roger de Clinton's

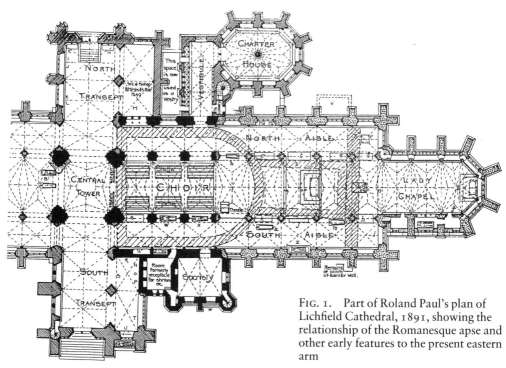

FIG. 1.   Part of Roland Paul's plan of Lichfield Cathedral, 1891, showing the relationship of the Romanesque apse and other early features to the present eastern arm

episcopate (1129–48); and he concurred with the previously expressed view that the rebuilding of the eastern arm did not begin before *c.* 1195–1200, despite the presence of several diagnostically late Romanesque architectural embellishments.[5]

This two-stage development, although basically correct, fails to take into account all the archaeological evidence recorded by Willis, as well as several surviving architectural features in the choir. These include the remains of a late 12th-century arcade of three bays embedded in the south aisle wall, and visible from within the consistory court (Pl. IIA). There is also some early and hitherto unexplained masonry preserved in the triforia above the choir arcades. Finally, a deflection in the alignment of the north aisle wall, near its mid-point, has often been noted but not explained. Clearly, a reconsideration of the detailed development of the eastern arm of the Cathedral, prior to the 14th century, is overdue. With a view to clarifying these problems, the Dean and Chapter of Lichfield commissioned an archaeological-architectural study of the Consistory Court and chapel complex in 1985, and of the Early English choir in 1986–7.[6] This paper summarises the results of the latter project.[7]

Any reconsideration of the earliest remaining work in the choir must take cognisance of its predecessors, and thus a reappraisal of the archaeological evidence recorded in the last century is necessary. Willis's published plan of the foundations beneath the choir is an amalgam of evidence recorded by various observers between 1856 and 1860. Unfortunately, the plan makes no distinction between foundations that were actually observed, and those presumed to have existed. There are several manuscript copies of Willis's plan preserved at Lichfield, as well as two original field plans: one is by John Hamlet (stonemason, 1856), and the other is probably by the clerk of works in 1860.[8] Both plans show evidence which is not

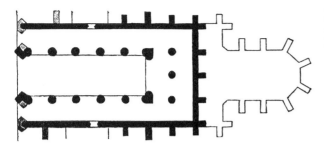

Fɪɢ. 2. Willis's reconstructed plan (1861) of the choir and presbytery of Lichfield Cathedral in *c.* 1200

on Willis's, and there are some manifest disagreements concerning the precise positions of pier bases, wall thicknesses, and so on.

Finally, there is a single plan, dated 1880, by J. T. Irvine (clerk of works under Scott, from the 1870s), which shows buttress foundations discovered during drainage works alongside the south choir aisle.[9] All these documents were evidently known to the anonymous compiler of a publication in 1883 entitled *Ground Plan of Lichfield Cathedral.*[10]

A new measured plan of the choir has been prepared, on to which all the available archaeological evidence has been plotted with as much accuracy as existing records permit (Fig. 4). In addition to the material accrued from Victorian sources, fresh information gleaned through detailed examination of the extant fabric has been added to the plan.

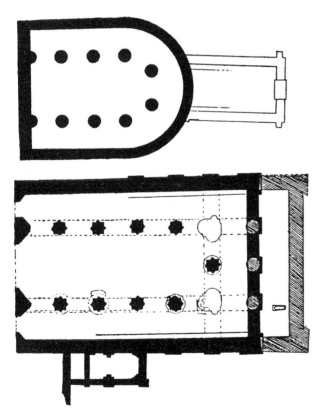

Fɪɢ. 3. The development of the eastern arm of Lichfield Cathedral in the 12th and 13th centuries, as reconstructed by St John Hope and Irvine, and published by Paul, 1891

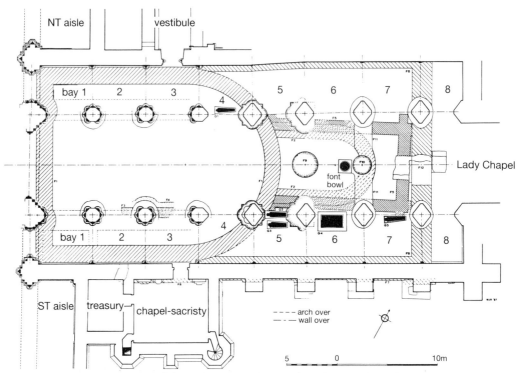

FIG. 4. Outline plan of the 14th-century choir and presbytery of Lichfield Cathedral, onto which has been plotted archaeological evidence for foundations and features of all periods (obliquely hatched)

OUTLINE DEVELOPMENT OF THE CHOIR

1. *Early Norman*, c. *1085–1100* (Fig. 5.1)

Parts of the outer wall defining the apsidal choir and presbytery have been found, together with the east side of the crossing. Hamlet's plan shows a pair of semicircular projections on the crossing foundation, which are clearly the abutments of the north and south choir arcades. The aisles were very narrow, probably *c.* 1.8 m at floor level, and formed a continuous ambulatory around the inside of the apse. The choir must have been of three bays, defined by massive drum columns, with the apsidal sanctuary to the east. In all, there were possibly ten free-standing columns, although no specific evidence of these has yet been located. Willis, evidently unaware of Hamlet's recorded evidence for the width of the Norman aisles, attempted to locate putative arcade bases by digging holes inside the present choir, instead of outside it (i.e. within the present aisles).

Willis and most later commentators have assumed that the eastern arm terminated in a single large apse, *c.* 19.2 m (63 ft) in diameter, externally. On some plans, putative apses have been shown on the transepts too, although no specific evidence for these has been reported.[11] Not only would a single large apse with a narrow ambulatory on the eastern arm have constituted an unusual arrangement, but its outer wall footing was only 1.52 m wide, whereas the north and south side walls were 1.75 m in width. Clearly, there are structural complications at the east end that were unrecognised in 1860.

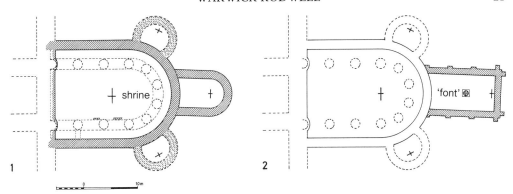

FIG. 5.   Reconstructed foundation plans of the Romanesque choir and eastern chapels.
New work is hatched, while retained earlier masonry is shown in outline. Suggested
altar and shrine positions are indicated
1. Early Norman, *c.* 1085–1100.   2. Later Norman, *c.* 1150–60

The most likely reason for the different footing widths is that the ambulatory was ringed
by a suite of subsidiary apses, probably three in number; Willis even mentioned the
possibility of such an arrangement, but failed to relate it to his own evidence. Nor did he
appreciate that the foundation of the central apsidiole was encapsulated in the slightly later
Lady Chapel of rectangular plan. Dufty was the first to observe this.[12] Sufficient is known of
the central apsidiole to ascertain that it was of elongated form, as at Norwich. Its altar is
most likely to have been dedicated to St Mary the Virgin, although there is no express
evidence to this effect.

The central chapel was not perfectly aligned on the axis of the choir, but was skewed by
about three degrees to the south-east. No explanation can be offered with certainty, but the
discrepancy could have arisen as a result of the triplet of subsidiary chapels being
constructed after the body of the choir had been completed. The high altar would have been
positioned on or close to the chord of the apse, and St Chad's shrine presumably lay to the
east, but this is no more than supposition. It is not unlikely, at the period under consideration, for the shrine to have been physically attached to the back of the high altar. Access to
the shrine would have been from the ambulatory.

The site of the Anglo-Saxon Cathedral at Lichfield is unknown, and there is no hint of it in
the plan or fabric of the present structure, which is a development of the Norman period,
and later. There is, unfortunately, no documented date for the building of any part of the
Romanesque Cathedral at Lichfield, but it may reasonably be assumed that work on the
choir and sanctuary was accorded the first priority, and this was most likely in hand in 1088,
when it is recorded that Bishop Robert de Limesay (1085–1117) took a great quantity of
silver from Coventry, allegedly to pay for building work at Lichfield.[13] A date in the 1080s
would accord with the plan-type. The eastern arm was presumably completed by *c.* 1095–
1100, with work thereafter being concentrated on the transepts and nave.

The Romanesque eastern arm can now be seen as comparable in plan with other buildings
dating from the late 11th century, and Lichfield must surely be part of the contemporary
family of great churches in the west of England, which included Worcester, Gloucester, Bath
and Winchester. In scale, however, Lichfield was somewhat smaller than its sister churches,
approximating more nearly to the size of Leominster priory church.[14] Worcester,
Gloucester and Winchester were all provided with elaborate crypts beneath their choirs, in

which the apsidal forms of their sanctuaries were also reflected. But this does not appear to have been the case at either Lichfield or Leominster. Willis expressly searched for a crypt, and failed to find one. Moreover, the approximate level of bedrock is known beneath the choir (*c.* 2 m below pavement), and this militates against the existence of a substantial crypt. The possibility of a small crypt beneath the high altar and shrine of St Chad is remote but should not be altogether overlooked.

2.   *Later Norman, c. 1150–60* (Fig. 5.2)

The first alteration to the Romanesque east end comprised the enlargement of the centrally projecting chapel (Lady Chapel?). The new structure was of rectangular plan, slightly wider and longer than its predecessor, and was finished with clasping buttresses at its eastern corners; structurally, it was probably of three bays. The slightly skewed alignment of the previous chapel was perpetuated.

A curious feature discovered near to the centre of the new Lady Chapel, and clearly aligned with it, was the square bowl of a large, early Norman font. The bowl was found in 1856, but its discovery was only reported to Willis four years later.[15] Willis referred to the bowl as being inverted when found, but Hamlet's contemporary plan shows the basin with mouth uppermost; the latter is more likely to be correct. Willis suggested that the bowl may have been buried as a receptacle for some important relics, and this is undoubtedly the most plausible explanation.

The bowl and its contents would not, however, have been buried in isolation, but would have been sited beneath an altar or shrine. Unfortunately, there are several uncertainties that cannot now be resolved. First, the date of manufacture of the font is unknown: the bowl was described as plain, 4½ ft square, and made of common sandstone; it had also been reddened and cracked by fire. The font is unlikely to be earlier than the latter part of the 11th century, and how long it had been in use before being damaged and buried is beyond conjecture. No record of a major fire at Lichfield in the 12th century has survived, and no other physical evidence for one has been noted.[16]

If the burial of the font took place in the later Norman (rectangular) chapel, it probably did not mark the site of the altar to the Virgin, which would have been nearer to the east end. Equally, it is unlikely to have been a deposit beneath the shrine of St Chad which, at this period, should still have been close to the high altar.

An alternative worth considering is that the font was buried during the first half of the 12th century and was inside the original apsidal chapel. That being so, it would have lain neatly beneath an altar or shrine in the centre of the apse. This latter explanation is, on balance, to be preferred.

Although Bishop Roger de Clinton (1129–48) is recorded as a munificent builder at Lichfield — and he is said to have constructed the Romanesque nave — he was probably not responsible for the enlarged Lady Chapel, since both the plan and the plinth moulding recorded by Willis are unlikely to date before *c.*1150. The new Lady Chapel was presumably built in response to the increasing popularity of the cult of the Virgin in the 12th and early 13th centuries; this phenomenon received architectural expression at Leominster, Gloucester and Norwich in a manner exactly similar to that at Lichfield.

3.   *Norman Transitional I, c. 1170–80* (Fig. 6.3)

This marks the beginning of a complex rebuilding of the choir and presbytery, executed in several consecutive phases, for which only partial evidence survives. The reasons for

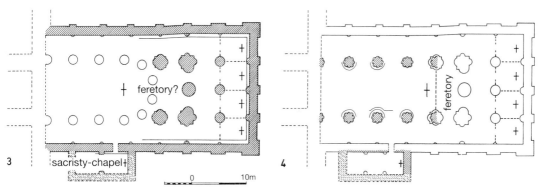

FIG. 6.   Reconstructed plans of the Transitional choir, feretory and eastern chapels.
New work is hatched, while retained earlier masonry is shown in outline
3. Transitional I, c. 1170–80.   4. Transitional II, c. 1180–90

carrying out the reconstruction are not difficult to appreciate: stumpy, apsidal sanctuaries encircled by narrow ambulatories were out of fashion by the later 12th century; more choir space was required for the canons; and a suitably commodious and dignified feretory for the enshrinement of the relics of the local saint was necessitated by the burgeoning cult of St Chad and the increased flow of pilgrims which that generated.

It is worth observing that there is no documented evidence for a 'revival' in the cult of St Chad in the 13th century, which was already strong by the time it appears in surviving medieval records. It is therefore argued that the Normans did not suppress the local cult at Lichfield, as happened elsewhere: Chad remained popular throughout. Indeed, it may be further argued that it was primarily the cult which supplied the motivation for rebuilding and extending the eastern arm in the later 12th century, bearing in mind the fact that Lichfield had then been demoted from the status of Cathedral to college of secular canons.[17]

The rebuilding of the Cathedral again started at the east end, where the greater part of the new shell could be erected outside the existing structure, thus avoiding long-term dislocation of services. The new choir and presbytery of seven bays just fitted around the old presbytery and Lady Chapel. In fact the fit was so tight that the eastward-projecting buttresses of the chapel must have been shorn off in order to accommodate the foundation for the new east wall.

It would appear that the south and east walls were laid out first, with shallow buttresses defining the seven bays and the range of four eastern chapels. The plan was evidently based on a grid using a module of 17½ ft. It would, of course, have been necessary to demolish the south-east apsidiole in order to lay out the new south wall, and one might have expected a similar course of action on the north side too. But that does not appear to have been the case. The sixth and seventh bays on the north synchronised perfectly with the grid, and were most likely laid out in the same operation as the east end. Then, it would appear, the foundations were laid for the first, second and third bays on the north, without sufficient care being taken to align them accurately with bays six and seven. The implication must be that there was an obstruction in the area which, in due course, would be occupied by bays four and five. That is precisely the position where it is argued the north-east apsidiole lay.

Thus, the foundations for the north wall must have been laid in two lengths, abutting the apsidiole to east and west. When the apsidiole was eventually demolished, and the builders came to lay the foundation for the remaining section of wall, the discrepant alignments would have been revealed. Evidently, it was too late to realign the whole of the north wall, and it was accepted that a kink would have to be introduced at this point. Willis first observed the kink in the foundations of the Transitional choir; curiously, the same feature was perpetuated in the 14th-century rebuild.

It is not difficult to explain the longer retention of the north-east apsidiole: it is likely to have temporarily housed an altar of particular importance (perhaps the Lady Altar) while construction work on the range of chapels at the east end was in progress.

The old Lady Chapel had to be demolished at an early stage, so that the piers for the new retrochoir and eastern range of chapels could be constructed. Then the ambulatory and outer wall of the Romanesque choir were removed, leaving only the apsidal arcade surrounding the sanctuary. This was, apparently, to remain for some time to come. The discoveries of 1856 and 1860 included only parts of the piers of the retrochoir, and some details must remain conjectural. The general arrangement, though, is not seriously in doubt. The new plan provided for the choir in the first three bays, and the sanctuary in the fourth. The fifth bay appears superficially to have been narrower than the rest, on account of its being defined by a quartet of massive piers of compound form. There can be little doubt that this was the new feretory, where St Chad's relics would have been housed in a shrine carried upon an elaborate pedestal. The shrine structure, and its accompanying altar, may have been entirely independent of the sanctuary and high altar, being separated by a screen.

The junction between the fifth and sixth bays marked the end of the main vessel of the presbytery, and the large circular pier base discovered in the centre of the building would have supported the high east gable. Beyond that, and with a much lower roof line, was the eastern aisle which connected the north and south aisles, to form a continuous ambulatory. Beyond again, in the seventh and final bay, lay a line of four small chapels. The form of the piers and responds, and the arrangement of the screening in this area is not known; only the circular base of the pier which occupied the central position has been found.

The square eastern termination containing four chapels was not common: one other example has survived amongst English cathedrals, namely Southwark, where the eastern arm of the former priory church comprises eight bays. The Southwark retrochoir was built soon after 1212.[18] The closest comparison for Lichfield is, however, to be found at Glasgow, with its seven-bay choir and presbytery.[19] Here, not only is the plan similar, but the 17½ ft module is also in evidence. To the south of the new choir at Lichfield lay a rectangular appendage alongside the second and third bays. The position is indicative of a sacristy, but the structure may have had a dual function as a chapel. Laterally projecting sacristies designed to service the high altar were not uncommon, and since the structure at Lichfield was built alongside the third bay, rather than the fourth or fifth, it may imply that there was no perceived intention of moving the high altar eastwards to any great extent during the rebuilding of the presbytery. The alternative explanation for its position — that the sacristy had an earlier origin — is plausible but not supported by extant evidence. A similarly positioned sacristy is found at Selby Abbey, and was built in the early 14th century.[20]

Scarcely any of the masonry of the first Transitional phase at Lichfield remains visible today, apart from the wall-benches in the aisles. These survive, more or less intact, in bays 1, 2 and 3 (north and south), and in bay 6 (south); the lower parts of the benches, with new tops added, remain in bay 4 (north) and bay 7 (south). The work of this period was all in the local red sandstone.

4. Norman Transitional II, c. 1180–90 (Fig. 6.4)

In this phase — which was essentially a continuation of the previous one — the nucleus of the old choir was remodelled. The three original bays, together with the apsidal sanctuary, were replaced by four new bays, following a plan that had been previously determined. But certain changes appear to have been introduced, with the result that it was only the basic structural form and ground plan that were followed, not the architectural detailing. A change of master mason is possibly indicated.

First, the design of the arcade piers was streamlined. The plan of the piers of the retrochoir was based on a square core with large, semicircular shafts attached to each face, essentially a later Romanesque type. The new choir piers were, however, of clustered form, with triplet shafts arranged around an octagonal core. Still surviving from this period are the responds adjoining the crossing, the first and second pairs of choir piers, and the western half of the third pair of piers. Evidence recorded by Willis suggested that the junction between the two transitional phases actually occurred in the middle of the fourth pair of piers. The visual effect of this juxtapositioning of styles would have been lessened by the presence of a reredos at the end of the fourth bay, dividing the sanctuary from the feretory.

The new work was truly Transitional in style, with filleted shafts and water-holding bases which looked forward to Gothic, but with capitals decorated in a style overtly reminiscent of later Romanesque sculpture. All this work was executed in a fine sandstone of pale greenish colour. The mouldings of the arches and piers of the choir arcades at Lichfield have been compared by Pevsner and others to those of the choir at Wells, which is also dated to c. 1180.[21] While the mouldings may bear comparison, the capitals do not. The Wells capitals are all ornamented with stiff-leaf sculpture of the earliest Gothic style, whereas the Lichfield capitals more closely resemble those of Christchurch, Oxford, in terms of decorative detail but not form.[22] Again the date is c. 1180–90 for the choir at Oxford; further comparisons may be made with contemporary work at Canterbury.

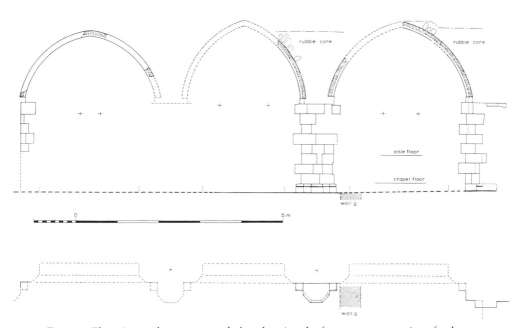

FIG. 7.   Elevation and reconstructed plan showing the fragmentary remains of a three-bay wall arcade belonging to the Transitional sacristy–chapel adjoining the south choir aisle

An ancillary structure belonging to this building period at Lichfield was the second phase of the sacristy-chapel adjoining the south side of the choir. It has already been noted that the foundation plan of the south aisle accommodated a sacristy of two bays: either this structure was not built above ground level, or it had a very short life. The former is perhaps more likely, reflecting a change of plan in mid-build. Whatever the reason and time interval, it is clear that the foundations were adapted to accommodate a building of three vaulted bays, the remains of which are still visible in the sacristy and adjoining vergers' room (Pl. IIA). The outline of the wall arcade supporting the sacristy-chapel vault is shown here in elevation in Figure 7. The three bays are all slightly different in pitch. The base of the pier between the second and third bays is preserved in a heating duct beneath the Victorian floor (Pl. IIB). The doorway leading from the choir to the sacristy-chapel was probably off-centre in the easternmost bay, but was seemingly not the present doorway.

5. *Transitional III*, c. *1190–1200* (Fig. 8.5)

In this phase the Transitional choir was completed. The work seems, in so far as the evidence survives, to have been concerned very largely with refacing the internal walls of the aisles, and beginning the new transepts. The latter had their own eastern aisles, or chapels. The refurbishment of the choir may have taken place in two stages, the north aisle being tackled first, followed by the south aisle. There are various minor stylistic and technical differences between the work in the two aisles, as well as different sets of masons' marks; either two separate gangs were involved, or the work was not carried out contemporaneously.

The benches along the outer walls were retained, but the masonry above seems to have been reduced slightly in thickness, and trefoil-headed blind arcading was introduced. This still remains in three bays on the north (Fig. 9) and two on the south. The arcading was probably once continuous to the end of the fourth bay of the choir. Integral with this work

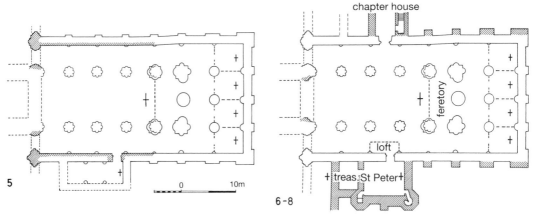

FIG. 8.   Reconstructed plans of the Transitional and Early English choir, feretory, eastern chapels and St Peter's Chapel. New work is hatched, while retained earlier masonry is shown in outline
5. Transitional III, c. 1190–1200.   6. Early English I, c. 1200–20 (reconstruction of crossing arches and triforium).   7. Early English II, c. 1220–30 (St Peter's Chapel, crypt below, and watching loft).   8. Early English III, c. 1230–40 (treasury, St Chad's Head Chapel, Chapter House vestibule, high vaults and flying buttresses)

west east

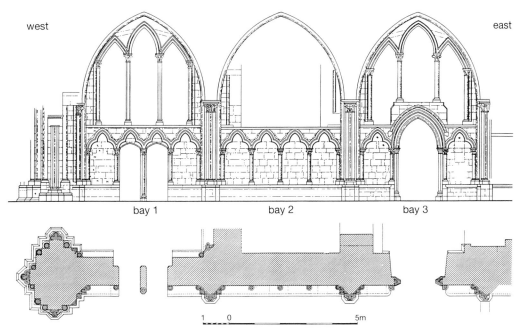

bay 1 bay 2 bay 3

1 0 5m

FIG. 9. Elevation and plan of the first three bays of the north choir aisle, showing
extant 12th- and 13th-century masonry

was the construction of the present wall-shafts: these now carry the aisle vaults, but must
originally have supported a wooden roof structure. The arches which open from the aisles
into the transepts are part of the same work; and this includes the fine chevron arch in the
north choir aisle.[23] Finally, the round-headed doorway giving access to the sacristy-chapel
was built (Fig. 11), presumably as a replacement for a small doorway on the same site.

This doorway was very inconveniently situated from the point of view of its integration
with the new arcading in the south aisle, in consequence of which a special arrangement had
to be contrived for the third bay. Undoubtedly, the master mason would have preferred to
centre the door within the bay, but was prevented from doing so by the arrangement of the
recently constructed vaulting in the sacristy-chapel. Had the original two-bay plan for the
sacristy been adhered to there would have been no difficulty, but the three-bay design was
out of step with the aisle.

Above the wall-arcading in the choir is a string-course which forms a common sill for the
various window arrangements which now obtain. There have been several changes in the
fenestration since the late 12th century, but there is just sufficient evidence remaining to
enable a reliable reconstruction of the final Transitional arrangement. It is now clear that
there were no windows in the first bay of the aisles, and that the present openings are later
modifications. There probably were original windows in the second bay, but virtually all
relevant evidence has been removed, both on the north and on the south, by the existing late
14th-century fenestration. The third bay, however, on both sides of the choir, retains all the
vital evidence to enable a reconstruction.

The arrangement is better preserved on the north side (Fig. 9). The window opening was
in the form of a tall lancet, flanked externally by a pair of detached shafts with annulets

c

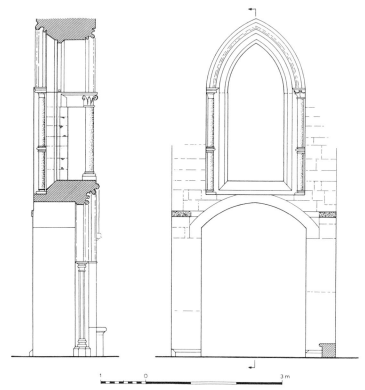

FIG. 10.   Section and
north elevation of the
Transitional window
in the third bay of
north choir aisle. The
sill was raised when
the doorway to the
Chapter House
vestibule was cut
through the wall,
c. 1230–40

(Fig. 10). These shafts were surmounted by Transitional capitals with square abaci. As may be seen from the main elevation drawing, the window has been reduced in height, the sill having been raised by one course. This occurred when the entrance to the chapter house vestibule was cut through the wall, *c.* 1230–40 (p. 33).

Internally, the window opening occupied the central bay of a rear-arch of triple lancet form (Fig. 9). The arches are supported on four free-standing columns which carry Transitional capitals with square abaci. The central pair of capitals are cut on oblong blocks of stone (bridging capitals) that span the void between the rear-arch and the outer skin of the wall, tying the whole arrangement together. The central shafts were obviously shortened when the vestibule doorway was intruded. The heads of the existing triple arches of unequal and squinted form appear to belong to a later phase, when the aisle vaulting was added.

In the third bay of the south aisle, only the lancet-headed opening of the window survives, together with its external shafts and capitals: again, they are much reduced in height. The rear-arch was wholly removed by the 14th-century gallery at the entrance to St Chad's Head Chapel. Although cut off flush with the wall face, the remains of the bridging capitals may still be seen (Fig. 11A). A reconstruction of the original internal elevation of the third bay in the south aisle has been attempted in Figure 11B.

There are sufficent tell-tale traces in the extant masonry around the sacristy-chapel doorway to indicate that it was originally of two orders (the outer one having later been cut away) and that there were two specially contrived, narrow bays of wall arcading to the west. It is uncertain whether this arcading was of plain lancet form (as shown in Fig. 11B), or

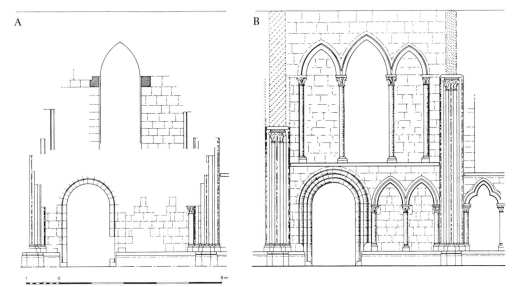

FIG. 11. Internal elevation of the third bay of the south choir aisle
A. Surviving late 12th-century masonry. The pair of hatched stones flanking
the window opening are the cut-back remains of the bridging capitals of the destroyed
rear-arch. **B.** Suggested reconstruction of the same elevation. Two possible
alternatives are shown for the relationship between the tops of the wall-shafts and the
roof structure

cusped as it is in the surviving wider bays. The triple rear-arch above the string-course is reconstructed from the evidence already described for the north aisle.

One major uncertainty is the original height of the wall-shafts dividing the aisle bays. Two alternatives are offered in Figure 11B: on the left the wall-shaft is shown at its present height, with the capital supporting a putative cross-arch in the aisle; on the right the wall-shaft has been taken up to the springing level of the windows, where its capital could have supported the foot of a timber roof truss. On balance, it is perhaps more likely that the second arrangement obtained, and that the wall-shafts were all reduced in height when the vaulting was added. The original capitals would then have been reset at a lower level.

In all the work of this phase, a fine, pale greenish sandstone was employed for moulded masonry, while red stone was used for the plain ashlar of the blind arcading; it is also found in the window recesses, and on external wall faces.

6. *Early English I, c. 1200–20* (Fig. 8.6)

Having completed the eastern arm, the rebuilding of the crossing and transepts was naturally the next part of the Cathedral to receive attention. These areas fall largely outside the present study and need only be mentioned in so far as they are relevant to the development of the choir. The crossing piers were not entirely renewed, even though the four major arches were reconstructed; the central tower, with its wall passages and corner vices, was however a completely new structure. Linked to this work, and evidently of the same date, were the triforia of the transepts. The masonry of this phase is almost entirely in red coloured sandstone, which contrasts with that of the previous phase. A change of quarry is indicated.

The stair vices in the north-east and south-east corners of the central tower not only gave access to wall passages at triforium and clerestory level, but also embodied doorways which opened on to the choir aisle roofs in an unusual manner. The aisles must have been reroofed in this phase, and at the same time were given stone vaulting. The aisles were covered by double-pitched roofs, rather than the usual monopitched arrangement which is found over most triforia. Thus the Early English triforium, both in the transept and in the choir, comprised a wall-passage flanked by window openings to the exterior. Externally, at the base of each line of windows, was a valley gutter which trapped rainwater both from the inner pitch of the aisle roof and from the high roof of the choir.

The valley gutter took the form of a continuous stone trough, integral with the choir wall and projecting from it at the base of the triforium. Portions of this trough still remain *in situ* within the present roof spaces of the north and south aisles. The valley gutter discharged its water, at each bay division, into another gutter which ran transversely across the aisle vault, to an outlet (spout or gargoyle) on top of each external buttress. The remains of this arrangement are shown in Figure 12. The transverse gutters must have run open-topped through the roof spaces in the same way as a 'deadman's gutter' did in recent times.

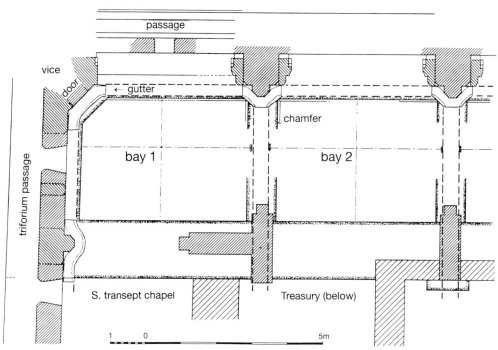

FIG. 12.   Plan of the first and second bays of the south choir aisle at triforium level: the top of the aisle wall is shown, with the flying buttresses standing on it. The south transept triforium is on the left. Shaped gutter blocks survive around the bases of the pilasters to the choir and transept: the intervening missing sections are indicated by broken lines

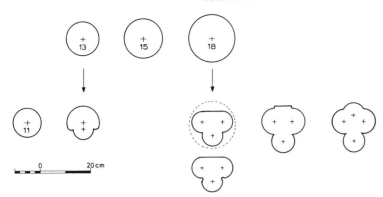

FIG. 13. Cross-sections of stone shafting used in the choir aisles. The Transitional phases employed circular shafts of green sandstone: 13, 15 and 18 cm in diameter (top row). In the early Gothic work more complex forms were employed, in red sandstone. Some new shafts were made by recutting old ones, as indicated by the arrows

Obviously the stone troughs had to be fully supported along their length, and that was achieved by building them into the crowns of the vaults over the aisles.

The evidence is unequivocal in demonstrating that the crossing tower, the vaulting of the aisles, the new triforium, and the unusual roof and gutter arrangements were all of one build. Vaulting the aisles had consequences for their fenestration. The triple rear-arches, described above (pp. 28, 29), had to be modified in order to make room for the attachment of the wall-ribs. Thus the rear-arches were rebuilt in the stepped and canted fashion that still survives in the third bay of the north aisle (Fig. 9). Then, with a view to achieving symmetry throughout the aisles, false rear-arches were created in the first bay, both to north and south. These were blind at first: the extant openings through the aisle walls, into the transept chapels, are of later date.

All the sculptured detail associated with this phase is of distinctive early Gothic form (mainly stiff-leaf capitals); and the shafts introduced with the new window arches are not of circular cross-section, as the Transitional ones are, but are of trefoil or quatrefoil section (Fig. 13). Close examination shows that some of the early Gothic shafts were made by recutting older ones to new profiles.

7. *Early English II, c. 1220–30* (Fig. 8.7)

A total rebuild of the sacristy-chapel took place in the 1220s, a project which is confidently attributable to William of Mancetter, dean from 1222 to 1254. The old single-storey building was demolished and replaced by a new structure of different plan: only the Transitional doorway to the south aisle was retained. The chapel complex has been the subject of a separate study.[24]

The new structure was conceived as multi-purpose from the outset: it was a sacristy, treasury, and chapel; it also housed the chantry and place of sepulture for Dean Mancetter himself. A subterranean crypt of barrel-vaulted form was first constructed.[25] Above it was built a rib-vaulted chapel, dedicated to St Peter, with octagonal turrets at the south-east and south-west corners (Pl. IIc). The former housed a spiral stair that led down to the crypt-treasury,

FIG. 14. Elevation and plan of
the third bay of the south choir
aisle. The dashed shading
indicates the suggested
abutment of a 13th-century
watching loft with integral
staircase. The floor of the loft
would have been at window
sill level. The existing steps
leading up from the sill,
through the former aisle
window opening, to the floor
of St Chad's Head Chapel, are
indicated by broken lines

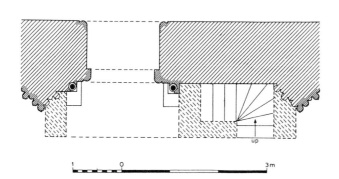

and the latter contained a well chamber. There was no means within the structure of gaining access to an upper storey, and the original design probably did not allow for one.

Nevertheless, St Chad's Head Chapel was built directly above St Peter's, and without any apparent form of access prior to the construction of the present stair in the 14th century. Attention has not previously been focused on this fundamental problem; indeed, its very existence seems to have gone unnoticed hitherto. Examination of the third bay of the south aisle shows that there is a small amount of relict evidence for early 13th-century work here: this provides the only clue to the original means of access to the upper chapel.

It is discernible that the outer moulded order of the doorway between the aisle and St Peter's Chapel was removed, and a pair of flanking shafts introduced instead: these now carry the 14th-century vaulted gallery, but must previously have supported some other structure. The wall-shafts at the east and west ends of this same bay have also suffered modification, and have subsequently been repaired. Both have lost their Transitional capitals and, on the eastern shaft, at least, a 13th-century plain bell-shaped capital was substituted (and restored in the 19th century).

The various alterations and scars are consistent with the evidence that might well remain after the removal of a structure that had been built into the aisle, filling much of the third bay. This structure must have incorporated a stair giving access to the upper chapel, via a doorway which was adapted from a former aisle window. It is suggested that the structure was more than just a stair: it was possibly a watching loft, from which vigil could be kept over the high altar and St Chad's shrine in the sanctuary. A basic reconstruction of such an arrangement is given in Figure 14. The floor of the loft, which was presumably carried over the aisle on a stone or wooden vault, would have been at the level of the existing window-sill;[26] a steep stairway rising in the western part of the structure would have given access from the aisle floor to the loft. Later, it served St Chad's Head Chapel, too. The doorway to St Peter's Chapel had to be respected by the new structure.

A somewhat comparable arrangement is seen in the early 15th-century watching loft at St Alban's Abbey, there situated on the north side of the feretory, under the aisle arcade.[27]

8. *Early English III, c. 1230–40* (Fig. 8.8)

Many alterations and additions to the choir and transepts took place in this period, and their precise sequence has yet to be determined. The south transept was completed, and the small space between it and St Peter's Chapel was infilled by the construction of a new stone-vaulted treasury (Fig. 1). The Chapter House vestibule was erected against the north choir aisle: it was a two-storey structure with an attached stair turret. Its original purpose and relationship to the Chapter House are unclear.

The chapel of St Chad's Head was added as an upper storey to St Peter's Chapel, and access was gained via the posited watching loft, and through a former window in the choir aisle. The architecture of St Chad's Head Chapel is plain externally, and conforms with the structure below (Pl. IIc), but internally it is very elaborate.[28] It is undoubtedly the result of a change of plan. Although it has been argued (p. 32) that there was originally no intention of building a second chapel above St Peter's, it is likely that there would have been a modest chamber between the roof and the stone vault below. Being difficult of access, this chamber would have been a secure and appropriate place for the storage of relics. The space may have been comparable to that above the Berkeley Chapel adjoining the south choir aisle at Bristol.[29]

Changes were also made at a high level in the choir, with the rebuilding of the triforium and clerestory. The double-pitched roofs of the aisles, along with their extraordinarily complex and inefficient gutter arrangements, were short-lived. The triforium was re-designed with a series of openings leading off the wall-passage into the void beneath a new monopitched roof (an arrangement which still obtains). The buttresses along the aisles were rebuilt and were adapted to receive fliers from the high roof of the choir. Thus, the choir was undoubtedly vaulted at this stage, although perhaps in timber rather than in stone. Surely this is what Henry III admired in the late 1230s and ordered its replication at Windsor in 1243?[30]

ACKNOWLEDGEMENTS

I am deeply indebted to the Dean and Chapter of Lichfield for providing every facility necessary to carry out this and other studies since 1982. The personal interest shown, and support given, by all members of chapter has been greatly valued. Thanks are also due to the Head Verger, Mr G. P. Hives, and his staff, who have always been most helpful. Finally, I am particularly grateful to Canon and Mrs G. M. Smallwood (now retired) for their kind hospitality whilst I was working on this project.

REFERENCES

1. 'Ground Plan shewing the positions of old foundations discovered during progress of excavations for hot air flues 1856', Lichfield Cathedral Library MS.
2. R. Willis, 'On Foundations of Early Buildings recently discovered at Lichfield Cathedral', *Archaeol. J.*, XVIII (1861), 1–24.
3. R. Paul, 'Lichfield Cathedral', *The Builder*, LX (1891), 108–9.
4. A. R. Dufty, 'Lichfield Cathedral', *Archaeol. J.*, CXXII (1963), 293–5.
5. N. Pevsner and P. Metcalf, *The Cathedrals of England: Midland, Eastern and Northern England* (1985), 182, 187–8.
6. W. J. Rodwell, 'Lichfield Cathedral: St Chad's Head Chapel: A Report upon the Investigation of a Burial found in the South Wall . . .' (1982); 'St Chad's Head Chapel and related Structures at Lichfield Cathedral: An Archaeological Survey' (1985); 'The Norman and Early Gothic Quires of Lichfield Cathedral Church: An Archaeological Study' (1987). Lichfield Cathedral Library, MS reports.
7. See also: W. J. Rodwell, 'The Norman Quire of Lichfield Cathedral: Its Plan and Liturgical Arrangement', *Friends of Lichfield Cathedral. Fiftieth Annual Report* (1987), 10–14. The plan has been reproduced in *VCH Staffordshire*, XIV (1990), fig. 9. For a general summary of the archaeological investigations carried out at the Cathedral since 1982, see W. J. Rodwell, 'Archaeology and the Standing Fabric: Recent Studies at Lichfield Cathedral', *Antiquity* 63 (1989), 281–94. It is proposed in due course to publish a monograph on *The Archaeology of Lichfield Cathedral*.
8. For Hamlet's field plan of 1856, see n. 1; this has additions and annotations dated 12 July 1860. The other field plan, which is unsigned and undated, is in LJRO (Accn Tp 1441); it is probably the work of Mr Clark, and must date to 1860.
9. Plan signed by J. T. Irvine, titled 'Plinths and ancient buttresses of south aisle of quire, Lichfield Cathedral, laid open April 22 1880', LJRO.
10. Anon., *Ground Plan of Lichfield Cathedral, with refrence to its various objects of interest* (1883). A. C. Lomax, Lichfield. There is a draft of this plan, dated 1881, in Lichfield Cathedral Library.
11. Ibid.
12. Dufty (1963), op. cit., 293–4.
13. *VCH Staffordshire*, III (1970), 143 and reference.
14. E. A. Freeman, 'Excavations at Leominster Priory Church', *Archaeol. J.*, X (1853), 109–15. E. Roberts, 'On Leominster Priory Church', *JBAA*, XXVII (1871), 438–45.
15. Willis (1861), op. cit., 8.
16. The earliest recorded fire at Lichfield was in 1291, and that appears to have been confined to the town: *VCH Staffordshire*, XIV (1990), 11. However, a reference to the bishop's palace in the 12th century being 'ruined during the time of war', may point to an otherwise unrecorded disaster in the Close: *VCH Staffordshire*, III, 141.
17. In 1075 the see was transferred from Lichfield to Chester, and thence to Coventry in 1102. However, the first known statutes of the Cathedral date from Bishop Nonant's time (1185–98). Lichfield recovered its status as a see in 1228. *VCH Staffordshire*, XIV, 9–10.
18. N. Pevsner and P. Metcalf, *The Cathedrals of England: Southern England* (1985), 150.
19. T. L. Watson, *The Double Choir of Glasgow Cathedral* (1916), fig. 2.
20. C. C. Hodges, 'The Architectural History of Selby Abbey', *Yorkshire Archaeol. J.*, XII (1893), 344–94.
21. Pevsner and Metcalf (1985), op. cit. (n. 5), 188.
22. Pevsner and Metcalf (1985), op. cit. (n. 18), 220.
23. Illustrated in C. Harradine, *Hand Guide to Lichfield Cathedral* (sixth edn., 1899), 34. A. C. Lomax, Lichfield.
24. See n. 6; also, W. J. Rodwell, 'Archaeology at the Cathedral: A New Study of St Chad's Head Chapel', *Friends of Lichfield Cathedral: Forty-Eighth Annual Report* (1985), 10–14.

25. Illustrated in Rodwell (1989), op. cit., fig. 7. The significance of this crypt was hitherto unrecognised.
26. This is also the floor level of the extant 14th-century gallery.
27. RCHM *Hertfordshire* (1911), 186–7 and pl.
28. St Peter's Chapel is also relatively plain internally, heightening the contrast with St Chad's Head Chapel.
29. Conveniently illustrated in R. Paul, 'Bristol Cathedral', *The Builder*, LXI (1891), 86–7.
30. *VCH Staffordshire*, III, 149 and reference. It has usually been assumed that Henry III was inspired by the south transept at Lichfield, but the eastern arm is a more likely candidate.

POSTSCRIPT

Since writing this paper, an archaeological excavation has been carried out in the south choir aisle (1992), revealing much additional detail about the Romanesque foundations. For a preliminary note, see W. Rodwell, 'Revealing the History of the Cathedral: Archaeology in the South Quire Aisle', *Friends of Lichfield Cathedral: Fifty-Sixth Annual Report* (1993), 23–34.

Croxden Abbey

By Lawrence Hoey

Croxden Abbey is undoubtedly one of the least known of England's monastic ruins.[1] Although in the Middle Ages an important Cistercian house of the north-west Midlands, Croxden exists today in isolation in northern Staffordshire, remote from major urban centres and lacking the companionship of other important medieval sites such as have made the Cistercian monasteries of Yorkshire centres of study and tourism. Isolation from urban areas was, of course, a conscious Cistercian preference and would have been as true of the Middle Ages as of the present, but Croxden's current remoteness from other monastic sites is illusionary and the result of their poor preservation in this part of the country. Only St Werburgh's, Chester (now the Cathedral) remains in use and in anything like a complete state of preservation, and of Cistercian houses only Valle Crucis in Wales retains as much standing fabric as Croxden. Most of the other monasteries of the area have almost completely disappeared, a state of affairs that makes the remains at Croxden of particular importance for an understanding of how the north-west Midlands fit architecturally with the other parts of England in the first half of the 13th century. Croxden is interesting in itself as well, however, and presents a number of historical, archaeological and contextual problems that have been only fitfully treated in earlier literature. Although there is much we will never know about Croxden, what remains suggests a design that does not fit easily into the usual moulds of English Gothic in the second quarter of the 13th century and thus raises the question of Croxden being the sole survivor of a distinctive group of monastic churches in the north-west Midlands.

While Croxden remains an impressive ruin, much of the fabric has disappeared, including virtually all of the inner elevations. The primary remains are the west (Pl. IIIA) front and the south (Fig. 1, Pl. IIIB) and west walls (Pl. IVA) of the south transept, and between them, an incomplete stretch of the south nave aisle wall. There is also a fragment of the north-west ambulatory chapel of the choir (Pl. IVB) and some foundation walls of the north transept, including a pier base. The foundations of the other ambulatory chapels and the north nave aisle wall were mostly cleared in the 19th and 20th centuries,[2] but nothing is known of the main elevations of any part of the building except what survives against the south transept south wall (Fig. 2, Pl. IVC) and against the interior of the west front. In spite of such serious losses, however, enough remains to make some interesting observations on the building's place in 13th century English Gothic architecture.

The foundation and early history of Croxden have several problematic implications for the site's architectural history. The founder and patron of Croxden was Bertram de Verdun, whose career was typical of the men Henry II utilised in administering his widespread kingdom.[3] Bertram was sheriff of Leicester and Warwick from 1170–84, he served in a judicial capacity on the Curia Regis and he seems to have been seneschal in Ireland during John's expedition there in 1185.[4] In 1190 he went on Crusade with Richard I and died at Acre in 1192.[5] Bertram's foundation for Cistercians at Croxden was also typical of his class, where a monastic foundation was considered essential for baronial prestige, as well as a way of developing unused land, and, not least, providing a form of religious insurance for the founder and his family.[6] Bertram may have received the land at Croxden from an advantageous second marriage, but the sources here are far from clear.[7]

The first grant of land was made in 1176, but the monks do not seem to have congregated and elected an abbot until 1178.[8] The convent first settled at 'Chotes', which is usually

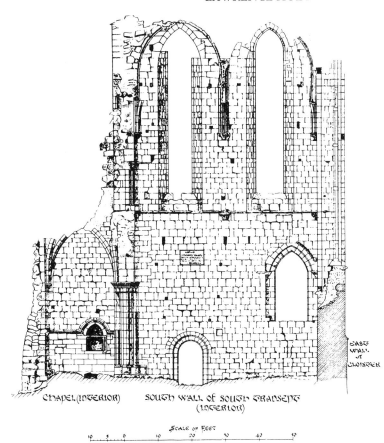

FIG. 1.   Croxden Abbey, south transept south wall elevation. From C. Lynam, *The Abbey of St Mary, Croxden, Staffordshire*, pl. 6

CHAPEL (INTERIOR)   SOUTH WALL OF SOUTH TRANSEPT
                                    (INTERIOR)

SCALE OF FEET

identified with Cotton or Cawton, and moved to Croxden itself in 1179.[9] It is not clear whether this move was intended from the first, Chotes having simply provided lodgings and facilities until construction had progressed far enough at Croxden to move there, or whether circumstances now unknown had forced the monks to move.[10] The proper interpretation of this problem has implications for the early architectural history of the monastery, because the Chronicle of the abbey records a dedication two years later in 1181. This is a 'dedication of the place of Croxden' (*dedicatio loci*).[11] If the site alone was being dedicated, why did the monks wait until two years after they had occupied it? Although the use of the work *locus* definitely clouds the issue, it seems more logical to surmise that the dedication of 1181 took place because certain monastic buildings had reached some appropriate stage of completeness. What these buildings may have been is impossible to know, but it seems likely they perhaps would have included a chapel or even the east end of a first church. Two years would admittedly be a short time to construct the eastern half of a stone church (although it need not have been completely finished or roofed), but if construction had begun in 1176 or shortly thereafter the possibility becomes less unlikely.[12]

The nature and date of the first church at Croxden could only be elucidated by an excavation of the site. It is important to assert that there was a first church, however, because most commentators on Croxden, including R. K. Baillie-Reynolds and Pevsner

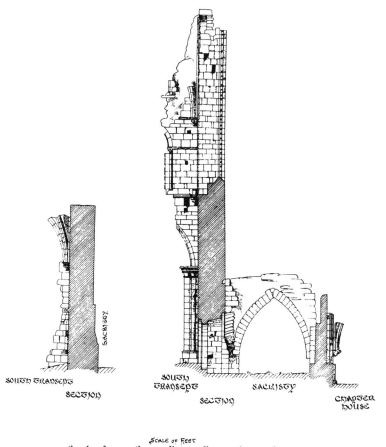

FIG. 2. Croxden
Abbey, south
transept east wall
elevation. From C.
Lynam, *The Abbey of
St Mary, Croxden,
Staffordshire*, pl. 8

SOUTH TRANSEPT
SECTION

SOUTH
TRANSEPT
SECTION

SACRISTY

CHAPTER
HOUSE

SCALE OF FEET
10 . 5 . 0   10   20   30   40   50

have assumed a single gradual campaign of construction from 1179 to the dedication of the
church recorded in 1253/54.[13] The standing remains are clearly all 13th-century in style,
however, and accord best with the three decades before 1253. There must have been a first
church which these replaced, but its dates and appearance remain unknown.

The documentary evidence for the construction of the second church is also ambiguous,
except for the 1253/54 dedication which must mark the end of the work on the church.
There is no starting date, although the Chronicle tells us the first abbot, Thomas, 'erected
very many buildings' without specifying what they were.[14] Abbot Thomas died in 1229 and
was buried, as usual for Cistercian abbots, in the chapter house.[15] On the other hand,
Nicholas de Verdun, the son of the founder, died in 1231 and was buried in front of the high
altar.[16] This is likely to have been in the choir of the second church, given the lateness of the
date. While the Chronicle itself does not record this burial, it does record a somewhat
ambiguous dedication for the church in the year 1232.[17] Is it possible this was connected
with the burial of Nicholas and represents the completion or near-completion of the eastern
half of the new church? Another piece of documentary evidence reinforces this conclusion.
Abbot Walter of London, who acceded to office in 1242, built 'half the church' that was

dedicated in 1253/4.[18] This is best interprepted to mean that Abbot Walter built the nave or nave and transepts onto the already existing choir. After the completion of the church Abbot Walter went on to rebuild most of the monastic buildings, including a gate and the precinct wall, before his death in 1268.[19] The second, partially surviving, church at Croxden, then, was probably begun c. 1220–5 by Abbot Thomas some thirty years after the completion of the first church (also built by him). The choir seems to have been finished by about 1232 and the whole church by 1253/4. There is nothing in the architectural remains to contradict this dating.

It remains to determine if any of the 12th-century church remains in the present fabric. Peter Fergusson, the only scholar to have postulated a 12th-century church preceding the present one, has suggested that the north transept pier base and some of the exterior courses of the south transept survive from the original building.[20] The pier base is a monolithic slab in the form of an eight-shaft cluster with keeled shafts in the cardinal directions and round shafts in the diagonals. This is one of the many variations of clustered pier that appear all over the north in the 12th and 13th centuries, forms by no means confined to Cistercian churches. Identical piers can be found at 12th-century Byland or 13th-century Whitby, and there seems no reason why the Croxden base should not go with the extant ruins rather than being a remnant of the first church.[21] The clustered form of this plinth is unusual, because clustered piers more typically have square, stepped, or round plinths. Two parallels for the Croxden plinth are in the naves of Shap Abbey and Repton Priory. The Shap piers are eight-shaft clusters like those at Croxden.[22] The Repton piers are more complex and include detached shafts in combination with clustered forms (the result, probably, of Lincoln influence), but Repton is only some fifteen miles away from Croxden.[23] Both these parallels suggest, in any case, that the Croxden pier is 13th-century. Fergusson also rightly remarks on the strange lack of individual bases for the pier shafts so clearly set out by incised lines on the plinth.[24] One can only point out that unmoulded shaft bases seem a bizarre speciality of Croxden masons, appearing in still cruder form under the nave west respond (Pl. IVD) and the south nave aisle vault shafts.[25]

The south transept south wall is a more complex matter (Fig. 1, Pl. VA–C). The simple unmoulded round arch door from the transept to the adjoining sacristy has struck some writers as an early feature.[26] Beginning just above the eastern haunch of this door and continuing for six courses is a stepped seam rising to the west on both the interior and exterior of the transept wall.[27] The stones adjoining it to the east are cut to fit the stepped seam above the door, implying that the door and the six courses of wall above it are earlier than the transept wall to the east. This latter wall includes the south respond of the transept arcade on its interior and the chasing for the east dormitory wall on its exterior, both of them clearly part of the 13th-century church. At the level of the arcade respond capital is a levelling course that runs straight across the wall above the stepped seam and indicates that everything above this level is 13th century. It is clear, however, that the arcade spandrel was built before the wall adjoining it to the west, for there is a very jagged break two or three feet west of the junction of south and east transept walls that rises from just above the arcade capital to the sill of the great lancets.[28] This time it is the stones of the courses to the west that are worked to fit their fellows to the east and must therefore post-date them. To the west of the round arch door the coursing of the interior of the lower south wall continues into the lower west wall of the transept. On the exterior the rebuilt barrel-vaulted book cupboard makes it difficult to follow the coursing around the corner, but there is a clear break at the junction of the transept west wall with the nave south wall, just east of the east processional door. It seems possible, then, that the lower west wall and lower west half of the south wall of the south transept may be remnants of the first building. On the other hand, the quality of

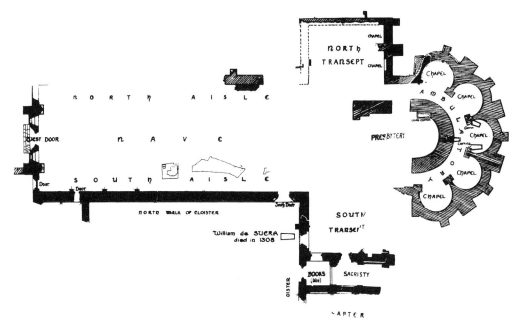

FIG. 3.   Croxden Abbey, plan of existing walls and foundations as of 1911.
From C. Lynam, *The Abbey of St Mary, Croxden, Staffordshire*, plan no. 3

masonry, sizes of stones and of mortar joints do not seem to differ significantly in the different parts of the south transept (it is possible, of course, that many 12th-century stones were reused in the 13th century church).

Professor Fergusson has also suggested that the 13th-century transepts were rebuilt on the plan of their 12th-century predecessors and that this accounts for the awkward junction with the French-style chevet.[29] This seems quite likely, but it must be emphasised that the transepts were entirely rebuilt. What remains of the base moulding of the north transept is identical to that of the remaining choir chapel, and the details of the south transept (with the possible exceptions noted above) are all 13th-century.[30]

The choir plan of Croxden is a major problem, however (Figs 3, 4). Croxden was one of those rare English Gothic buildings that adopted the French plan of an ambulatory with radiating chapels.[31] At Croxden there were five chapels separated from one another by heavy buttresses. Each chapel had two windows separated by a smaller central buttress, and was vaulted with a five-part vault. The chapels were rounded rather than polygonal on both exterior and interior. While the ambulatory continues the choir aisles in the usual fashion, the chapels themselves are not integrated into the choir plan in any way typical of contemporary French churches.[32] Instead they sprout abruptly beyond the single straight bay separating them from the transept exterior walls. The chapels and ambulatory do indeed look as though they were added on to an earlier plan or at least built by a master unaccustomed to thinking in terms of integrated choir designs.

The source for the plan of the Croxden chevet has traditionally been attributed to Croxden's mother house of Aunay-sur-Odon in Normandy.[33] Established on its present site by 1151, the church at Aunay was dedicated in 1190.[34] The site has not been investigated

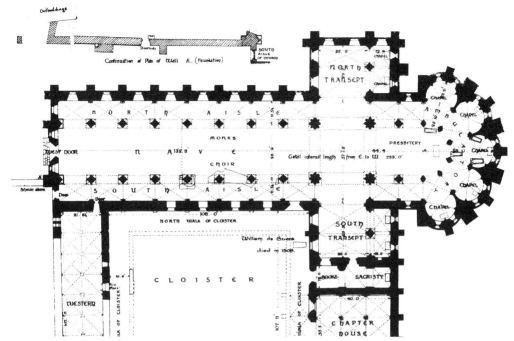

FIG. 4.   Croxden Abbey, plan of church, as reconstructed by C. Lynam, *The Abbey of St Mary, Croxden, Staffordshire*, plan no. 4

archaeologically, but the north choir wall of a late 13th- or early 14th-century reconstruction remains and this preserves a 90° return at its east end, indicating that the choir of Aunay was square-ended, at least by 1300.[35] As Lindy Grant and Nicola Coldstream have indicated, it is extremely unlikely that an ambulatory plan in France would have been replaced by a flat east end later, or that Aunay would have had an ambulatory plan to begin with as early as 1151.[36] It seems very unlikely indeed, then, that the 12th-century choir at Aunay could have been the model for Croxden.

In any case, the usual chevet plan for Norman Cistercian churches later in the 12th century followed Clairvaux III and bore little similarity to the plan of Croxden. In these buildings the ambulatory chapels do not project independently but form a polygonal ring around the ambulatory. In Normandy the chapels are usually square internally and separated by triangular buttresses; Bonport and Breuil-Benoit are characteristic examples.[37] It is significant that King John's foundation of 1204 at Beaulieu in Hampshire also used the plan with non-projecting chapels, and shows no similarity to the plan of Croxden.[38] The first French Cistercian church to adopt the High Gothic plan of projecting chapels was Longpont, begun *c.*1220, to be followed by Royaumont, but these buildings have seven chapels integrated with double-aisled choirs and have three windows and two intermediate buttresses per chapel, an arrangement quite different from the Croxden plan.[39]

On the other hand, there is one important Cistercian house in Normandy that does resemble Croxden in its choir plan. This is the abbey of Mortemer, with a choir laid out in 1174–9.[40] The fragmentary remains of the east end indicate that Mortemer had an ambulatory with seven radiating chapels, rounded externally and internally, with two windows per chapel and a central division between them, just as at Croxden.[41] The westernmost chapels at Mortemer abut directly on to the transept east aisle east wall, as would have been the case at Croxden also had there been seven instead of five chapels. These western chapels at the Norman abbey are actually smaller than their fellows to the east and set rather awkwardly in their transitional positions, and one might imagine the designer at Croxden, faced with a pre-existing transept plan, deciding that omitting the western chapels was simpler and more satisfying than squeezing them into an uncongenial corner.

Mortemer had early attracted royal patronage, and both the nave of c. 1160 and the choir begun in the 1170s were made possible by generous grants from Henry II.[42] Lindy Grant has suggested that the plan of the choir may have been a conscious appropriation of the plan of Saint-Denis and its progeny in the Ile-de-France, an attempt by the Angevins to rival the new buildings across the River Epte patronised by the rival Capetian dynasty.[43] We know Bertram de Verdun served in Normandy with Henry II and he may well have seen the new chevet at Mortemer under construction.[44] On the other hand, the choir at Mortemer was complete by c. 1200 and the Croxden east end does not seem to have been begun until c. 1220. By that date there were more up-to-date plans for Cistercian ambulatories available in France, not to mention royal Beaulieu in England. Did the de Verduns have some personal connection with Mortemer or some special feeling for Henry's favourite Norman abbey that persisted even after the fall of Normandy in 1204? If so, the knowledge of these ties is now lost to us, and whether Mortemer was really the source for the Croxden choir plan must remain hypothetical, but it is, in the present state of research, the most likely candidate.[45]

Although the plan of the Croxden chevet is clearly French, the detailing is not. The respond between the surviving north-west ambulatory chapel and the choir aisle wall provides large, keeled shafts for the support of the transverse arch of the aisle and the entrance arch to the chapel; between these are small, coursed shafts for the support of the diagonal ribs of aisle and chapel (Pl. IVB). The respond, in other words, is a variant of the type of clustered pier evidenced by the north transept base. The responds of the transept (Pl. VB) and nave arcades (Pl. IVD) are similar, though not identical, in that a chamfered section separates the main and subsidiary shafts.[46] All these surviving forms are similar enough in type to make it virtually certain that the entire building contained clustered piers for the support of its elevations. Whether these all matched the surviving north transept base, however, is impossible to know. Eight-shaft clusters are the most common type of pier in the northern Gothic buildings to which Croxden is most closely related, and there are enough cases of such piers being used with responds of slightly (or radically) different form to make their use throughout Croxden very likely.[47] It is also possible, however, that the piers of either south transept or nave followed literally the shape of their responds: keeled shafts in the cardinal directions separated by three-sided chamfered sections in the diagonals. Such piers are not common but exist in the contemporary nave of St Albans and, more apropos of Croxden, in the contemporary Cistercian church at Netley.[48] Whatever their precise form, the Croxden piers were distinctively English. The same is true of all details such as the abaci of the piers, the stiff-leaf foliage capitals used as corbels for rib springers, and the moulded profiles of arches and ribs, in so far as these survive.[49]

The only evidence for the reconstruction of the main elevation above pier level at Croxden is found in the stubs of the south transept east elevation gallery and clerestory protruding from that transept's south wall (Fig. 2, Pl. IVC). The gallery fragment shows that its opening into the roof space over the chapel vault was articulated in two orders. The outer arch was given a coursed shaft with a crocket capital, while the inner arch was supported by only a chamfered jamb. This difference of treatment makes it likely that the inner opening was subdivided as it is in many early Gothic buildings in England, particularly in the north. Of the clerestory above, only the outer south jamb of the window survives. Nothing remains of the interior treatment of the window, but it is clear here, as it is against the nave west front, that there was no clerestory passage in either place.[50] The great lancet windows of transept and west front have no openings in their jambs for temporary platforms to provide continuity of circulation at gallery or clerestory level, as is often the case in buildings with similar high windows, nor is there any obvious provision for staircase turrets at Croxden.[51] The anomalous nature of this 'thin-walled' elevation in English Gothic will be discussed below.

The south transept (Pl. IIIB) and west front (Pl. IIIA) lancet windows are surely the most spectacular surviving features at Croxden. In the south transept there are two windows in each of the surviving walls. The south wall windows have higher sills to clear the night stair door and are unarticulated by shafts on either their interiors or exteriors. The west wall lancets (Pl. IVA), on the other hand, had a single order of detached shafts on both inside and outside. The use of two, instead of three, lancets in the end wall is unusual, although there are parallels at Arbroath.[52] It is difficult to know whether the use of a single range of full windows in the south transept end wall, conditioned as it is by the adjoining cloister buildings, would have been expanded to two ranges in the end wall of the north transept, where there were no such hindrances.[53] The evidence of the south transept west wall and the west front of the building strongly suggest, however, that excessively attenuated lancets were a conscious aesthetic device of the Croxden master.

The west façade of Croxden is of a stunning simplicity (Pl. IIIA). Above a typical 13th-century shafted and moulded portal rise three unarticulated lancets of surpassing thinness. The centre lancet rises slightly higher than its neighbours, but these latter are actually longer, because they rise from just above the springing of the portal arch. Although in absolute height (about 35 ft) the Croxden lancets are surpassed by windows in larger buildings, in the ratio of thinness to height they are unlikely to have any rivals in Britain.[54] Tallness and thinness are the operative formal concerns here, and there is no approach to the proto-tracery of façades such as the north walls of the York or Hexham transepts, where only bundles of shafts separate the lancets, at least on the interior. At Croxden, on the contrary, there are substantial masonry panels between the windows.[55]

What distinguishes the Croxden façade from others that make use of large lancets is the lack of any competing feature or decoration. The west façade of Byland Abbey, for example, has three high lancet windows, but these are set within a shafted blind arcade and overtopped by a large rose window. Nor do they penetrate into the zone of the doorway below. At Brinkburn, the west façade again features three lancets, but, as at Byland, they are set in a shafted arcade. There was no rose window above, but below them is a high dado arcade of blind arches (there is no west portal at Brinkburn). The west front of Lanercost Priory, with its three stepped lancets, is perhaps the closest design to Croxden, but the windows are again set in an arcade prominently shafted with ringed monoliths and separated from the portal below by a lower zone of continuous blind arcading. At Croxden, by contrast, the windows begin as low as the doorway will allow and are completely unarticulated by shafts. The present austerity of the Croxden façade may, of course, have been mitigated by its missing parts: the gable above the lancets, and the half gables of the adjoining aisle façades.[56] Still, enough survives to indicate a composition quite different from the more richly decorated and subdivided façades typical of the second quarter of the 13th century.

Croxden was vaulted in stone in all its lower zones, including the choir chapels and ambulatory, the transept east chapels, and the nave aisles. The nave and transept aisles had

D

chamfered ribs, but the choir ribs were moulded. Those in the ambulatory exhibit a characteristic central roll flanked by hollows, but the ribs of the chapels had a very peculiar profile with a fillet set in a broad concavity.[57] The rib springing from between the chapel windows was supported by a shaft rising from the floor, as were those ribs springing from the responds of the chapel entrances (Pl. IVB). The ribs springing from the outer sides of the chapel windows, on the other hand, were supported on foliage corbels with square abaci. This emphasis on the central axis of the chapel is amplified by a selective use of wall arches. Those framing the two windows and springing from the vault shaft between these windows are moulded with a roll, while those framing the outer sections of blank wall are only chamfered. Such a subtle manipulation of arch mouldings and vault shafts is not unknown in English Gothic, but it may here be that having to articulate the unaccustomed form of an ambulatory chapel provided an extra fillip of inspiration to the English master.[58]

The ribs of the transept aisle vaults were supported by full shafts, so far as can be ascertained from the single remaining one in the south transept. The nave aisle vaults were also supported by a single, keeled shaft dividing each bay. These have the peculiar, unmoulded bases that seem characteristic of parts of Croxden.

The remains of the south transept at Croxden afford clear evidence of high vaults (Pl. IIIB) and if the transepts were vaulted it is likely the choir was as well.[59] There is no evidence to indicate, however, whether or not the nave was vaulted. The transept vault ribs were carried against the south wall by en délit shafts which rose from corbels set at window-sill level. Against the west wall (Pl. IVA), on the other hand, is a single, keeled shaft, coursed rather than en délit, that again rises from the (here lower) window-sill level of the great lancets. It carried a moulded triple capital for the support of transverse and diagonal ribs. The use of such a triple capital above a large keeled shaft seems to hark back to a building such as Roche Abbey, over fifty years earlier, although the detailing of these forms at Croxden is entirely 13th century.[60] The south compartment of vaulting in the south transept had an extra rib rising from between the two south wall lancets to form a five-part vault. Such extra ribs in terminal bays with lancet windows can also be found at Tynemouth Priory, Southwell Minster, and in the Nine Altars Chapel at Fountains Abbey.[61]

What, then, are the filiations of the Croxden design, in so far as we can reconstruct it? The broadest and most obvious connections are with the early Gothic architecture of the north, including both Cistercian and non-Cistercian buildings. Large lancet windows and clustered piers are the most generically northern features. Some parallels for the Croxden windows have been adduced above, and one could add many more. Tall lancets were not limited to the north, of course, as the east transepts of Worcester Cathedral demonstrate. Much closer to Croxden is Lichfield Cathedral where the contemporary north transept north wall sported five tall lancets in a pattern reminiscent of the York Five Sisters.[62] Like York and unlike Croxden, the Lichfield lancets are heavily articulated, set behind a wall passage, and ranged close together to eliminate as much of the wall surface as possible. There are very few other significant connections between Lichfield and Croxden, and it seems more likely that both reflect the influence of northern buildings, although the specific sources and their interpretation are different in the two cases.

Clustered piers of the Croxden type were far more common in the north at this period than anywhere else, although some were finding their way south by 1220; witness the St Albans choir or, closer to Croxden, Much Wenlock Priory and Southwell Minster. It is also interesting that the later Cistercian churches at Hailes and Tintern used variations on the clustered forms, as did Benedictine Chester in its late 13th-century reconstruction.[63] The north remained the locus classicus of the clustered pier in 1220, however, and it seems the logical place to derive the Croxden forms.

The rest of the Croxden elevation, with one important exception, also seems to derive from northern buildings. The use of a false gallery with a subdivided arch opening in two orders (if that was indeed the case at Croxden) can be seen at Arbroath, Hexham, Jedburgh, or Lanercost. Such a design is perhaps conservative by 1220 when the further multiplication of units had become more common (York, Whitby, or the Lincoln nave) and when the articulation of openings with shafts and mouldings tended to be much heavier and complex, even in Cistercian buildings, as Rievaulx demonstrates. Croxden, with Rievaulx, is among the last Cistercian buildings in England in the 13th century to have a separate middle storey,[64] and it is the elided upper elevations of Netley and Tintern that becomes the Cistercians' preference.

What really sets Croxden apart from its northern relatives, and from virtually all other contemporary buildings in England, is its lack of a clerestory passage. At Croxden the clerestory lancet window(s) was set in a thin wall just as were the south and west wall windows, and was probably just as modestly articulated. Although the first Cistercian buildings in England show some hesitation in adopting this typical Anglo-Norman Romanesque feature, it becomes common in Cistercian Gothic churches designed after Byland, as it is in all other Gothic churches of any pretension in England. The 13th-century Cistercian churches of Fountains, Rievaulx, Netley, and Sweetheart all continue the tradition; only at Tintern at the end of the century is there another Cistercian elevation without passages.[65] In its lack of passages Croxden harks back to the earlier Cistercian tradition of Roche and Dundrennan, but the Gothic thinness and detailing of the former bear little resemblance to those 12th-century designs. The lack of a wall passage at Croxden is of a piece with the simply articulated lancets and gallery, and seems best interpreted as a rejection of the emphasis on wall depth and heavy articulation common in English Gothic in the second half of the 13th century.

The tall lancets, clustered piers, and gallery design are all major features of Croxden best put down to northern influence, although their very ubiquity there makes identifying any specific sources difficult. Architectural detailing at Croxden, on the other hand, is not so clearly related to the north. While the simple chamfered plinth at Croxden might be considered a reduction of the more elaborate examples of the Fountains or Rievaulx choirs, the rib profiles do not seem particularly northern. The high vault of the Croxden south transept had an unusual profile with two side-by-side beaked half-rolls, and beaked half-rolls are an important motif at Beaulieu, in Hampshire.[66] The chamfered ribs of the Croxden nave and transept aisles can be found in the north as well as just about everywhere else, but their use in a building of Croxden's size and sophistication suggest a parallel with up-to-date Netley, also in Hampshire, rather than northern buildings such as Brinkburn or Lanercost. The use of chamfered ribs at Croxden may indeed be another indication of a conscious eschewing of more elaborate forms. The single vault shaft used for the Croxden nave aisle appears in the north in the 12th century at Furness, but corbels or corbeled shafts remain more popular, at least until the choir of Rievaulx.[67] Closer parallels again come from the southern Cistercian houses of Beaulieu and Netley, as well as Tintern later in the century. The Croxden masons were seemingly aware of these southern buildings, but in any of the larger measures of design, such as elevation or fenestration, Croxden has little in common with Beaulieu, Netley, or their progeny at Hailes.

Some of the Croxden details have local parallels. The foliage capitals seem close to work in the Lichfield transepts, and the concave octagonal shafts of the east processional door — an unusually florid effect for Croxden — have parallels at Lichfield as well as at Ashbourne parish church and Chester Chapter House.[68] Ashbourne exhibits another intriguing parallel to Croxden in the form of the parish church's arch responds between choir and transept aisles. These have keeled shafts set against chamfered responds as at Croxden. The Ashbourne responds are likely to be later than Croxden, however, and probably represent the influence of the abbey on the neighbourhood rather than vice versa.[69]

It may be, then, that Lichfield masons were brought in to do some of the detailed work on capitals, door jambs, and arch mouldings, such as those of the east processional door.[70] Far more striking than these minor connections, however, is the stylistic gulf between the Cathedral and Croxden. The Lichfield choir and transepts represent a development of the rich West Country style of Early English Gothic, with complex multi-shafted piers and arch mouldings, an innovative upper elevation combining triforium and clerestory, and a design making use of the full panoply of Early English articulation and decoration.[71] Ashbourne and Chester are firmly in the Lichfield camp, and all make a striking contrast with the general austerity of Croxden. Even the foliage capitals of Croxden are restricted to subsidiary positions as corbels for vault shafts or ribs, while the main pier and respond capitals are all moulded.

The great unanswerable question in assessing both the sources and influence of the Croxden design is its relation to the lost abbeys of the north-west Midlands. What did Cistercian Combermere, Hulton, Garendon, or Dieulacres look like? Or Augustinian Norton, Trentham, Darley, Repton, or Ulverscroft? The pier bases of Repton have already been mentioned; at Dieulacres fragments of two crossing piers remain, but their design seems to relate more closely to the Lichfield group than anything at Croxden.[72] More is preserved of the Welsh Cistercian houses at Basingwerk and Valle Crucis, but neither seems to have much to do with Croxden. One can, of course, draw up similar lists of lost medieval buildings for most parts of England, but the losses in the north-west Midlands seem particularly severe for monastic architecture. If more were known of these designs Croxden might not seem so idiosyncratic.

Croxden remains an elusive design. The strongest impression left by the standing fragments is of an elegant austerity that inevitably raises the question of whether Cistercian ideals of architectural simplicity persisted into the 13th century at Croxden in ways they do not at, say, Fountains or Rievaulx. On the other hand, the French-inspired plan of the east end does not argue for austerity at all. Perhaps the plan was the result of the de Verduns' Norman connections or of connections or preferences of Abbot Thomas now lost to us; it was, in any case, definitely a patron-determined feature. The overall design of the elevations seems the result of a general brief derived from the early Gothic architecture of the north; architectural details suggest wider awareness, however. There were some connections with the local episcopal workshop, but they do not appear to have been particularly significant. Whatever connections may have existed with other local monastic workshops are now impossible to uncover. In addition to the intrinsic beauty of its remains, Croxden Abbey church stands as a reminder of the dangers and difficulties of generalisation, not only about Cistercian buildings, but about 13th-century English Gothic as a whole, when so much has been lost.

REFERENCES

1. The only monograph on Croxden is C. Lynam, *The Abbey of St Mary, Croxden, Staffordshire* (London 1911), which is particularly useful for its illustrations and drawings. An important predecessor to Lynam is G. Hills, 'Croxden Abbey and Its Chronicle', *JBAA*, XXI (1865), 294–315. The only recent architectural descriptions of Croxden are P. K. Baillie-Reynolds, *Croxden Abbey* (London 1946); idem., 'Croxden Abbey', *Archaeol. J.*, CXX (1964), 278; and N. Pevsner, *B/E Staffordshire* (Harmondsworth 1974), 111–13.

There are also some valuable comments in P. Fergusson, *Architecture of Solitude: Cistercian Abbeys in Twelfth-Century England* (Princeton 1984), 122–3. Important for the history of the abbey are M. Laurence, 'Notes on the Chronicle and other Documents relating to St. Mary's Abbey, Croxden', *TNSFC*, LXXXV–LXXXVII (1951–3), 1–27, 27–50, 51–74; and the account in *VCH Staffordshire*, III (London 1970), 226–30.

2. For the 19th-century excavations and repairs see Lynam, *Croxden*, v–vi. More consolidation was done when the government acquired the site in the 1930s, and Baillie-Reynolds, 'Croxden', 278, alludes to excavations (or 're-excavations') in the north transept and monastic buildings, but there is no other publication of this work.

3. For the life of Bertram de Verdun, see Lynam, *Croxden*, appendix V ('Sketch of the Earlier Verduns'), vi–xv.

4. Ibid., vi–vii.

5. Ibid., viii.

6. For the patrons of 12th-century English monasteries and their motives for founding them see C. Platt, *The Abbeys and Priories of Medieval England* (New York 1984), and B. Hill, *English Cistercian Monasteries and Their Patrons in the Twelfth Century* (Urbana 1968).

7. For a discussion of this problem see Lynam, *Croxden*, appendix V, ix–xiv.

8. *VCH Staffordshire*, 226.

9. Ibid.

10. For the theory that 'Chotes' was always meant to be a temporary site see F. Hibbert, 'The Date of Croxden', *TNSFC*, XLVIII (1913–14), 129–41. There are, of course, many examples of 12th-century monastic founda-tions moving from their initial sites, for a variety of reasons. Byland, Jervaulx, Kirkstall, and Louth Park are all Cistercian examples from the 12th century.

11. *VCH Staffordshire*, 226. This dedication of the site has no parallels known to this author in the records of other monasteries.

12. Could the first church have been constructed of wood? This seems unlikely in the late 12th century. See below for possible remnants of a first stone church in the present fabric.

13. Baillie-Reynolds, *Croxden*, 1, and Pevsner, *B/E Staffordshire*, 111.

14. The Chronicle of Croxden Abbey was composed by a monk of the abbey in the 14th century. See Lawrence, 'Notes', and Lynam's translation of relevant entries in *Croxden*, appendix IV, 'Translation of "Chronicle" as relating to the Abbey'.

15. Ibid., iii.

16. Lynam, *Croxden*, appendix V, xix. Bertram de Verdun's father Norman was at some point placed in a tomb in the north chapel of the south transept, but the date is not recorded. See Hills, 'Croxden', 306.

17. The only author to mention the 1232 date is Fergusson, *Architecture*, 122. Lynam, in *Croxden*, appendix IV, iii, translates the entry for 1232 as follows: [Abbot Walter] 'by requesting obtained from the king that the church should be dedicated in honour of the Blessed Mary'.

18. Ibid.

19. Ibid.

20. Fergusson, *Architecture*, 123.

21. Eight-shaft clustered piers with keeled cardinal shafts and round diagonal ones are also found in Hartlepool church in County Durham, in the north nave arcade.

22. For the Shap nave see H. Colvin and R. Gilyard-Beer, *Shap Abbey* (London 1963), 12. The east nave piers are early 13th century; the west ones are from the end of the century.

23. Repton Priory is a poorly studied building. For the nave piers see N. Pevsner, *B/E Derbyshire* (2nd edn, rev. E. Williamson, Harmondsworth 1978), 306–7. The east nave piers are no longer visible today.

24. P. Fergusson, 'Notes on Two Cistercian Engraved Designs', *Speculum*, LIV (1979), 15, n. 33.

25. It is hard to imagine pier bases being set in place unfinished, yet that is exactly the impression the nave bases, at least, give. On the other hand, the south transept respond base is fully moulded.

26. Pevsner, *B/E Staffordshire*, 111.

27. Another anomaly of the south transept south wall, inexplicable to this author, is the beginning of a second range of voussoirs above the east haunch of the door arch. Only three stones were set, however, and there is no indication these were to continue around the arch.

28. On the exterior the break is just west of the ragged edge of the dormitory east wall.

29. Fergusson, *Architecture*, 123.

30. Only the lower two courses of the plinth remain in the north transept and even these are incomplete. The best preserved sections are the buttress between the two east chapels and the north wall. The chamfered lower course is identical to the same on the ambulatory chapel, however.

31. The only example that precedes Croxden is at Beaulieu, for which see below. The most famous 13th-century example is of course Westminster Abbey, which seems to have inspired the Cistercian examples at Hailes and Valey-Royal later in the century.

32. The usual French High Gothic procedure was to add a second aisle to the choir straight bays to correspond to the projecting chapels. See Reims and Amiens Cathedrals, or Longpont and Royaumont Abbeys. At Soissons Cathedral rectangular chapels attached to the choir aisles achieve the same goal.

33. Hills, 'Croxden', 307; Baillie-Reynolds, *Croxden*, 2; Pevsner, *B/E Staffordshire*, 111.

34. For Aunay see L. Grant, 'The Architecture of the Early Savignacs and Cistercians in Normandy', *Anglo-Norman Studies*, X (1989), 137.

35. The north-west crossing pier and parts of the north nave wall and north transept walls remain from the original building. The later north choir wall seems to be an extension of the earlier north wall of the north transept.

36. Ibid., 137, and N. Coldstream, 'Cistercian architecture from Beaulieu to the Dissolution', in C. Norton and D. Park (eds), *Cistercian Art and Architecture in the British Isles* (Cambridge 1986), 145.

37. For the plans of these Norman Cistercian churches see C. Bruzelius, 'Cistercian High Gothic: Longpont and the Architecture of the Cistercians in France in the Early Thirteenth Century', PhD Dissertation (Yale University 1977), 114–15; and V. Jansen, 'Architectural Remains of King John's Abbey, Beaulieu (Hampshire)', in M. Lillich (ed.), *Studies in Cistercian Art and Architecture*, II (Kalamazoo, Michigan 1984), figs 4 and 5.

38. Ibid., fig. 2. At Beaulieu, however, the chapels are wedge-shaped instead of square internally.

39. Bruzelius, *Longpont*, 89–123, and fig. 1.

40. For Mortemer see Grant, 'Architecture', 113–24, and P. Gallagher, 'The Cistercian Church at Mortemer: A Reassessment of the Chronology and Possible Sources', in M. Lillich (ed.), *Studies in Cistercian Art and Architecture*, I (Kalamazoo, Michigan 1982), 53–70.

41. For plans of Mortemer see Grant, 'Architecture', 116, pl. 4, and Gallagher, 'Mortemer', fig. 1.

42. Grant, 'Architecture', 114–15, and Gallagher, 'Mortemer', 60–1.

43. Personal correspondence from the author conveying information from her unpublished PhD dissertation, 'Gothic Architecture in Normandy c. 1150–1250', London, 1987. I want to thank Dr Grant for providing this information and for discussing the problems of Mortemer and Aunay with me.

44. Lynam, *Croxden*, appendix V, vi; Laurence, 'Notes', B21. If Bertram had seen the new choir of Mortemer in the 1170s or 1180s, is it possible that the original and contemporary choir of his new foundation at Croxden copied it and that the 13th-century rebuilding simply duplicated the plan of the first church? Such a chevet plan would be even more unusual in England at that date than forty years later, and in the absence of any archaeological evidence for it whatsoever, it seems better to stick with the hypothesis of a typical Cistercian square east end for the first Croxden church.

45. If the Croxden chevet was indeed laid out c. 1225–30, then it is the earliest Gothic building in England with radiating chapels untrammelled by a containing wall, as at Beaulieu. Westminster Abbey, begun in 1245, is of course the most famous example of such a plan, but there is no detailed similarity between its plan and that at Croxden. For the Westminster chevet plan, adapted from Reims Cathedral, see C. Wilson in C. Wilson *et al.*, *Westminster Abbey* (The New Bell's Cathedral Guides) (London 1986), 37–9. The plan of Croxden seems to have been an anomaly without issue.

46. Only the plinth of the north transept north respond remains and this has had its eastern subsidiary shaft broken away. The south transept south respond has an extra base which carries no shaft attached to the west side of its plinth. This must have been intended for the corner high vault shaft which, in the event, was set on a corbel at window-sill height.

47. Examples of clustered piers used with non-matching arcades can be found at Hexham, Whitby, and Dryburgh Abbeys, among others.

48. The nave of St Albans dates to the 1230s, contemporary with Croxden. Netley was founded in 1239. At Netley, however, the diagonal chamfers of the piers are broader and the cardinal shafts proportionally smaller than at Croxden.

49. The outer order of the south transept arcade had a slight bevelled edge, but the inner orders do not survive. The beginning of a chamfered order is preserved on the aisle side above the west nave respond, but this does not necessarily mean the side toward the nave was also chamfered. Many English arcades have moulded orders toward the main vessel and chamfers toward the aisle. The soffit order of the nave arcade has disappeared as it has in the south transept.

50. The solid core of the wall remains abutting the clerestory level in both south transept and west front.

51. Provisions for planks to connect wall passages across high lancets can be found at Arbroath (with two lancets per wall as at Croxden), in the nearby Lichfield north transept north wall, on a smaller scale in the Chester Chapter House, and in the east transepts of Worcester Cathedral, as well as in many other contemporary buildings.

Stair turrets are frequently found in the outer west corners of transepts, but there is none in the surviving south transept west corner at Croxden. The north transept north corner is destroyed almost to foundation level, although the height of the rubble core here seems to militate against any hypothetical stair turret. There is no sign of any stair in the west corners of the nave either (the north-west corner is completely destroyed). Yet surely there must have been some access to the roofs; from the cloister ranges only?

52. The windows of Arbroath, which was founded in 1178, are earlier than those at Croxden, and there is certainly no historical connection between the buildings. Arbroath is the closest surviving parallel to Croxden, however, with two tall lancets in the south wall and two still taller lancets in the west wall. The windows are round arched, as befits their earlier date.

53. Generalizations about the symmetry or asymmetry of transept façades is difficult when so many buildings retain only one such façade. Kilwinning and Arbroath, for example, both have a single tier of windows in the south transept like Croxden, but both, again like Croxden, have lost their north façades. At Whitby only the north transept survives. At Dryburgh both façades survive, the south with a single tier, the north with three tiers. The north transept at Hexham also has three tiers, but here the south façade also has two tiers set above the east cloister range. At Rievaulx, in contrast, both surviving façades have only a single tier.

54. In absolute height, the Croxden lancets are exceeded, for example, by those of the York north transept north façade, which are approximately 50 ft high.

55. These may, of course, be the result of their designer's concern for structural stability.

56. The buttresses flanking the nave façade at Croxden are not symmetrical. The southern is broader at its base and steps back twice in its ascent while the northern does not vary in size, which is that of the upper third of its southern counterpart. The reason for this discrepancy may be the fall in ground level to the south.

57. The closest parallel to this profile I have been able to find is the vault shafts of the lavabo at Cistercian Mellifont Abbey in Ireland. See R. Stalley, 'Mellifont Abbey: At Study of Its Architectural History', *Proceedings of the Royal Irish Academy*, 80C (1980), 311, Fig. 19, no. 4. Stalley, 312, dates the lavabo to c.1210.

58. Such a manipulation of moulding profiles for architectural emphasis can be found at the contemporary Cistercian chapter house at Margam Abbey, in southern Wales. There only the interior east window of the chapter house has a moulded arch while the others have simple chamfers (presumably the abbot sat under this window). On the exterior the two windows adjacent to the east window have moulded arches as well as the latter, while the rest have chamfers.

59. Rib fragments of what appears to have been the choir high vault show a centre filleted roll flanked by two unfilleted rolls. The vault bosses had stiff-leaf foliage, as did those of the south transept vaults.

60. The Roche vault shaft has the waterleaf capitals and semi-octagonal abacus typical of the 12th century. See P. Fergusson, 'Roche Abbey: The Source and Date of the Eastern Remains', *JBAA*, XXXIV (1971), pls VIII, IX.

61. At Tynemouth two tiercerons rose from between three lancets against the east wall of the presbytery while at Southwell the ridge rib of the choir sprang from between four lancets. At Fountains, as at Tynemouth, two tiercerons originally sprang from between three lancets in the north and south façade walls. The Fountains keystones survive and I am indebted to Mr Stuart Harrison for showing them to me. Mr Harrison is working on a reconstruction of the Fountains vaults.

62. The Lichfield lancets are a reconstruction by J. O. Scott, for which he seems to have found evidence during his removal of the existing Perpendicular window. See M. Thurlby, 52 and R. Lockett, 125.

63. Hailes was founded in 1246 (the chevet was built 1270-7), Tintern was rebuilt 1270-1301, and Chester from the 1270s.

64. Coldstream, 'Cistercian', 149.

65. Even at Tintern there is a clerestory passage in the north transept east and west walls and the south transept west wall. It is impossible to tell now if Beaulieu or Hailes might have lacked clerestory passages.

66. For an analysis of this motif see V. Jansen, 'Beaulieu', 84-7.

67. At Furness the single vault shaft is used in the south nave aisle. It also appears in the chronologically more apropos Cistercian churches at Beaulieu, Netley, and Tintern.

68. For the foliage capitals see M. Thurlby, 59. For the fluted polygonal shafts see V. Jansen, 'The Architecture of the Thirteenth Century Rebuilding of St Werburgh's, Chester', PhD dissertation (University of California, Berkeley 1975), 94.

69. A later 13th-century example of this form can be found in the west nave responds of the parish church in Nantwich.

70. See Thurlby, 59, 60.

71. Ibid., 50-3.

72. Dieulacres is a particularly unfortunate loss. Founded in 1214, it was the closest Cistercian house to Croxden. Although relations between the houses were often uneasy, it would be logical to suspect some architectural connection. It might even be that the beginning of Dieulacres in a more up-to-date style inspired the reconstruction at Croxden. The fragments of crossing piers at the former, however, have small coursed shafts set in stepped cores in the tradition of the Lichfield transept piers, although there is hardly enough evidence to say anything definite about the filiations of Dieulacres.

The Early Gothic Transepts
of Lichfield Cathedral

By Malcolm Thurlby

DOCUMENTATION

In 1241 Bishop Patteshull was buried before the altar in St Stephen's chapel in the east aisle of the north transept.[1] It will be demonstrated that for the most part the north transept is later than the south and therefore that both transepts were finished, or at least were close to completion, by 1241. Other documentation indicates that work was in progress in the 1220s and 1230s. In 1221 King Henry III gave twenty oaks from Cannock Forest for rafters and timber for the church.[2] In 1231 he gave timber for ladders from Ogley Hay,[3] and in 1235 and 1238 permission was granted to use the quarry in Hopwas Hay.[4] Then, in 1243 the king ordered for his chapel at Windsor a wooden vault to be constructed in imitation of stone like the new work at Lichfield.[5] Unfortunately, the document is not specific about the location of the wooden vault(s) at Lichfield, but the candidacy of the transepts will be discussed below.

PROBLEMS CONNECTED WITH RECONSTRUCTING THE EARLY GOTHIC TRANSEPTS

The transepts extend three bays from the crossing and have richly decorated portals in the north and south façades (Pl. VIA, B). The first bays in each arm open into the choir and nave aisles, while the second and third bays have aisle chapels to the east, those in the north transept being somewhat larger than in the south. The present form of the transepts comprises the core of the Early English fabric with Perpendicular modifications and subsequent reworking and restorations (Pls VIC, D, VIIA, B).[6] The post-medieval work does not significantly inhibit our understanding of the early Gothic design. However, the Perpendicular rebuilding has left us with evidence not easily interpreted with regard to the original appearance of the upper parts of the 13th-century transepts. Both two- and three-storey schemes have been reconstructed.[7] Careful scrutiny of the stonework is therefore necessary if we hope to provide a definitive answer to this question. We have to determine whether there was a separate triforium and clerestory, or whether they were integrated in some way. Was the original design like Netley Abbey with a single arch on the inner plane of the wall embracing the division of the triforium and clerestory on the rear wall?[8] Or was it like the choir of Pershore with a triple arched screen on the inner plane?[9] Perhaps the arrangement at Christ Church, Dublin, would provide the closest parallel, with the clear articulation of triforium and clerestory.[10] And what of the vault; is it original or a Perpendicular insertion? Did the elevation of the transepts follow that of the choir? What is to be made of the design variety, including changes in pier design and arch mouldings, not only from one transept to the other, but also within each transept? Perhaps the changes are indicative of a rapid turnover of master masons and/or skilled craftsmen. Or is it feasible that the variety resulted from a consciously planned aesthetic? Finally, we have to consider the possible design sources and the place of the transepts in the development of Early English architecture.

THE BAY DESIGN OF THE EARLY GOTHIC TRANSEPTS

In spite of detail differences between the two transepts, and even differences between individual bays in each arm, the two arms are sufficiently similar in their basic form for it to make sense to start our investigation by considering the broader design issues. With the essentials established we will then be in a position to proceed with the examination of the finer details.

The main arcade and vault shafts with their stiff-leaf and moulded capitals clearly belong to the Early English build (Pls VIc, VIIA). The reticulated tracery of the clerestory windows that slips down over the rear wall of the triforium is quite obviously Perpendicular. With regard to the vault, the depressed trajectory of the wall arches, especially over the terminal window in the south transept (Pl. VID), the foliage bosses and the crenellated blocks above the vault capitals all speak in favour of a Perpendicular date. The position of the bosses at the junction of the wall arches and the transverse vault ribs confirms that the wall arches and vault belong with the Perpendicular clerestory windows. Therefore, in spite of the fact that the complete mouldings of the wall arches appear to be early Gothic, and that many, if not all, of the stones may be reused from the early Gothic fabric, we must discount the trajectory of the wall arches from our consideration of the early Gothic elevation. Similarly, although many of the *en délit* shafts and their stiff-leaf and moulded capitals are Early English, their placement may not be original and therefore they must be interpreted with due caution.

In the south transept the bay immediately next to the crossing on the east side (S1E) preserves more of the original Early English upper storey than the other bays (Pl. VIIc).[11] There are two arches in the upper storey of bay S1E. The arch next to the crossing is filled in with large Perpendicular stones which include two panels of blind tracery. The back of the second arch is now occupied by the Perpendicular clerestory window, while the front plane is asymmetrical in that it springs from a higher point on the left than on the right. This asymmetry is conditioned by the retention of the original 13th-century trajectory for the left arc, but the substitution of a Perpendicular arc on the right.[12] Other than the Perpendicular infill there is no indication of later medieval tampering with the first arch. It is therefore important to note certain details for comparison with other bays. First, the front shaft of each stepped group is carried on a corbel.[13] Secondly, the shafts are monolithic and are held by a ring at the halfway point. Thirdly, the front shaft of the left jamb is fluted octagonal rather than round.[14] Fourthly, the stiff-leaf capitals with their rounded abaci are of the same type as in the crossing with sharply delineated stems and leaves clinging to the bell.

Turning to the exterior of bay S1E, on the north jamb of the clerestory window we find the moulded base of the original Early English window jamb set slightly in front of the shaft of the present window (Pl. VIID). Above the right arc of this window is preserved the scar of the head its narrower Early English predecessor. With reference to the left arc of this Early English lancet we may project the placement of the left (south) jamb of the Early English window through to the interior. It is clear that it would have been flanked by a narrow arch as on the north side of the bay. The bay would therefore have been symmetrical with a screen of three pointed arches on the front plane of the wall with the central arch aligning with the window. This arrangement would agree with the evidence in the wall at the back of the passage in this bay. Here there is a centrally placed chamfered arch which opens into the roof space. The reconstructed rhythm of the front arcade aligns perfectly with the placement of this opening. The tripartite division of this front screen is also paralleled elsewhere in the Cathedral, in the windows in St Chad's Head Chapel (Pl. VIIIA), in the west bays of the north and south choir aisles, and in the east windows of the south transept chapels (Pl. VIIIB). It is significant that the choir aisle and south transept chapel triplets are carried on grouped shafts as in the south transept upper storey. Furthermore, in south transept chapel 1 the front shaft of each central group is carried on a corbel at sill level as in the upper storey of the south transept.

The design of the upper portion of bay S1E represents a change from the scheme in the choir.[15] Originally it was intended to continue the choir design, with its precocious glazed triforium, into the south transept. The evidence is in bay S1E in the roof space above the chapel and on the exterior immediately above the roof and below, and to the south of, the clerestory window in this bay (Pls VIID, VIIIC). In the roof space the valley gutter continues from the base of the south choir triforium below the blocked opening from the stair vice within the south-east crossing pier, to make its way below the south transept triforium. In the wall of the triforium there are two blocked openings, the evidence for which continues above the roof to the sill of the Perpendicular clerestory window. The bay is then terminated by a semi-octagonal buttress as in the choir. At this point this scheme was abandoned in favour of a somewhat more conservative and more substantial design. The two openings planned for the rear wall of the triforium were blocked and the revised arrangement was conceived with a single central opening in the rear wall and a tripartite screen on the front plane of the wall.

The tripartite rhythm of the upper elevation of bay S1E was in essence followed in the second and third bays (S2E and S3E) of the transept. On the exterior in both bays the arcs of the Early English lancets are visible above the present clerestory windows (Pl. VIIID). Their trajectory equates with a tripartite division of the bay in which the heads of the side lancets are placed slightly lower than the head of the central lancet. It seems likely that all three lancets would have been glazed as in St Chad's Head Chapel (Pl. VIIIA). Inside, at the back of the wall passage in both bays S2E and S3E, there are three arched openings which accord with the tripartite division in each bay (Pls VID, IXA). Confirmation of this rhythm is found in bay S3E in the form of a clear mark of a base on the outer ledge of the passage floor, the placement of which coincides with the right jamb of the centre rear wall opening. This mark indicates that the outer shaft of the group of three would have projected beyond the floor of the passage to have been supported on a corbel as in bay S1E and in south transept chapel 1. The placement of this subdivision would result in an approximately 1:2:1 rhythm for each bay.[16]

So far it is clear that above the main arcade in the Lichfield transepts there was a tripartite screen of tall lancets. It would appear, then, that it looked like the choir of Pershore Abbey, as Catherine Milburn has suggested.[17] However, neither Milburn, nor Willis before her, mention the evidence for a separate clerestory passage.[18] From each of the stair vices there are blocked openings to such a passage, and in a number of bays in both the north and south transepts there are blocked clerestory passage openings (Pl. IXB).[19] Therefore, in my previous reconstruction of the Lichfield transept elevation I opted for a three-storey scheme with superimposed triforium and clerestory passages which were integrated with single shafts running from the sill of the triforium to the capitals of the clerestory arches.[20] I was aware that there was no trace of the cutting back of the spandrels of the triforium arches next to the vaulting shafts. However, given the restored condition of the fabric and the apparent tampering with the 13th-century stonework elsewhere in the transept, I was quite happy to attribute this loss to the reworking of the ashlar. I therefore ended up with something closer to the nave of Christ Church, Dublin. This scheme must now be modified. I have in mind an arrangement like the north window of the Lichfield north transept which was created by Scott to replace a large Perpendicular window (Pl. VIIA). According to Canon Lonsdale's contemporary account, Scott's work was 'in every sense a restoration: for on taking out the Perpendicular window, and removing such of the stonework as was defective on either side, the headings of the five Early English lights ... were discovered'.[21] Whether or not Scott found clear evidence for the exact arrangement of the pseudo-clerestory passage is not known, but such a scheme is not uncommon elsewhere in Early

English churches. It is found inside the west front of Bolton Priory, in the south transept at Arbroath Abbey, and, most interestingly, in the Lady Chapel of Worcester Cathedral (Pl. IXc), where we even see the 'temporary' wooden floor in place.[22] I would therefore modify my reconstruction to appear like the outer bays of the eastern transepts or the east bay of the Lady Chapel at Worcester Cathedral, and include the provision of a removable wooden floor at clerestory level.[23]

The scars of the heads of the clerestory side lancets in bays S2E and S3E show that the arches came close to the top of the wall (Pl. VIIId). At first sight it is difficult to equate this evidence with the trajectory of the original 13th-century vault. Had the side lancets of the front screen risen to the same height as the heads on the outer wall then the stilting of the vault springers would have been extreme. Fortunately the answer to the problem is close at hand in the Chapel of St Chad's Head (Pl. VIIIa). Here the lancet windows all rise to the same height, and yet inside the tripartite screen has staggered arches so as to accommodate the vault springers. Although the south transept clerestory side windows were not so tall as the central lancet of the triplet, further stepping of the inner screen would have been necessary to allow room for the vault.

It seems likely that the Lichfield transepts originally had high wooden vaults. Referring to the 1243 document in which Henry III ordered for his chapel at Windsor a wooden vault like the new work at Lichfield, Willis suggests that the date would 'suit the transepts better than the choir'.[24] At the same time, however, given the precocious skeletal structure of the early Gothic choir, a wooden vault there would make good sense.

RELATIVE CHRONOLOGY AND DESIGN VARIETY IN THE TRANSEPTS

It is significant that the transepts differ considerably in matters of detail, not just from one transept to the other but from one bay to the next in each transept. Both transept façades have centrally placed portals with double doors (Pl. VIa, b). The portals share details like syncopated *en délit* shafts with dog-tooth behind the outer shafts and foliage pyramid voussoirs. However, the south portal archivolts are composed solely of foliage whereas the north portal has an elaborate iconographic programme with a Tree of Jesse.[25] The south portal has to each side two niches with gabled nodding trefoil heads. Above there is a row of renewed statues in trefoil-headed niches. By contrast the north portal has a single statue niche to either side of the arch. Whether the south transept façade originally boasted a range of five lancet windows like those restored by Scott in the façade of the north transept is not known. At any rate, the gable designs differ. In the south transept there is a rose window flanked by trefoil-headed niches and surmounted by a vesica; in the north transept there is a central window with Y-tracery flanked by blind arches of similar form.[26]

The arches of the crossing and the east arcades of both transepts have the inner order carried on stepped triple-coursed shafts, but in the crossing piers the other shafts are detached monoliths with shaft rings (Pls VIc, VIIa, c, IXa).[27] In keeping with the design of the crossing piers, the outer two orders of the arches to the north and south choir aisles are carried on detached shafts (Pl. IXa). The outer responds of these arches, however, have coursed shafts throughout, and the use of coursed shafts remains consistent in the other east arcade piers of both transepts (Pls VIc, VIIa). The arches to the choir aisles and to the south nave aisle (Pls VIc, VIIa) differ from the others in the transepts in having the capitals of the soffit triplet set lower than the capitals of the two outer orders. Also, the capital of the outer order on the north respond of the arch to the south choir aisle and the outer capitals of both responds of the arch to the north choir aisle are square rather than round. The mouldings of the arches to the choir aisles are different; the south arch mouldings are finer and have a greater profusion of fillets than the north. Moreover, the east side of the north arch boasts a deeply undercut chevron ornament which is absent on the south.

The next piers in both transepts (SII and NII) are broader than SIII and NIII (Pls VIc, VIIa, Xa–d). This is conditioned by the alignment of SII and NII with the outer walls of the choir aisles, as opposed to SIII and NIII which align with the narrower division between the chapels. The greater width of SII over SIII is immediately obvious in the space to either side of the high vault shafts. The design of the latter is the same in SII and SIII with a stepped coursed triplet, the central shaft of which is filleted. The shafts for the wall arches are also filleted. In SII there is a space to either side of the stepped triplet but in SIII the triplet is more completely integrated into the design of the pier. Aside from this, the basic design of piers SII, SIII and SIV is the same (Pl. Xa, b). However, there are detail differences. The bases on SII, where original, are proto-water holding; in SIII they are water holding, and in SIV they have triple rolls. Also, in SIV the rounded subsection of the base sits directly on the plinth, whereas in SII and SIII there is an intervening block of the same square plan as the plinth. The stiff-leaf capitals on SII are taller than on SIII. Furthermore, the abaci change from a double roll in SII to a single roll in SIII. The capitals on SIV are moulded. The single outer shafts of SIV are unlike SII and SIII in being plain rather than filleted. On SII and SIII there are quadrant rolls between the shafts but this changes to a chamfer on SIV. The arch mouldings in bays 2 and 3 are also different from those in bay 1.

Pier NII, unlike SII, has squared stones rather than quadrant rolls between the shafts (Pl. Xa, c). These piers also differ in a number of other ways. NII has heads incorporated into the stiff-leaf capitals carrying the two outer orders of the arch of bay 2, while the capitals of the soffit triplet are moulded. There is no fillet on the central shaft of the soffit triplet respond, and the base and arch mouldings differ in detail from SII.

Further changes occur between piers NII and NIII (Pl. Xc, d). In NIII the stepped plinth is abandoned. Instead, the plinth has straight sides on the diagonal while the front is chamfered off in front of the high vault shafts. Moulded capitals are now used exclusively on the pier, and coursed shafts appear between and behind the front coursed shafts to give a syncopated rhythm in contrast to the squared stones between the shafts on NII. The high vault shafts are now grouped as a triplet rather than a quintuplet.

NIV is essentially the same as NIII, even to the arch mouldings and the plinth. However, there are minor changes: the profile of the moulded capitals is slightly different, the central shaft of the soffit triplet is filleted like the north face of NIII.[28] Also, the triplet as a whole is set apart from the rest of the pier by a squared stone rather than a quadrant roll.

The arches from the north and south transepts to their respective nave aisles are very different in form (Pls VId, VIIb). The arch from the south transept to the south nave aisle has alternating continuous and non-continuous orders and the stiff-leaf capitals of orders 1 and 3 are set at different heights. The shafts of the north respond and the inner shaft of the south respond are *en délit*. The counterpart to this arch in the north transept has moulded capitals set at one level and shafts disposed on the core as in pier NIV.[29]

The west walls of the transepts match neither on the interior nor on the exterior (Pls VId, VIIb, XIa, b). The high vault shafts in the south transept west wall follow the basic five-part form of the east side of the transept, although the lateral shafts on the west wall are narrower and they also lack fillets. In the north transept the west wall vault shafts adopt the triplet design as on pier NIII, and they are backed with a slim dosseret. The interior dado arcade in the south transept has five pointed arches in the middle bay and three in the south bay,[30] while in the north transept there are four trefoil pointed arches per bay. In the south transept there is also an exterior dado arcade, but there is not one on the north transept. The south transept has paired lancet windows, whereas in each bay of the north transept there was a tripartite division with a centrally placed window with a Y-tracery blind arch to either side. The clerestory windows in both transepts are Perpendicular replacements. On the exterior of the south transept there is no indication of the form of the Early English originals. In the interior, however, the blind arch on the north side of bay S1W and the trajectory of the adjacent north arc of the window suggests that originally there would have been a tripartite arrangement to match that in bay S1E. On the exterior of the north transept the scars of the former arch heads suggest that there were triple lancets in bays N2W and N3W.

Turning to the clerestory on the east side of the transepts, bays S1E and N1E appear to be compatible. In the interior, bay N2E has a narrow blind arch on the south side which is a device for articulating the wall space above the wide pier (NII) below. It is probable that bay S2E was originally like this. However, in view of the use of a more compact pier for SIII and NIII it is unlikely that the blind arch would have been used in the clerestory above these piers. The clerestory in these bays would therefore have been asymmetrical. From the scars on the exterior of the clerestory it is seen that the trajectory of the side lancets was steeper on the north than on the south (Pl. VIIID).[31] In contrast to the south transept, it seems likely that the lancets of the north transept east clerestory would all have risen to the same height. In bays S2E and S3E there are single central lancets at the back of the triforium passage, while in bays N2E and N3E the central lancets are paired. Bays S1E and N1E are executed primarily in green sandstone, but this is abandoned after the north respond of pier SII and the south respond of pier NII. The differences in the mouldings of the arches leading from the transepts to the choir aisles have been observed above. The lower voussoirs of the two outer orders of bay N2E which spring from pier NII are also executed in green stone and have the same profile as the arch of bay S1E. This suggests that the mouldings of bays N2E and N3E were planned from the first to match bay S1E, and consequently to contrast with bay N1E. While this may indicate that the north transept followed immediately after the construction of bay S1E, other changes in the detailing of the transepts suggest that, in the main, the north transept was constructed after the southern arm.[32] The more compact treatment of the high vault responds in NIII and NIV is related to the nave piers, which suggests that the north transept came after the south (Pl. XB, D). This sequence is supported by the design of the plinths. In the south transept the plinths are all stepped, as is the plinth of NII, but NIII and NIV have flat plinths on the diagonal which presage the nave piers. Moulded capitals are used in SIV and in NII, NIII and NIV. The capitals on NIII and NIV come closest to examples in the Chapter House and Chapter House vestibule and are therefore later in date than those in the south transept.

Aside from these basic chronological observations, care must be taken not to make too much of detail design differences in determining the sequence of the building, especially with regard to the matter of building breaks and the number of campaigns of construction. Details of the stiff-leaf capitals remain fairly consistent throughout the transepts.[33] Arch mouldings may change but the basic vocabulary remains essentially the same. Professor Hoey has mustered convincing evidence to show that 'Variety was clearly the spice of life for Early English masons designing piers'.[34] In the Lichfield transepts this variety went beyond pier design to the design of arch mouldings and the clerestory. Analogous variety in transept design is found, for example, at Abbey Dore, Hexham Abbey, York Minster and Rochester Cathedral, while in a single space the design of the choir of St Mary de Haura at New Shoreham (Sussex) provides an extreme example of asymmetry.[35] Whether or not this variety was planned from the start, at the very least it was tolerated and it may well have been viewed as a very desirable aesthetic.[36]

SOURCES OF THE TRANSEPTS

On the placement of the Lichfield transepts in context, Brakspear included the choir among the works of the West Country School of Masons, but he considered that 'the transepts and nave were apparently never finished by the school'.[37] On the other hand, Stalley grouped the choir and transepts together and observed that 'the low massive piers, with their groups of triple shafts recall those at Wells and Pershore, and the relative lowness of the arcade, which gives great emphasis to the intricately moulded soffits, is reminiscent of the same two buildings'.[38] There can be no doubt as to the basic validity of Stalley's judgement, but neither Wells nor Pershore fully prepare us for the variety of pier forms in the Lichfield transepts.[39] The Lichfield choir arcade piers are composed of groups of triple shafts around a core, and as such they compare closely with the arcade piers at Wells, Pershore and Cwm Hir.[40] In the Lichfield transepts, however, triple shafts are only used for the inner order of each arch, while the other elements change from pier to pier.[41]

   Although variety in pier design is not a hallmark of individual West Country buildings, the elements of the Lichfield patterns may be paralleled in a West Country orbit. To start with the crossing piers which differ from the main arcade piers in incorporating *en délit* shafts. Brakspear considered that the absence of detached columns was symptomatic of the West Country School of Masons. He observed that they occur 'only in the work of presumably one master ... in Glastonbury Lady Chapel and the porches of Wells and Bishops Cleeve'.[42] However, detached shafts are not quite so rare in the West Country School as Brakspear would have us believe. They are used on the west front of Llandaff Cathedral, in the inner north porch of St Mary Redcliffe at Bristol, in the nave arcades at Deerhurst, Gloucestershire, in the doorway to the Bishop's Palace at Exeter, in the choir of St Mary de Lode at Gloucester, in the doorways at St Mary at Shrewsbury and in the north doorway at Holy Trinity at Coventry. By the 1220s they are standard — Wells west front, Pershore Lady Chapel and phase 1 of the choir, Worcester eastern arm, Bristol Elder Lady Chapel, and Chepstow Castle Keep. The Lichfield crossing piers are unusual, however, in combining coursed and detached shafts. It is true that this juxtaposition is encountered at Pershore and Worcester, but these are probably not early enough to have influenced the Lichfield crossing piers.[43] More interesting are the west responds of the nave arcades at Coventry Cathedral-Priory where on the aisle side of the responds we find a single *en délit* shaft alongside coursed shafts.[44] Relative dating, however, is once again a problem. But this is not so with the former Benedictine Nunnery at Nuneaton.[45] Here on the east responds of the north and south crossing arches a coursed triplet carried the soffit of the arch (Pl. XIIA). Then, working out to either side, there is a quadrant roll, a detached shaft and another quadrant roll. The final design is quite different from the Lichfield crossing piers, but individual elements at Nuneaton speak in favour of its importance for Lichfield. Quite apart from the detached shafts and the juxtaposition of a soffit triplet and single side shafts, the Nuneaton responds incorporate a fluted octagonal shaft as the central element of the triple shaft group as in the Lichfield transept clerestory.[46] Even closer are the north and south responds of the eastern crossing arch at Nuneaton with a coursed soffit triplet flanked by ringed *en délit* shafts (Pl. XIIA). Typologically these Nuneaton responds are far in advance of the other crossing responds, and even of the Lichfield crossing, for behind and between the *en délit* shafts there are coursed filleted shafts, which give a syncopation to the responds like the Lichfield north and south transept doorways.[47]

The responds of the north, south and west crossing arches at Nuneaton introduce the concept of variety of pier design (Pl. XIIB). The basic design remains the same, but the east responds of the north and south crossing arches go together and yet they differ in detail from north-west and south-west crossing piers. Each respond is symmetrical and has a quadrant roll at the back and a stepped triplet against quadrant rolls at the front. Between the back and front quadrant rolls on the east piers there is a coursed shaft on a base followed by an *en délit* shaft on a base. The central element of the soffit triplet is fluted octagonal. On the west piers the soffit triplet uses circular shafts throughout. Then the coursed shaft next to the back quadrant roll has no base and rather than following this with an *en délit* shaft there is a coursed shaft on a base.[48]

The high vault responds of the Lichfield south transept may be read as a refinement of the central element of the Nuneaton north-west and south-west crossing pier responds. At Nuneaton the stepped triplet is set on a pilaster with quadrant edges. Related forms occur in the high vault responds in the transepts at Abbey Dore and in the west bays of Worcester Cathedral nave which rise uninterrupted from floor to vault as at Lichfield.[49] The main arcade piers in the Worcester west bays are also related to the Lichfield transept piers in that the outer two orders carried on single shafts.[50]

The arch from the south transept to the south nave aisle adopts the West Country theme of the alternation of continuous and non-continuous orders (Pl. VID).[51] Also within a West Country orbit the complex section of the inner order support should be specifically compared with the entrance jambs to the Becket Chapel in the north transept of St David's Cathedral.[52]

The semi-octagonal plan of the buttresses at Nuneaton presages those of the Lichfield choir and phase one of the transept, and this form is also used in the refectory at Merevale Abbey, Warwickshire (Pls VIID, XIIC). The form and close setting of the buttresses at Merevale and Nuneaton led Brakspear to suggest that the Merevale refectory was executed by the same masons as Nuneaton.[53] It is therefore interesting to observe that inside the Merevale refectory there are shafts with fillets which continue into the moulded capital, just as at Lichfield in the inner shaft of the soffit triplet in bay N3E and in the enclosing arch to the south transept gable rose inside the roof space.

Reference to a West Country background also helps our understanding of the integration of the triforium and clerestory in the Lichfield transepts. There is a fine pedigree for the integration of storeys in the west of Britain. The giant order embraced the first two storeys of the elevation in the Romanesque choir at Tewkesbury Abbey, in the Great Church at Glastonbury Abbey and at Waterford Cathedral.[54] The unification of triforium and clerestory appears in the naves of St David's Cathedral, Llanthony Priory and possibly Abbey Dore.[55] When this tradition is embellished with complex early Gothic mouldings, detached shafts and stiff-leaf and moulded capitals, the elements for the creation of the Lichfield design are at hand.

The grouping of the five lancets on the Lichfield north transept façade invites comparison with the famous Five Sisters window in the north transept of York Minster.[56] The relative dating here is problematical and it may well be that Lichfield precedes York. However, tall lancet windows are normally considered in the context of northern Gothic; Hoey refers to the York north transept lancets as 'unreservedly northern Early English'. It is true that there are examples of tall lancets in the north which pre-date York, such as Tynemouth Priory presbytery and Arbroath Abbey south transept. But tall lancets are not exclusive to the north; they appear in the western transept at Peterborough Cathedral, in the transepts at

Abbey Dore, and, grouped into a stepped triplet, in the west front of Llandaff Cathedral. Furthermore, the early Gothic choir at Lichfield had a glazed triforium and therefore the lancets there would have stretched from the triforium floor to the top of the clerestory.[57]

AFFILIATIONS OF THE TRANSEPTS

Chester Chapter House

The Chapter House of St Werburgh's, Chester has numerous details in common with the early Gothic form of the Lichfield transepts (Pls XIID, XIIIA).[58] The skeletal handling of the upper section of the walls immediately recalls the treatment of the original triforium/ clerestory in the Lichfield transepts, as does the internal division of each bay of the side walls by triple stepped lancets. The unusual form of the stiff-leaf capitals, the round abaci and the use of fluted polygonal *en délit* shafts as the front member of the doubtlets and triplets in the lancet screen are intimately related to Lichfield.[59] Indeed, the details are so close as to suggest that we are dealing with the work of the same architect. This suggestion is confirmed when we see in the Chester Chapter House that there are openings behind the vault springers for a 'clerestory' passage, but no permanent floor to the passage itself. The arrangement must therefore have been like Worcester Lady Chapel (Pl. IXC) and indeed identical to Lichfield. Two further details are especially telling: first, the intermediate triple shafts in each bay are tied to the back wall with moulded 'transoms'; examination of the openings in the south transept triforia and the north transept west triforium at Lichfield shows that these 'transoms' have been reused as lintels in the Perpendicular remodelling (Pls VIC, VIIA–C, IXA).[60] Secondly, the lancet windows in the Chester Chapter House stretch almost to the top of the wall, and yet the height of the side lancets on the inner plane of the wall is curtailed by the trajectory of the vault. The upper section of the side windows is therefore not fully perceived inside. The same must have been true in the Lichfield north transept in which the clerestory windows rose almost to the top of the wall. The strong vertical emphasis on the exterior of the Chester Chapter House would be in keeping with the design of the transept clerestorys at Lichfield. In the second and third bays of the Lichfield transept clerestory there were three windows per bay, as in the second bay of the Chester Chapter House. In both cases there is the desire to perforate the wall surface which, along with the verticality, may suggest a French rather than an English attitude towards Gothic. Nevertheless, when the Chester work is put alongside the original early Gothic choir at Lichfield there can be little doubt that this daring perforation derives from Lichfield.

The articulation of the exterior of the Chester Chapter House is also allied to buildings we have cited as possible sources for Lichfield; Nuneaton and Merevale. The octagonal 'buttresses' between the windows at Chester relate to Nuneaton choir and transepts and the Merevale refectory (Pl. XIIC, D). Similarly, the design of the plinth, including the way the top string is interrupted by the buttresses, is the same in each case.

The relative dates of the Chester Chapter House and the Lichfield transepts are not easily determined. The earliest reference to burial in the Chapter House at Chester is in 1208.[61] It then remains the traditional burial place for the abbots of St Werburgh's in the 13th century, except for Abbot William Marmion who died in 1222 and was buried in the cloister.[62] Could the present structure have been completed before 1208, or does the fact that Abbot William was not buried in the Chapter House in 1222 mean that it was under construction at that time? It has also been suggested that the Chapter House may date soon after the increase in the number of monks to forty between 1240 and 1249.[63] A date in the 1250s for the Chapter House has much to recommend it, and it may even be supported with reference to dated work at Croxden Abbey.[64] However, it is possible that construction took place considerably earlier. The capitals of the Chester Chapter House find their closest parallels in the crossing piers and the transepts rather than in the choir at Lichfield (Pls VIIC, XA, XIIIA). If the transepts were in building in the 1220s and we suggest that the tall lancets and the daring skeletal design at Chester derive from the Lichfield choir, then a date around 1222 for the Chapter House may not be unreasonable.

Shrewsbury, St Mary

The easternmost window of the north choir wall at St Mary's, Shrewsbury, is a triple grouped lancet with an inner triplet lancet screen.[65] The capitals are in the form of a foliage frieze which stretches straight back to the rear wall exactly as in St Chad's Head Chapel (Pl. VIIA) and in the north and south choir aisle west bays at Lichfield.[66]

Ashbourne

Our reconstruction of the Lichfield transept upper elevation is also supported with reference to the internal detailing of the east windows of the north transept at Ashbourne parish church, Derbyshire (Pl. XIIIB).[67] Here we encounter the hollow walls with triple lancet screens in each bay as in the Lichfield and Chester Chapter House. In all three cases 'transoms' tie the *en délit* shafts to the back wall. Two shafts are used at the edge of the bay and triplets in the middle and in each case the front shafts are octagonal while the back shafts are round. The octagonal form of these front shafts is reflected in the moulded capitals at Ashbourne, and this was probably the case in Lichfield transept clerestory bay S3E where octagonal moulded capitals sit on renewed *en délit* shafts (Pl. IXA). The round abacus is a consistent feature for the vast majority of the capitals in all three buildings.[68]

Croxden Abbey[69]

Although the apse–ambulatory plan with radiating chapels, the three-storey elevation and clustered piers of Croxden have nothing in common with Lichfield, many details in the two buildings are intimately related. The form of the stiff-leaf capitals in the south transept and Chapter House and on the east processional doorway with sharply delineated flat stems and sparse foliation at the top of the bell relates closely to the Lichfield crossing and transept capitals (Pls VIIC, XIIIC). In addition to the general family resemblances, particular reference should be made to the similarity between the deeply undercut upright trefoil leaves on Lichfield clerestory bay N2E south capital and the south-east angle vault capital of the south transept chapel at Croxden (Pls IXB, XIIID). In both places round abaci predominate and there is a distinct resemblance between the moulded capitals. The syncopated rhythm of the bases for the detached shafts of the east processional doorway at Croxden is analogous to the north and south transept doorways at Lichfield. Similarly the necking on the better preserved bases of this doorway at Croxden indicate that the shafts would have been fluted octagonal as in the upper storey of the Lichfield transepts. The façade of the Chapter House relates closely to Lichfield. The inner order of the entrance and side arches is carried in each case on a triple shaft group as in the Lichfield main arcades. Similarly, the mouldings of the Chapter House façade are cut in a relatively shallow manner for the 13th century and they have a profusion of fillets, the juxtaposition of which is closely related to Lichfield transept arcades bays N2E and N3E (Pls XD, XIIIC). Details of the west doorway at Croxden also relate to the Lichfield transepts; the moulded capitals are most closely paralleled with pier

E

SIV at Lichfield while the narrow rolls between the shafts develop from the quadrant rolls on Lichfield piers SII and SIII. The allegiance of the two monuments is secured with reference to the rebate for the wooden frame for the glass in the Croxden lancets, which is best preserved on the south jamb of the south window in the west wall of the south transept, and in the former choir clerestory lancets at Lichfield. It is in the context of the skeletal treatment of the former clerestory windows in the Lichfield choir and the lancets in the Chester Chapter House that the extreme height of the Croxden south transept and west front lancet windows must be seen. The steep trajectory of the vault springers in the south transept at Croxden is a feature that was probably employed in the Lichfield choir and transepts in order to maximise the scale of the side lancets of the clerestory. Furthermore, such trajectory relates closely to the vault of the Chester Chapter House.

These detail parallels speak of a close link between the Lichfield transepts, the Chester Chapter House and the Croxden workshops. There can be little doubt that at least some of the same personnel worked at all three places. But how are we to interpret the major differences of plan, elevation and pier form? If these elements are strictly dictated by the patron, then it may be argued that the master mason of Croxden was trained at Lichfield but that he conformed to the patron's desire for a French plan along with clustered piers which enjoyed such popularity in Cistercian churches in northern England. On the other hand, one may suggest that there was either a north English or a Norman master mason and that he employed skilled craftsmen who had worked nearby at Lichfield. Given the constructional parallels of window rebates and steep trajectories of high vaults, the evidence would seem to be in favour of a local master mason. However, at the present stage of research perhaps the question should remain open.

Unfortunately, the documentation relating to the building of Croxden does not allow for final clarification on the relative dating of Lichfield, Chester Chapter House and Croxden itself. There is reference to burial in the Chapter House at Croxden in 1229 and to work on the church and Chapter House, as well as other buildings, after 1242.[70] Given that the stiff-leaf capitals and other details of the Croxden Chapter House are closely related to the Lichfield transepts and the Chester Chapter House, the following chronology may be suggested: Lichfield transepts in the 1230s, Croxden Chapter House in the 1240s and Chester Chapter House in the 1250s. However, the same capital types are found in the south transept at Croxden, which was probably executed before the post-1242 building campaign, and this form was probably in use in the Lichfield transepts in the 1220s. It may therefore be argued that the Chester Chapter House can also be placed in the 1220s.

CONCLUSION

The Lichfield transepts are an excellent example of the richness and variations which are so characteristic of Early English Gothic design. While the precise chronology of the buildings allied to this work at Lichfield may be open to different interpretation, at least the affiliations speak clearly of a group of masons active in the diocese of Lichfield. Their work at Lichfield and in the Chester Chapter House is characterised by a daring skeletonisation of the upper elevation which finds further parallels in the choir of Pershore Abbey and in the east bay of the Lady Chapel and the outer bays of the east transepts at Worcester Cathedral. These designs are further allied through emphasis on the vertical, a verticality that is obvious not least in the tall lancet windows. Tall lancets are often associated with the northern school of Early English architecture, but it is clear that they are not confined to that school. Examination of this and other motifs in relation to the 'Lichfield Group' should provide an interesting area for future research.

ACKNOWLEDGEMENTS

Unlimited access to all parts of Lichfield Cathedral has been possible thanks to the kindness of Canon Graham Smallwood, Godfrey Hives (Head Verger), Christopher Craddock and Michael Sturgess (Vergers). Research for this article has been generously funded by the Social Sciences and Humanities Research Council of Canada.

REFERENCES

SHORTENED TITLES USED

BRAKSPEAR (1931) — Harold Brakspear, 'A West Country School of Masons', *Archaeologia*, LXXXI (1931), 1–18.
BRIEGER (1957) — Peter Brieger, *English Art 1216–1307* (Oxford 1957).
CLIFTON (1900) — A. B. Clifton, *The Cathedral Church of Lichfield*, 2nd revised edition (London 1900).
DUFTY (1963) — A. R. Dufty, 'Lichfield Cathedral', *Archaeol. J.*, CXX (1963), 293–95.
HOEY (1986a) — Lawrence Hoey, 'Pier Alternation in Early English Gothic Architecture', *JBAA*, CXXXIX (1986), 45–67.
HOEY (1986b) — Lawrence Hoey, 'The 13th-Century Transepts of York Minster', *Gesta*, XXV/2 (1986), 227–44.
HOEY (1987) — Lawrence Hoey, 'Piers versus vault shafts in Early English Gothic architecture', *JSAH*, XLVI (1987), 241–64.
JANSEN (1975) — Virginia Jansen, 'The Architecture of the Thirteenth-Century Rebuilding at St Werburgh's, Chester', unpublished PhD dissertation, University of California, Berkeley, 1975.
LYNAM (1911) — Charles Lynam, *The Abbey Church of St Mary, Croxden, Staffordshire* (London 1911).
MALONE (1973) — Carolyn Malone, 'West English Gothic Architecture 1175–1250', unpublished PhD dissertation, University of California, Berkeley, 1973.
MALONE (1984) — Carolyn Malone, 'Abbey Dore: English Versus French Design', *Studies in Cistercian Art and Architecture*, II (1984), 50–75.
MILBURN (1974) — Catherine Milburn, 'Pershore Abbey: The Thirteenth-Century Choir', *JBAA*, CXXXVII (1984), 130–44.
SAVAGE (1913–14) — H. E. Savage, 'The Architectural Story of Lichfield Cathedral', *TNSFC*, XLVIII (1913–14), 1–10.
STALLEY (1981) — Roger Stalley, 'Three Irish Buildings with West Country Origins', *BAA CT*, IV (1981).
STALLEY AND THURLBY (1974) — Roger Stalley and Malcolm Thurlby, 'A Note on the Architecture of Pershore Abbey', *JBAA*, CXXXVII (1974), 113–18.
STALLEY AND THURLBY (1989) — Roger Stalley and Malcolm Thurlby, 'The Early Gothic Choir of Pershore Abbey', *JSAH*, XLVIII (1989), 351–70.
THURLBY (1985) — Malcolm Thurlby, 'The Early Gothic Elevation of Lichfield Cathedral', *Transactions of the Third Canadian Conference of Medieval Art Historians* (London, Ontario 1985), 71–9.
THURLBY (1986) — Malcolm Thurlby, 'The North Transept Doorway of Lichfield Cathedral: Problems of Style', *RACAR*, XIII/2 (1986), 121–30.
WILLIS (1861) — Robert Willis, 'On Foundations of Early Buildings, Recently Discovered in Lichfield Cathedral', *Archaeol. J.*, XVIII (1861), 1–24, reprinted in *idem.*, *Architectural History of some English Cathedrals*, II (Chicheley 1973).
WILSON (1975) — Christopher Wilson, 'The Sources of the Late Twelfth-Century Work at Worcester Cathedral', *BAA CT*, I, 80–90.

1. H. Wharton, *Anglia Sacra* (London 1691), 439.
2. *Rotuli Litterarum Clausarum* (Rec. Comm.), I, ed. T. Hardy (London 1833), 465.
3. *Close Rolls*, 1227–31, 471.
4. *Close Rolls*, 1234–7, 103; 1237–42, 46.
5. H. M. Colvin (ed.), *The History of the Kings Works*, I (London 1963), 123, II, 868; *Close Rolls*, 1242–7, 39.
6. On the Perpendicular remodelling and the Victorian restorations see J. M. Maddison, 'Master masons of the diocese of Lichfield: a study in 14th-century architecture at the time of the Black Death', *Journal of the Lancs. and Cheshire Antiquarian Society*, 85 (1988), 161–5, and Richard Lockett's paper in this volume. On restoration in general see, *VCH Staffordshire*, III (1970), 175–6, 187–9, 193–5.

7. The two-storey elevation was suggested by Milburn (1984), 138–40; the three-storey scheme by Thurlby (1985), 71–9, fig. 44.

8. A. Hamilton Thompson, *Netley Abbey* (London, HMSO 1953).

9. The reconstruction of a triple-arched screen was originally suggested by Willis (1861), 11–12, and in this he was followed by Milburn (1984), 138–40. On Pershore choir, see Stalley and Thurlby (1974), 113–18; Milburn (1984), 130–44; and Stalley and Thurlby (1989), 351–70.

10. Stalley (1981), 71–5, pl. XVIIIA.

11. The inner plane of the equivalent bay in the north transept (N1E) preserves a similar amount of the Early English fabric, but because the organ is located in this bay it is more difficult to study than bay S1E.

12. The opposite bay on the west wall of the south transept (S1W) is similarly asymmetrical.

13. The stiff-leaf foliage on these corbels is 19th century. The shafts next to the crossing piers are arranged as a pair, while the next group forms a triplet. We may therefore conclude that the detached shafts at the ends of each bay of the Early English clerestory would have been paired while the intermediate shafts were triplets.

14. The fluted front shaft is also preserved in the opposite clerestory bay (S1W). In bay S3E the outer columns that carry the wall arch have moulded octagonal Early English capitals which suggests that the original 13th-century shafts would probably have been fluted octagonal. On this point see below, p. 59, for the discussion of the Ashbourne (Derbyshire) north transept windows.

15. On the design of the early Gothic choir see the paper by Warwick Rodwell in this volume.

16. Milburn (1984), 139–40, refers to round holes on the east and west edges of the north transept clerestorys (visible on Pl. IXB) which she equates with the location of the intermediate shaft groups in each bay. However, their location does not coincide with the openings in the back wall of the passage and it would appear that the holes have nothing to do with the 13th-century clerestory.

17. Milburn (1984), 138–40.

18. Milburn (1984), 138–40; Willis (1861).

19. In the north transept blocked clerestory passage openings occur on both the north and south splays of bays N2E and N3E. In the south transept they are present on the south splay of bays S1E and S1W. In all the other bays the masonry courses with the Perpendicular window jambs.

20. Thurlby (1985).

21. Canon J. G. Lonsdale, *Recollections of the work done in and upon Lichfield Cathedral from 1856 to 1894* (Lichfield 1895), quoted in Clifton (1900), 68. I should like to thank Canon Graham Smallwood for information on Lonsdale's original publication.

22. Brian Eacock, Clerk of Works at Worcester Cathedral, informs me that this 'temporary' wooden floor has occupied its present position for as long as he can remember. Similar openings to pseudo-passages also occur in the jambs of the main west window at Worksop Priory and Kelso Abbey.

23. For the elevation of the eastern transepts at Worcester, see Charles Wild, *An Illustration of the Architecture and Sculpture of the Cathedral Church of Worcester* (London 1823), pl. 8.

24. Willis (1861), 18.

25. The sculpture of the north transept doorway is discussed in detail in Thurlby (1986).

26. The buttresses on the two transepts are of different form, but those on the south transept date from Wyatt's restoration (1787–93).

27. On the north-east face of the north-west crossing pier coursed filleted shafts are used.

28. The central shaft on the south side of pier NIII is plain. This results in an asymmetrical design for the pier. However, symmetry is achieved with reference to the design of the bay in that the central shaft on the north of pier NII is plain but the central shaft on NIV is filleted. An analogous arrangement of bay symmetry, as opposed to pier symmetry, occurs in the nave of Castle Acre Priory (Bridget Cherry, 'Romanesque Architecture in Eastern England', *JBAA*, CXXXI (1978), 1–29, especially, 12–14, figs 6 and 7).

29. The south respond of the arch from the north transept to the north nave aisle has chamfered stones between the shafts, but on the north respond there are shallow shafts between the main shafts as on pier NIV.

30. The south end of the south bay is occupied by the doorway to the stair vice.

31. Milburn (1984), pl. XXXc.

32. Willis (1861) believed that the transepts followed the same general design but that the south transept was earlier than the north, dating them *c.* 1220 and *c.* 1240 respectively. He added that the latter belonged to the same work as the vestibule of the Chapter House and the Chapter House itself. Clifton ((1900), 6, 67–8) followed Willis's sequence but this was challenged by Savage ((1913–14), 3–4) who suggested that the construction of the north transept preceded the south. Brieger ((1957), 184) and Dufty ((1963), 294) both adhered to Willis's sequence and dates, while Pevsner (*B/E Staffordshire*, 177) saw the early Gothic fabric as a whole starting about 1220 with the transepts being constructed about 1230–40 with the south 'more likely to be a little earlier'.

33. The majority of the stiff-leaf capitals at Lichfield are of an unusual type in which the leaves grow to the side at the top of the capital and cling to the bell rather than growing into space to form pronounced crockets. There

are also examples of a more straightforward, simple crocket type, and one case of upright trefoil leaves in the clerestory of bay N2E (Pl. IXB).

34. Hoey (1986a), 61.

35. On Abbey Dore, see RCHM *Herefordshire SW*, 1–9; Malone (1984), 50–75; and the important remarks by Lawrence Hoey (1987), 259, n. 87–8. For Hexham, see C. C. Hodges and J. Gibson, *Hexham and its Abbey* (Hexham 1919). On York Minster, see Lawrence Hoey (1986b), 227–44. For Rochester, W. H. St John Hope, 'The Architectural History of the Cathedral Church and Monastery of St Andrew at Rochester', *Archaeologia Cantiana*, XXIII (1898), 194–328, especially 254–68. For New Shoreham, Edmund Sharpe, *The Architectural History of St Mary's Church, New Shoreham* (Chichester 1861).

36. In this connection see the important remarks by Lawrence Hoey (1986b), especially 232–3 and 239–40. Aesthetic variety in Early English Gothic architecture is presaged in many English Romanesque buildings; see Hoey (1986a), 45–7; Malcolm Thurlby and Yoshio Kusaba, 'The Nave of St Andrew at Steyning: A Case Study in Design Variety in 12th-century Architecture in Britain', *Gesta*, XXX/2 (1991), 163–75.

37. Brakspear (1931), 11.

38. Stalley (1981), 73.

39. Hoey (1986), 48.

40. The north nave arcade at Llanidloes (Powys) was re-erected from Cwm Hir Abbey. On Cwm Hir and Llanidloes see the *Royal Commission on the Ancient and Historical Monuments and Constructions in Wales and Monmouthshire*, III, *County of Radnor* (1913), 3–7; C. A. Ralegh Radford, 'The Cistercian Abbey of Cwm Hir, Radnorshire', *Archaeologia Cambrensis*, CXXXI (1982), 58–76.
    The intermediate piers of the Llanidloes north nave arcade use triple shaft groups throughout while the east and west responds have alternating single and triple shafts. Similarly, in the south arcade of Pershore choir piers with groups of triple shafts in the cardinal directions and larger single shafts on the diagonals alternate with a pier having triple shaft groups on all faces (Hoey (1986a), 48, pl. XVIIIA). Hoey (1987), 260, observes that 'Lichfield Cathedral choir, like Wells, has piers with eight groups of triple shafts, but unlike Wells they are arranged around a lozenge core, and the forward group originally rose up the choir wall'.

41. Ibid., 260–1 n. 96.

42. Brakspear (1931), 7.

43. The eastern arm of Pershore was probably commenced around 1220 (Stalley and Thurlby (1974), 113). The eastern arm at Worcester is precisely dated 1224–32 (Barrie Singleton, 'The Remodelling of the East End of Worcester Cathedral in the Earlier Part of the Thirteenth Century', *BAA CT*, I, 105–15, with further bibliography).

44. On Coventry, see *VCH Warwickshire*, III, 125–9; Brian Hobley, 'Excavations at the Cathedral and Benedictine Priory of St Mary, Coventry', *Transactions of the Birmingham and Warwickshire Archaeological Society*, 84 (1967–70), 45–139. Hobley's date of the second half of the 13th century for the west responds of the nave arcade seems too late (ibid., 91).

45. On Nuneaton, see *VCH Warwickshire*, II, 66–70; David Andrew *et al.*, 'The archaeology and topography of Nuneaton Priory', *Birmingham and Warwickshire Archaeological Society Transactions*, XCI (1981), 55–81.

46. Jansen (1975), 94, observes that 'Polygonal fluted shafts appear everywhere in the first work at Lincoln' — i.e. the early Gothic work commenced in 1192. She traces their use to the clerestory and west front at Selby, the clerestory at Beverley, to the north transept at Ashbourne and the transepts at Lichfield and finally to the Chester Chapter House. The Nuneaton polygonal fluted shafts would appear to pre-date St Hugh's choir at Lincoln and to be the direct influence on the Lichfield transepts and the related work at Ashbourne and in the Chester Chapter House.

47. It seems likely that the responds of the east crossing arch at Nuneaton should be dated in connection with the 1237 and 1238 gifts from the king of 10 and 15 oaks respectively (*Close Rolls*, 1234–7, 502; *Close Rolls*, 1237–42, 103).
    For further discussion of the jambs of the Lichfield north transept doorway see, Thurlby (1986), 128–9.

48. Brakspear (1931), 10, observes that 'the continuous roll moulding between the jamb shafts at Nuneaton and at Glastonbury is started directly off the plinth course without a stop of any kind, which is a trick of workmanship that must have been due to the same hand, as there is no logical reason why it should have been so treated'. However, the motif does occur elsewhere in the West Country, in the responds of the entrance arch to the Becket Chapel in the north transept at St David's Cathedral, in the north-east and south-east piers of Pershore Abbey choir and in the crossing piers of Margam Abbey (Stalley and Thurlby (1989), figs 4, 8, 15 and 16).

49. On Abbey Dore see Malone (1984), 50–75. On the west bays of Worcester nave see Wilson (1975); Malone (1973), 73–91; Hoey (1987), 259.

50. The piers of Worcester nave west bays are illustrated in Hoey (1987), fig. 25.

51. Brakspear (1931), 6–7.

52. Stalley and Thurlby (1989), fig. 15.

53. Harold Brakspear, in Mrs Hilary Jenkinson, *Some Account of St Mary's Priory, Nuneaton, and of the Restored Church* (London 1922), 27. The heads of the Merevale refectory buttresses are illustrated in *VCH Warwickshire*, IV (1947), 143.

54. On the Giant Order at Tewkesbury and its affiliations, see Richard Halsey, 'Tewkesbury Abbey: some recent observations', *BAA CT*, VII, 20–9. On Glastonbury Great Church, see Robert Willis, *The Architectural History of Glastonbury Abbey* (Cambridge 1866). For Waterford Cathedral, see Stalley (1981), 66–71.

55. On St David's, see E. W. Lovegrove, 'St Davids Cathedral', *Archaeologia Cambrensis*, LXXVI (1922), 360–82, which Lovegrove reworks and expands in 'The Cathedral Church of St Davids', *Archaeol. J.*, LXXXIII (1926), 255–83; on Llanthony, idem, 'Llanthony Priory, Monmouthshire', *Archaeologia Cambrensis*, XCIX (1946–7), 64–77. See also Virginia Jansen, 'Superposed Wall Passages and the Triforium Elevation of St Werburgh's, Chester', *JSAH*, XXXVIII (1979), 223–43; Thurlby (1985), 73–4.

56. Hoey (1986b), 239, figs 4 and 5.

57. These lancets may be seen as forerunners of those in the south transept and west front of Croxden Abbey.

58. Jansen (1975), 90–8. My thanks to Larry Hoey for this reference, and to Roger Stalley for first drawing my attention to Chester Chapter House in connection with the Lichfield transepts.

59. In contrast to the Lichfield transepts, a polygonal form is also used in the Chester Chapter House for the front shaft of the vault respond triplet.

60. I should like to thank Warwick Rodwell for pointing out the reuse of the 'transoms' in the Lichfield transept triforia.

61. William Dugdale, *Monasticon Anglicanum*, II (London 1819), 373.

62. Ibid.

63. Jansen (1975), 97–8. *B/E Cheshire*, 14, 137, also gives about 1250–60 for the date of the Chapter House. Charles Hiatt, *The Cathedral Church of Chester* (London 1898), 71, gives a date of 1240 for the Chapter House.

64. See below.

65. Jansen (1975), 92, 93, observes stylistic links between St Mary's, Shrewsbury, Chester Chapter House and the Lichfield transepts.

66. In the St Mary's, Shrewsbury, window the marble shafts and the 'transoms' linking the shafts to the back of the wall are 19th century.

67. Jansen (1975), 92, 93, 94, 95, 97. Ashbourne church was dedicated by Hugh Patteshull in 1241 (Thomas Rickman, *An attempt to discriminate the styles of Architecture in England, from the Conquest to the Reformation*, 7th edn (Oxford and London 1881), 170).

68. The mouldings of the east arcade of the Ashbourne north transept are closely related to Lichfield north transept bays N2E and N3E. Similarly the continuation of the fillet from the shafts to the capitals of the Ashbourne north transept piers is paralleled in the shafts and capitals supporting the soffit of Lichfield north transept bay N3E.

69. For a detailed discussion of Croxden Abbey, see the paper by Lawrence Hoey in this volume. See also, Lynam (1911), especially for documentation and illustrations. The plan of the east processional doorway on pl. 61 shows hexagonal fluted shafts. However, the evidence of the bases *in situ* indicates that they were of octagonal fluted form.

70. Thomas of Woodstock, the first abbot of Croxden, died on 4 December 1229, and was buried in the Chapter House (BL Cotton MS Faustina B VI, f. 73ᵛ, transcribed in Lynam (1911), iii). Walter London, the fifth abbot, took office in 1242. 'He wonderfully enlarged the convent of Croxden and the very beautiful buildings there, namely, gates of the monastery, the halves of the church, of the chapter house and of the frater. The kitchen, the dorter of the lay brothers, the infirmary and the cloisters thereof, the *probatorium*, and many other buildings, in his time he skilfully built, and these with other necessary offices 'he laudably furnished for his successor' (BL Cotton MS Faustina, B VI, f. 74ʳ; Lynam (1911), iii).

Building at Lichfield Cathedral during the Episcopate of Walter Langton (1296–1321)

By John Maddison

On the death in 1292 of Robert Burnell, Bishop of Bath and Wells and Chancellor of England, it was the Treasurer, Walter Langton, who assumed the mantle of the most trusted and influential counsellor of Edward I. Burnell is recognised as an important architectural patron of the late 13th century and his buildings at Wells — the Bishop's chapel and great hall, the chapter house staircase and undercroft — taken together with his church and fortified manor house at Acton Burnell, form one of the most coherent and interesting architectural sequences in the early Decorated style.[1] Can the buildings put up at Lichfield in the time of Walter Langton be granted a position of comparable eminence in the development of early 14th-century architecture? That this question has not so far been seriously addressed is no doubt attributable to the damaged and restored state in which the buildings have come down to us. Langton's great palace has been all but destroyed, and the vicissitudes of the Cathedral's post-Reformation history are described in other papers in this volume. But these factors have only partially obscured something which was, in its day, one of the most spectacular architectural compositions of medieval England; the mother church of a vast diocese and the palace of a great magnate.

Little is known of Langton's early origins. His date of birth is not recorded but the name by which we know him was a toponymic derived from the Leicestershire village in which he was born. His family name was Peverel.[2] In 1290 Langton appears in the royal accounts as a clerk of the king's Wardrobe. His rapid promotion from this time was probably due to his attachment to the service of Robert Burnell. In 1292 he became Keeper of the Wardrobe and on Burnell's death was given the custody of the Great Seal. Through the king's influence he began to acquire extensive lands and became a canon of Lichfield. In 1295 he was appointed Edward's Treasurer and on 20 February 1296 was elected Bishop of the See of Coventry, Lichfield and Chester.

Towards the end of his life Edward I made some powerful enemies and his growing unpopularity was soon to engulf the Treasurer who had, indeed, made numerous enemies of his own. In the early years of the new century there were repeated attempts to unseat Langton. In the Lincoln Parliament of 1301 the Barons, led by Archbishop Winchelsea, demanded his dismissal but the king refused. Shortly afterwards a series of weighty and in some instances bizarre charges were levelled against Langton by Sir John Lovetot. He was accused not only of living in adultery with Lovetot's stepmother but also of murdering his father. He was charged with pluralism, with simony and of paying homage to the devil. Langton was eventually cleared of these accusations but not before he had travelled to Rome to plead his cause with Boniface VIII. The papal absolution which he received in 1303 was by no means the end of the matter and Langton was to be beset by troubles for many years to come.[3]

THE BISHOP'S PALACE AND CLOSE FORTIFICATIONS

When Langton was summoned to Rome to answer the charges that were made against him the Dean and Chapter of Lichfield wrote a testimonial letter to the Pope denouncing the 'slanders' against their Bishop and emphasising his energy and generosity in the diocese. The letter includes a reference to his architectural projects:

A most notable service has been rendered by him to the Close of Lichfield which, with its ring of houses for the bishop and the greater part of the canons, extends to some length; and to the episcopal manors which had long ago fallen into decay; all of which he has repaired and fortified at a continual outlay which we believe could not have been covered by the revenues of the See which he has received since his appointment.[4]

In 1299 Langton had obtained licence to crenellate and the document describes how, in order to fortify his house and the houses of the canons in the Close of Lichfield Cathedral, Walter, Bishop of Coventry and Lichfield is licensed to enclose the area with a stone wall and that the said wall is to be crenellated.[5] This was not the first time that the Close had been fortified, but it is the earliest reference to building activity at Lichfield during Langton's episcopate. In addition to dating part of the curtain walls it probably also marks the start of work on the new episcopal palace, a building which formed an integral part of the north and east walls. Dr Tringham's article does much to illuminate the layout of the building, and in transcribing the building accounts of 1304–14 provides a detailed chronology of its completion. The accounts describe chiefly carpentry, plumbing, roofing, painting and a good deal of gardening implying, no doubt, that much of the masonry structure was complete by 1304. Master Walter the Carpenter appears to have been the senior craftsman at this stage but it is most possible that his work was preceded by that of a master mason who built the walls and towers between 1299 and 1304. This could have been Hugh de la Dale, the mason to whom Langton granted a tenement in Lichfield in 1307.[6]

The palace was severely damaged when the Close was twice besieged in the Civil War and eventually largely demolished. Only a small portion of it now remains above ground. We have to reconstruct its appearance from ancient descriptions and an annotated plan prepared by Henry Greswold in 1685 (see Tringham, p. 88, Fig. 1). It is clear from the plan that the palace, incorporated as it was with the walls and angle towers of the Close defences, must have presented a military aspect. More specifically its eastern wall standing over thirty feet high and articulated by polygonal towers, with the northern one standing at fifty-two feet was to all intents and purposes a castle. Fuller's *Church History of Britain* of 1648 described it as the 'invisible castle now vanished out of sight'.[7] Langton was part of the military culture of the reign of Edward I. This period, decisive for the development of what Thomas Rickman called the Decorated style was, so far as the king's masons were concerned, dominated by castle building.[8] When the first stones of Langton's palace were laid, Caernarvon and Beaumaris were half-built. The Lichfield diocese was the hinterland of Edward's conquest of the Welsh, and Chester, capital of the royal County Palatine at its northern end, was the chief marshalling point for the three campaigns of 1277, 1282 and 1294. So it is not surprising that this fortified palace, in its relationship to the Close as a whole, finds parallels in the fortified towns which Edward I laid out in North Wales. At Caernarvon in particular, begun in 1283, the south curtain of the castle forms part of a continuous *enceinte* with the town walls in a manner directly comparable to the Lichfield palace. Langton was not the only bishop to build in this way at the end of the century, for in 1287 Bishop Thomas Bek of St David's had walled his close and incorporated a fortified palace. But Langton's residence made deliberate use of a vocabulary which had been employed by Edward at Caernarvon to create the image of the castle as the palace of the Prince of Wales. Dr A. J. Taylor has shown that the polygonal towers of Caernarvon, which set it apart from most of the other royal castles in Wales, were not only carefully copied from the land walls of the imperial city of Constantinople, but were also intended to convey the

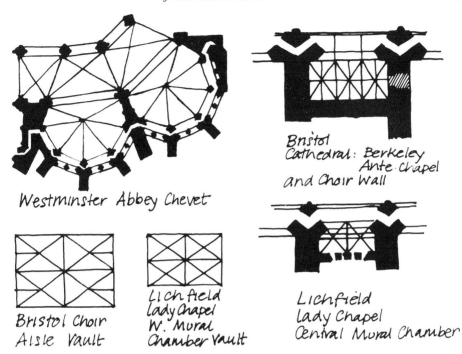

Westminster Abbey Chevet

Bristol Cathedral: Berkeley Ante-Chapel and Choir Wall

Bristol Choir Aisle Vault

Lichfield Lady Chapel W. Mural Chamber Vault

Lichfield Lady Chapel Central Mural Chamber

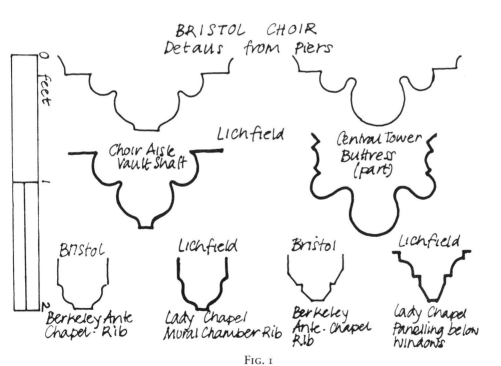

BRISTOL CHOIR
Details from Piers

feet

Choir Aisle Vault Shaft

LICHFIELD

Central Tower Buttress (part)

Bristol

Lichfield

Bristol

Lichfield

Berkeley Ante Chapel: Rib

Lady Chapel Mural Chamber Rib

Berkeley Ante. Chapel Rib

Lady Chapel Panelling below Windows

FIG. I

idea of a palace.[9] This distinction was acknowledged by the master of the king's works in Wales, James of St George, in the palace of Edward's vassal, Count Philip of Savoy, at St-Georges-d'Esperanche. This building was similarly marked out by its polygonal towers from the other castles which Master James built for the count prior to his employment in Wales and was referred to in the Court Rolls of Savoy as 'palacium'.[10]

That the Lichfield palace was in a real sense a record of Langton's association with the Edwardian achievement in Wales and Scotland is confirmed not only by surviving architectural evidence but also by Samson Erdswick's description of its mural decoration in 1603, quoted in full by Dr Tringham.[11] Langton had covered his walls with a cycle depicting the main events in the life of Edward I, including scenes from the wars in Wales and Scotland. Erdswick could make out the figures of knights and nobles engaged in combat in Wales: 'Roger de Pewlesdon..., Almaric de Balgioll, Burnell, Valence Earl of Pembroke' and others including 'the Lord Badlesmere' fighting the Scots.

The lower parts of the Close walls which bounded the north and east sides of the palace remain intact, and the most impressive survival of Langton's residence above ground — for certainly much of interest awaits excavation — is the lower part of the north-east angle tower which we know to have been the principal vertical accent in the silhouette. It stands now at less than half its height and is at the time of writing completely concealed by plant growth. Externally, however, the soft sandstone has for the most part been faced with brickwork (Pl. XIVA). It is octagonal and contains, at ground level, a vaulted octagonal chamber (Pl. XIVB). The vault is domical and of a type that is not common in Britain. Such vaults are frequently found in Byzantine architecture, and the fact that there are several at Caernarvon castle, in the Eagle Tower and the Cistern Tower, is wholly consistent with the more striking neo-Byzantine elements which Dr Taylor has already identified there.

Design elements of the palace were reciprocated in the Close walls themselves. Small polygonal turrets formed the south-east and south-west corners, where they were incorporated with two houses built by Langton, and there were other substantial mural towers, one of which, at the north-west corner, was once embellished with a statue of Langton. Moreover the recent excavation of the lower walls of the south-east gate show it to have been a powerful structure of twin semi-octagonal towers rising from a battered plinth. This building was, like the Lady Chapel, unfinished at the bishop's death in 1321 and the king ordered the completion of its western tower in 1322.[11]

ECCLESHALL CASTLE

The letter written by the Dean and Chapter to Boniface VIII stated that Langton had repaired and fortified the episcopal manors. This may mean that by 1299 Langton had begun to rebuild Eccleshall castle, the rural seat of the bishops of Lichfield, first built by Bishop Muschamp in about 1200. Camden's *Britannia*[12] relates that the castle was built by Langton in 1310 and the few remaining masonry details accord reasonably well with such a date, suggesting, by analogy with the Lady Chapel and choir of the Cathedral, that it was not being completed until 1315–21 (Fig. 3). There is no record of a licence to crenellate. The castle was slighted in the Civil War and this reduced it to the state indicated in a plan and elevations which were drawn up in 1687 (Pls XVB and XVC).[13] The castle was a rectangle — longest on its east–west axis — whose corners were marked by nine-sided towers (Pl. XVA). Surrounded by a moat, it was entered in the middle of the south front by a stone bridge which survives. Langton's apartments appear to have been ranged along the east front as at Lichfield.

The 1687 drawings show this front in plan and elevation. They present some difficulties of interpretation. For example it appears that the north-east tower was more dilapidated then than now, whereas the east curtain, penetrated by the windows of the principal apartments, has largely vanished. The most likely explanation is that when the present house was built by Bishop Lloyd, in about 1695, the east curtain was pulled down to form a terrace and open up the view, whereas the ruins of the north-east tower were consolidated to form a safe garden ornament. Parts of the stump of the south-east tower can also be discerned today. The elevations suggest, from the disposition of the windows, that all the principal rooms were at first-floor level above an undercroft, as was the case at Lichfield. The largest of the several substantial windows of the east front is that of the chapel and next to it is much smaller opening which, according to the plan, lit a small space contrived in the thickness of the wall. This could simply be a garderobe but could also have been a private pew of the type which was built next to the royal castle chapels at Conway and Beaumaris, perhaps another architectural expression of Langton's princely lifestyle.

The surviving tower at the north-east corner (Pl. XVA) has small windows rather than arrow loops and this feature, in conjunction with the large windows of the east front, shows how closely this building was allied in concept to many of the grander houses of the late 13th and early 14th centuries as a defensible manor rather than a castle. The military dress is usually fastidiously applied to make a good show and these martial flourishes are of course found at Acton Burnell (licence to crenellate 1284) where, in spite of the heroic four-towered silhouette, the large hall windows were vulnerable to attack. This was a period when several of the basic characteristics of the late medieval house in England were formulated. Just as Acton Burnell is one of the earliest tower houses, so Eccleshall is an early instance of the quadrangular, lightly fortified and moated residence of which Maxstoke in Warwickshire (licence to crenellate 1346) is the best preserved example. For Langton the polygonal towers of Eccleshall were probably intended to suggest high status and the whole plan is powerfully redolent of St-Georges-d'Esperanche.[14]

Langton was part-way through the construction of his great citadel around the Cathedral at Lichfield when the king's death brought about an abrupt change in his fortunes. Edward died in 1307 on a visit to the Scottish borders. The Treasurer's enemies, who included the new king, now had their chance to make redress. Langton accompanied Edward's cortège on part of its journey to London but left it at Waltham in order to hurry to Westminster to make arrangements for the funeral. He was intercepted by the servants of Edward II and arrested. Langton had never troubled to conceal his disapproval of the Prince of Wales while his father lived; he had been openly critical of his extravagance and of his association with Piers Gaveston. As a money lender he had antagonised a large group of significant and now potentially dangerous figures in both the spiritual and temporal spheres. Between 1307 and 1312 Langton therefore found himself under simultaneous investigation by the Exchequer and the Justices. The records of his trial are one of the best accounts we have of the dealings and interests of a great public official during this period.[15] Langton had clearly amassed a vast fortune, and the Chronicle of Walter of Guisborough records that he had lands worth 5,000 marks annually and treasure amounting to '50,000 librarum argenti preter aurum multum iocalia et lapides preciosos'.[16]

In the year of his arrest Langton's temporalities were seized and he was put under the personal charge of Gaveston, who went out of his way to insure the former Treasurer's discomfort and inconvenience. He was freed in 1308 by the protests of the new Pope, Clement V, but further accusations were made in 1309 and by 1311 he was again under arrest. He was finally released in 1312, his temporalities were returned and he was restored to the office of Treasurer to enable Edward II to resist the Ordainers who eventually, in

1315, managed to engineer Langton's dismissal from the Council. It was from this moment that Langton was able to turn his attention fully to the administration of the diocese. Even though he was reinstated to the Council of 1317/18 it is evident that he was no longer the dominant figure of earlier days. The remaining three years of his life were to be spent in relative tranquillity. These details of Langton's career form an historical backdrop to the building work at Lichfield and are a framework to which various elements of the Cathedral may bear some relation.

Langton left money for the continuation of the Lady Chapel on his death in 1321 and, while there is no documentary evidence for his involvement in other parts of the building, the architecture provides overwhelming evidence of sustained building activity in several different areas during the last twenty years of his life. The fact that only the Lady Chapel was mentioned in Langton's will does not preclude the possibility that other elements of the building benefited from his support if, as seems possible, these other projects were already complete by the time of his death. Discussion must, however, begin with the Lady Chapel and those parts of the choir which were evidently built as part of the same campaign.

THE REMODELLING OF THE CHOIR AND THE BUILDING OF THE LADY CHAPEL

The relevant clauses of Langton's will are as follows:

In primis lego animam meam deo et corpus meum ad sepeliendum in ecclesia cathedrali Lichfeldensis in novo opere ubi ordinavi.

Item lego ad continuacionem novi operis capelle beate Marie Lichfeldensis omnes florenos meos et omnia vasa mea aurea et argentea que ibidem habeo insuper et omnia vasa mea inclusa in quodam coffro existente apud Eccleshale in camera constabularii castri ultra portam sub custodia prioris de Routon qui habet unam clavem eiusdem coffri et Henrici de Crassewell qui habet aliam clavem.

Et volo quod Decanus et Capitulum Lichfeldensis habeant custodiam omnium florenorum et vasorum predictorum tam eorum que sunt Lichfeld quam eorum que sunt apud Eccleshale. Ita quod nec executores nec Decanus nec Capitulum Lichfeldensis habeant potestatem convertendi eo in alios usus quam in opus predictum sed executores mei de dictus bonis ministrent stipendia operariis dicte capelle et alias expensas pro eadem per visum et consilium dictorum Decani et Capituli.[17]

So Langton stipulated that neither his executors nor the Dean and Chapter could divert these funds to any use other than the said work. But in this his wishes were thwarted by Edward II, who in 1322 made the Dean and Chapter lend him £604 13s. 4d. which is said to have been the entire sum reserved for the Lady Chapel, as well as an additional £257 19s. 11d. from the Chapter funds, loans which were not repaid for half a century.[18]

Langton may have formulated the idea of rebuilding the eastern arm of the Cathedral several years earlier when he ordered, at considerable personal expense, a new shrine for the bones of St Chad. When he was arrested in 1307 his financial affairs had become the subject of a far-reaching investigation by the Exchequer. The books of his bankers, the Ballardi of Lucca, were called in for inspection and it emerged that they were accountable for a considerable amount of his fortune — some £2,120 18s. 2¼d. Against this figure, however, the Ballardi claimed allowance for the shrine of St Chad which Langton had ordered in Paris and for which they had already paid.[19] They did not specify the actual cost of the reliquary but the Lichfield Muniment Inventory of 1345 estimates its value at £2,000.[20]

The shrine cannot have been begun before 1303 because the testimonial letter which the chapter sent to the Pope in that year does not mention it, but was presumably finished by 1307/8 when the Ballardi cited it against their liabilities.

In the early years of the 14th century the choir was a largely 12th-century, seven-bay, aisled structure. The details of its plan were discovered by Willis in 1861 and it is described in Dr Rodwell's article.[21] By about 1350 most of this work had been rebuilt and this was accomplished in two principal phases, the first initiated by Langton before 1321 and the second directed by the royal mason, William Ramsey, between 1337 and 1349.[22]

The work set in hand by Langton can be distinguished from other phases through the occurrence of moulding profiles which resemble those used in the Lady Chapel (Fig. 2). These suggest that in addition to the chapel itself, Langton's mason built the eastern responds and the choir aisle walls back to the fourth bay on the south side and the third bay on the north. The piers and the upper levels of the work are almost entirely of Ramsey's period, but it seems that he followed a scheme proposed by Langton's master in all but the details. The piers, for example, copy the section of the western responds and the same is true of the arch mouldings. The fact that the eastern jamb of the eastern clerestory windows is part of the Lady Chapel build implies that the organisation of the upper elevation had also been generally determined before Ramsey's arrival.

Langton's work extended the whole choir by one narrow bay while the Lady Chapel continued the central vessel for three more full bays before closing it in a semi-octagonal apse (Pl. XVIA). Some of the dimensions of the remodelling were fixed by the earlier work. The aisles, for instance, are of the same volume as the early Gothic bays further west.

The new choir elevation was in two storeys with a passage along the clerestory window-sills, protected by an openwork parapet of interlocked pointed trefoils. The pitch of the aisle roofs necessitated a zone of blank wall beneath the clerestory windows and this is decorated with vertical panelling. The arcade piers are short and thick, corresponding in height and mass to the surviving supports of the early Gothic choir. The early 14th-century aisles have simple, continuously moulded wall arcades with well carved heads and foliage in the spandrels.

The elevation of the Lady Chapel is accomplished in one great vertical sweep of glass and stone. It is a design of great beauty, richly decorated at dado level by a wall arcade of nodding ogee arches beneath a parapet of the type used in the choir clerestory (Pl. XVIB). The parapet guards one side of a wall passage which cuts through the deep reveals of the windows. Immediately above this level the vault shafts blossom into dense foliated corbels supporting tabernacles which once held statues of the Wise and Foolish Virgins.[23] The vault is a tierceron design which appears, in its main lines, to be inspired by that of the nave.

The Cathedral is built on a south-facing slope whose angle of incline is steepest at the east end. On the exterior, therefore, the south walls of the choir and Lady Chapel are considerably taller than those on the north. The chapel vault needed deep buttresses, and the steep incline meant that on the south side the mason was able to accommodate a two-storey addition between them. This included a small crypt which runs the length of the flank, piercing the footings of the buttresses and roofed by a pointed tunnel vault. Built on top of this are three vaulted chambers expressed externally, it seems, as gabled tombs. Their roofs are formed by a solid stone slope which runs down from the sills on the main chapel windows like the *glacis* at the foot of a castle wall. All three chambers were much altered externally in J. Oldrid Scott's restoration of 1879 when the large middle one was converted to a memorial chapel for Bishop Selwyn. The elaborate cusping of the gables, the blank tracery, ballflower and heraldry all date from this time. Originally they were much plainer, as the drawings of Buckler and Mackenzie testify (Pl. XVIC).[24] The eastern chamber was in fact a porch. The original purpose of the vaulted chambers is open to question. It is possible that they may have been sacristies, but we have already seen that Langton may have incorporated a private pew in an analogous position next to the castle chapel at Eccleshall.

The Ste Chapelle in Paris (Pl. XVIIA) which was probably the key source for the Lady Chapel's design, has deep recesses in its dado to north and south which are similar in scale and which, it is thought, were built as royal pews. But a tomb function is also likely at Lichfield and the general design appears to have been inspired by earlier external tombs at the Cathedral, notably Dean Mancetter's monument on the south wall of St Chad's Head Chapel and the 13th-century gabled tomb fitted between the buttresses of the south transept (Pl. XXIII).

The choir aisles are, by contrast with the chapel, low and compact. Their eastern angles have the strongly projecting buttresses of the Lady Chapel, but the rest are simpler and smaller. The windows are small three-light compositions with two different tracery patterns above which the aisle parapets are formed of pierced trefoils.

Some of the tracery patterns in the eastern arm are Victorian designs, but the three windows of the Lady Chapel apse may be relied on so far as the design is concerned, and so may all the choir aisle windows, with the exception of the window in the fourth bay of the north aisle. The latter may possibly have once contained tracery of Ramsey's period because the wall beneath is his work. For the easternmost windows on the flanks of the Lady Chapel Scott copied the tracery of the apse, but the two westernmost windows are entirely his inventions. The former tracery of these windows was such a curious mixture of Perpendicular and Decorated forms as to suggest that it was in part at least an early restoration.

There can be little doubt that Langton's chapel was deliberately modelled on Louis IX's Ste Chapelle (1243–8). The tall narrow proportions, the deep buttresses and the polygonal east end were the critical elements for later emulators of this famous building. Lichfield also adopted the internal sculpture tabernacles of the Ste Chapelle and in the apse windows displayed a simplified version of its trefoil tracery. Although there are many English buildings whose design can be related to French Rayonnant of the mid-13th century and several Lady Chapels with polygonal ends, it is notable that there is perhaps no building in Europe which refers to the Ste Chapelle in such a direct and literal fashion as Langton's Lady Chapel. An English building of this period looking back to a French church built nearly seventy years earlier raises some interesting questions. Was Langton fulfilling a plan of Bishop Meuland (1257–95) to complete the choir in a way that would be consistent with the architecture of the nave?

When Langton was elected bishop in 1296 the new nave (Pl. XVIIB) had only recently been completed.[25] It is one of the best buildings of its period. The internal elevation is a successful cross-breed of Westminster Abbey (1245–69) and Lincoln Angel choir. Its rather thickset proportions were determined by an evident desire to conform with the clustered piers of the old choir. The Angel Choir may have provided the overall framework and some of the details, notably the manner in which the ornament is organised in the mouldings of the upper elevation, as well as the trefoils and cinqefoils in the spandrels of the nave arcade which can be related directly to Lincoln's wall arcades.[26] There is no doubt that Bishop Meuland, in whose episcopate (1257–95) the nave was commenced, knew Henry III's Westminster Abbey and shared his uncle the king's interest in French architecture. The spheric triangular windows of the Lichfield clerestory were used in the upper levels of Westminster Abbey, conceivably in imitation of the remodelled galleries of the nave of Notre Dame at Paris, or of the Ste Chapelle in which they were the most striking feature of the crypt. Langton's Lady Chapel, particularly when viewed from the midst of the Rayonnant nave, with its polygonal apse and, in silhouette, the piled-up trefoil tracery of its windows, contributes to an impression of wholeness and consistency that belies the building history of the Cathedral. But even if it is not beyond the bounds of possibility that the plan to build a Rayonnant east end was projected by Meuland and executed by Langton, it has also to be acknowledged that Langton may have had his own reasons for the adoption of the Ste Chapelle as the prototype for the Lady Chapel.

Langton's new shrine for Chad was ultimately to stand right in the centre of the area rebuilt and extended during his episcopate. Willis discovered what he supposed to be the foundations of the feretory in the eastern bay of the choir.[27] If it was Langton's intention that the shrine should stand at the mouth of the Lady Chapel, the architecture of the chapel gave him an opportunity to symbolise the enshrining function of the whole east end. The Ste Chapelle, built to house the Crown of Thorns, introduced a new type into the iconography of medieval architecture, the shrine church designed as though it were a giant reliquary. It was this aspect of the building which seems to have had a profound effect on the design of Westminster Abbey as the reliquary of St Edward writ large, and when Edward I began the new chapel of St Stephen at Westminster in 1292 it was, once more, the Ste Chapelle that provided the general model for the two-storey royal chapel. Langton, whose diplomatic missions for Edward I took him all over Europe, was familiar with Paris; we know that he paid for his two nephews to be educated there and, more significantly in the present context, that he had commissioned the shrine of St Chad from Parisian goldsmiths.[28] It is a fair assumption then that the form and decoration of the new Lady Chapel at Lichfield was intended to express the idea of great relics lying within the east end of the Cathedral.

The studious reference to a famous, if slightly out-of-date, prototype is only part of the story. The new east end also fits firmly into the picture of architectural design in early 14th-century England. We would expect that a new building connected with the patronage of one of the king's ministers would bear some relation to the architectural taste of the court. At Lichfield the range of decorative motifs connects almost exclusively to the court milieu and closely related buildings in Kent, East Anglia and elsewhere, some of which are associated with the Canterbury family of masons who were involved in the design of the Eleanor Crosses and of St Stephen's Chapel.[29]

First of all it is clear that there is a relationship between Lichfield and the internal elevation design of St Stephen's Chapel where the wall arcade of nodding ogees, combined with an openwork parapet also appears,[30] and where the ratio of wall to window is broadly similar. The walls of the upper chapel at St Stephen's were not begun until 1320. The gatehouse of St Augustine's Abbey, Canterbury (1301–9) has one of the first English instances of the zigzag parapet of interlocking trefoils found at Lichfield.[31] It would also be reasonable to compare the Lady Chapel's external parapet, a decorative and panelled form of crenellation, with the similar but earlier feature on the Canterbury gatehouse where the decorative motifs are inverted. The external parapet of the choir aisles (Pl. XVID) is also found earlier as the cresting of Prior Eastry's screen in the choir of Canterbury Cathedral (1304–5). The mouldings tell the same story (Fig. 2). The Lady Chapel window mullions have the same section as the Kentish traceried windows in the north arm of the cloisters at Westminster Abbey and the widespread use of the fleur-de-lis moulding at Lichfield surely has its origin in the repetition of the motif in the abbey and its cloister. East Anglia and particularly Norwich have also to be mentioned in any discussion of the court style around 1300, so the appearance at Norwich Cathedral of very similar profiles in the new east cloister arm in 1297 is to be expected, and it should also be noted that the tracery pattern of the early Norwich cloister windows is the closest surviving precursor of the fish-scale design used in the Lichfield aisles.

The choir of St Augustine's Bristol has a particularly interesting and perhaps unexpected kinship with the Lichfield work. This revolutionary design, begun perhaps as early as 1298, was the dynastic mausoleum of the Berkeleys, a military family closely connected with the court of Edward I. The building, which was sufficiently advanced in 1309 to accommodate

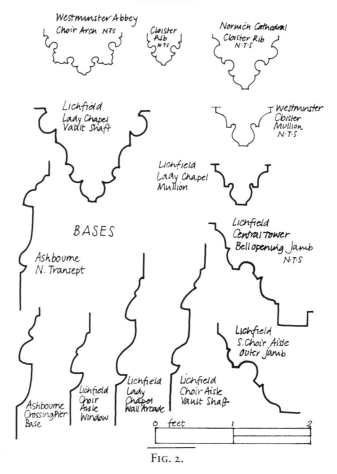

FIG. 2.

a burial in an arch in the south aisle wall, makes much use of the repertory of court ornament. It is not difficult to find many points of comparison with the Eleanor crosses, St Stephen's Chapel and Kentish early Decorated buildings. There is much heraldry, and military references are found in some of the ornament and in the severe face which Bristol choir presents to the outside world, an exterior of plain surfaces, powerful, slab-like buttresses and a silhouette of simple crenellation.

One could not pretend that Lichfield displayed the spatial ingenuity of Bristol or its sophisticated manipulation of rich ornament and austere surfaces. On the other hand the Lichfield design was formed by the shape of the building which it had to extend and it is argued that its repertory of ornament was to some extent governed by its architectural iconography as the shrine of Chad. There are, however, some important underlying points of comparison. The first is the way, in both buildings, that the Lady Chapel continues the main volume of the choir. Worcester and Beverley provide 13th-century antecedents, but the usual practice was to treat the Lady Chapel as a separate building entered through a low arch or retrochoir (e.g. Westminster, Tewkesbury, St Albans, Wells, Gloucester, Chester and Chichester). More significantly, however, is the similarity in the structure of the walls at

Lichfield and Bristol. This is one of the places where the Lichfield work departs significantly from the Ste Chapelle, for there is in Langton's chapel a wall passage at window-sill level. In possessing this feature Lichfield is closer to the western choir of Naumberg (c. 1250), itself possibly a derivative of the Ste Chapelle but more probably a scion of earlier Rayonnant buildings like Reims where such a passage was used in the chevet chapels (1211–20). The Reims wall passage was reproduced in the new east end at Westminster Abbey (1245–69) and this is probably why it came to be used at both Lichfield and Bristol (Fig. 1). When viewed in plan and compared with Lichfield, however, the Bristol choir walls reveal further analogies. The buttresses of both buildings are very deep and project into the interior as wedge-shaped wall masses. Where the wall passage runs through them, it is directed into the core of the buttress at an oblique angle before it re-emerges to pursue its normal course. This eccentricity which had no structural purpose at Lichfield or Bristol is probably derived from the Westminster chevet chapels where the oblique angles of their octagonal plans required it.

The second bay of Bristol choir holds between its southern buttresses a small, rectangular vaulted space which serves as the entrance and antechapel to the Berkeley family chantry and is very similar in scale and shape to the small vaulted chambers which are lodged between the buttresses at Lichfield. The vault of the Berkeley antechapel is remarkable for its early use of skeletal ribs, but if this extraordinary feature is set on one side, one can note that the main rib profile is the same in both buildings, and it must be of some significance that the vault of one of the chambers at Lichfield has a similar pattern to the vaults of the Bristol aisles. In the context of these important relationships in structure and planning, it is possible to pick out other key details at Lichfield which have their counterparts at Bristol. First of all there is a significant similarity between the nodding ogee wall arcades of the Lichfield Lady Chapel and the ogeed canopy of the niche in the Berkeley antechapel. Perhaps more interesting is the appearance in the Lichfield choir aisle vault shafts of the feature which helps to make the Bristol choir pier bases some of the most advanced of their kind in Europe (Pl. XVIIc, D).[32] This is the way in which the largest of the pier mouldings at Bristol are allowed to die into the sloping plinth. Dying profiles are common in the 13th century, but not in bases where horizontal mouldings were part of the canon inherited from antiquity. The same feature appears on a more modest scale in the aisle wall arcades at Lichfield and the application is strikingly similar, especially in the context of the continuous mouldings which form the arcade.

Langton would have known the Berkeleys; Thomas Lord Berkeley, whose military career in Wales and Scotland could well have assured him of a place in the wall paintings of the Bishop's palace, took the trouble to present an important jewel to Langton's new shrine for St Chad.[33] The relationship between the buildings is neither coincidental nor simply the expression of a kind of general period style. These are buildings which shed light on one another and which need to be considered together. First of all it is evident that the Berkeleys' militarisation of ecclesiastical architecture at Bristol belongs to the same climate of thought as Langton's patronage, in which secular and religious motifs are intermingled. We shall see in due course that the decorative crenellation of the Lady Chapel was originally repeated in more severe form in the crossing tower at Lichfield, and it has to be remembered that the whole east end was once girded round by the embattled walls and towers of the Close. Lichfield also usefully illuminates the controversy which must surround the extraordinary structural system of the hall choir of Bristol; the transfer of the thrust of the central vault to the buttresses by means of flying bridges in the aisles. These devices have their counterparts in a number of 13th- and 14th-century aisled barns and in timber halls like Nurstead Court. Jean Bony has also found a far-flung but impressive structural predecessor in the Franciscan

F

hall church of St Fortunato at Todi which was begun six years before Bristol.[34] It is, however, also acknowledged that the lower chapel of the Ste Chapelle has a miniature version of the aisle bridge complete with the pierced spandrels that are such a distinctive feature of the Bristol scheme. But could this small and ornamental feature in Paris really be regarded as a significant source for the spatial excitements of Bristol? Lichfield Lady Chapel, with its heavy dependence on the upper chapel of St Louis's famous shrine church, is another part of the Bristol story and provides powerful circumstantial evidence that the details of this mid-13th-century French building did help to give birth to the Bristol idea.

The exact dating of the Lady Chapel and the new choir bays is less than certain. They were unfinished in 1321, but when were they started and where do they fit into the general building chronology of the Cathedral? The completion of the nave and the lower part of the west front in the late 13th century meant that in the early 14th century there was still much to do at the west end of the Cathedral as well, and then there is the question of how to date the crossing tower and spire. Some of these issues need to be tackled before a closer dating of the Lady Chapel design can be attempted.

THE CROSSING TOWER

That the building of the crossing tower was concurrent with the remodelling of the east end, and was designed by the same master, is suggested by its details (Fig. 2) and perhaps corroborated by its close relationship with the crossing tower and spire of Ashbourne. The crossing tower (Pl. XVIIIa) is a relatively low structure which originally rose but one full storey above the crests of the surrounding roofs. Its square plan is augmented at the corners by polygonal stair turrets, abutted in their lower parts by blade-like, semi-hexagonal buttresses which continue the main axes of the tower walls and invest the whole with an impression of pyramidal stability. The repeated use of vertical mouldings on the buttresses and of miniature buttresses on the faces of the tower counterbalances the horizontality of the design and, with the four strong pinnacles at the corners, gives the building a powerful vertical drive which culminates in the spire. The upper parts of the tower and the spire itself have undergone some changes since the Middle Ages. The spire was knocked down in the Civil War but was rebuilt by Bishop Hacket in the 1660s, and the parapet which is now decorated with blind arcading was, before the Victorian restoration, plain and crenellated. For most of its height Hacket's spire is obviously 17th century, but at the base a certain amount of medieval masonry was retained, and the lowest lucarnes are clearly contemporary with the body of the tower. We can assume that the spire was part of the main tower build and not a later addition because of the interesting comparison furnished by the tower and the spire of Ashbourne (Pl. XVIIIb).

The crossing tower and spire of this large and important Derbyshire parish church combine, in one structure, the details of the Lichfield choir aisles, crossing tower and Eccleshall castle (Figs 2, 3). It is probably an exactly contemporary building, and may have been designed by the master mason of the new choir and Lady Chapel at Lichfield. The spire strings are very similar to those at the base of the Lichfield crossing spire; the parapet used is that of the Lichfield aisles; the arches of the wall passage around the crossing at Ashbourne are found at Eccleshall; and the solitary pier in Ashbourne north transept — evidently contemporary with the building of the tower — is made up of elements similar to the Cathedral's choir aisle vault shafts (Fig. 3).

Ashbourne seems to imply that the choir and crossing tower at Lichfield are contemporaries, and once this is accepted it is possible to pick up other affinities between these two major projects at the Cathedral. For example, each face of the Lichfield crossing tower has small

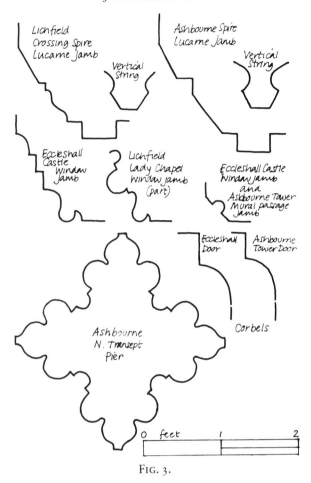

FIG. 3.

two-light windows flanked by narrow bays of blank Y-tracery. It is likely that this scheme was inspired by the original treatment of the north transept west elevation where, at ground level, mid-13th-century blank Y-tracery once flanked lancet windows (Pl. XIB). This tendency to incorporate and adapt elements from the 13th-century Cathedral is also apparent in the Lady Chapel where, as we have seen, the gabled forms of the south Lady Chapel wall are evidently inspired by 13th-century tombs. It has already been noted that the tower once had a plain crenellated parapet, so, like the Lady Chapel and the choir of St Augustine's Bristol, it made some reference to military architecture and in so doing played its part in reinforcing the embattled character of the Cathedral and its Close. In this connection it is interesting that the tracery of the tower windows can be found again in a military context in the king's works which provides very useful corroborative evidence of date.

The simple but distinctive quatrefoil pattern with enlarged side lobes, which also occurs in a window in one of the little chambers on the south side of the Lady Chapel, is precisely that which was used throughout the north curtain of Caernarvon castle in the early 14th century. Some of the main elements of the King's Gate at Caernarvon (Pl. XVIIIc), which has several of these windows, were nearing completion between March and April of 1320 and the master mason at this time was Henry Ellerton, who had been hard at work on the completion of the Eagle Tower since 1316.[35] Profiles suggest that the King's Gate was probably contemporary with the later work of the Eagle Tower and that its traceried windows can probably be dated between c.1316 and c.1320. Henry Ellerton's chantry chapel at Caernarvon, for which he obtained a licence in 1303 retains, despite extensive alterations, a window whose tracery is similar to the vesica pattern that occurs in the Lichfield choir aisles and is probably connected with a glazing date of 1316.[36]

THE WEST FRONT AND ITS TOWERS

The west end of Lichfield (Pl. XXIIA) is singular among 13th-century fronts in eschewing any significant form of relief. It would have been easy to provide additional articulation with buttresses as at Wells, or to have projected the porches as they did at Salisbury. Instead, the mason of the 13th-century nave thickened the terminal wall to provide the necessary abutment and gave himself a large flat surface which he could decorate with blank tracery and statue niches, finished at either end with a pair of substantial octagonal stair turrets. If the Angel Choir at Lincoln is to be regarded as the immediate forerunner of the nave then it is probable that the Gothic screen walls of the Lincoln west front provided the idea for the octagonal turrets and the rows of sculpture tabernacles which cover the Lichfield front.[37] There is no significant differentiation in the application of the decoration to walls or turrets and the portals are introduced with little ceremony. Even the great west door with its trumeau and figure sculpture retires modestly in the depth of the wall behind a cusped arch. Bishop Meuland's mason can only have reached the third string course which runs above the fourth tier of statues before the work came to a halt. Neither did he manage to construct a west window. This task, together with the raising of the central gable and the construction of the two towers and spires, was left to later hands. All the stylistic evidence points to the completion of the west front during Langton's episcopate, when it would no doubt have been perceived as a more urgent task than the rebuilding and extension of the 12th-century choir.

Sources of finance available to the Dean and Chapter for the fabric at the turn of the century were, it seems, modest and the construction of the upper parts of the front would have required large donations from other sources. By 1303 Langton had not made any significant contribution to the fabric of the Cathedral. The letter to the Pope of that year makes no mention of any such projects and certainly would have done so had they existed. Nor is there any reason to suppose, from the architectural evidence, that any large-scale works were undertaken at the Cathedral much before his arrest in 1307. But the design of the towers and central gable could be interpreted to indicate that the project was re-animated at the end of the first decade.

The tracery of the present west window is the work of Gilbert Scott (1869). He replaced the interesting, if rather ungainly, window donated by the Duke of York after the Restoration (Pl. XXIIA). The original window was destroyed in the Civil War but the medieval tracery is recorded in a drawing by Hollar (Pl. XIXA) who shows an intersected pattern with a number of quatrefoils. It is a curiously inconsistent design with a strange device in the centre. The two central lights are sub-arcuated so that they appear lower than their companions, and the result is that the larger arch which they form seems to split asunder. Hollar's less than competent draughtsmanship in all probability represents a window whose details are identical to those in St Katherine's Chapel at Ledbury (Pl. XIXB).[38] He had simply failed to read corectly the way in which the sides of two large quatrefoils press into the haunches of the main arches. King's drawing shows moreover that, as at Ledbury, the Lichfield mullions and tracery were studded with ballflowers. There is no reason to suspect a direct relationship and so one would hope to find a common source for these two designs. Such tracery, albeit in a slightly simpler form, is to be found in the second tier of the Hardingstone Eleanor cross (1291–4). The jumbled, interlocked trefoils of the west gable bear some resemblance to the distorted trefoils above the windows in St Augustine's gatehouse at Canterbury (1301–9). So we find here the sort of relationship to the court style that we might expect at Lichfield in the early 14th century. But dependence on the architecture of the court is perhaps the only characteristic that links the design of the west window to the architectural style of the Lady Chapel and crossing tower. It would be hard to demonstrate any close affinity in matters of detail, and the profiles do not appear to relate at all.

The west window was probably the contemporary of one or other of the western towers. Its jambs have the same profile as the bell openings. The western steeples at Lichfield form part of a sequence of important Decorated towers that are bound together by a common vocabulary of ornament. Further research is needed before we can explain why the towers of Lincoln, Grantham, Lichfield, Hereford, Salisbury and Pershore develop a series of decorative and design formuli which relate them as closely to one another as to the regional schools of which they also form a part.[39] It is self-evident that the Lichfield towers were intended as a pair, but there are small disparities which may well signify a slight difference in date. On these grounds the south-west tower has some claim to be considered the earliest (Pl. XXIIA). The use of ballflower ornament, miniature crenellation, and a band of cusped lozenges are features which are to be found on the towers of Hereford, Grantham and Salisbury. Grantham tower also has, at its base, a major intersected window in which both mullions and tracery are studded with ballflower, and in its middle stage the narrow bell openings are remarkably similar to those at Lichfield. There is no documented date for the tower at Grantham, but there must be some connection between it and the crossing tower of nearby Lincoln where similar tracery is to be found in the bell openings. The heavy delineation of the tracery at Lincoln with large cusps and swollen mouldings, and the deployment of ballflower in alternate arch mouldings, has much in common with the handling of similar features on the south-west tower at Lichfield. The Lincoln tower was built by the mason Richard of Stow in 1306/7–11. Stow was the builder of the Lincoln Eleanor Cross, and it is interesting to note that the shaft of this cross was made by the Master William of Ireland who supplied the same component for the Hardingstone cross.[40] Finally it should be observed that the statue tabernacles above the bell openings at Lichfield have the same bunched-up quality as the canopies that jostle together on the front of St Augustine's gatehouse. There are, therefore, several reasons to suppose that at least the south-west tower belongs to the same epoch in the building of the Cathedral as the lost west window, but that this phase may be distinct from the construction of the Lady Chapel and crossing tower.

J. T. Irvine suggested that the differences in design between the two western towers were partially the result of a rebuilding which took place in 'late Perpendicular times' and was led to this opinion by the knowledge that the vaulting of both towers, at aisle level, was not added until 1522–32. This is a possible explanation but it may also be legitimate to regard the north tower as the immediate successor of the southern one.[41]

The north tower is several feet shorter than its partner; a perplexing disparity. The gablets above the bell openings are not as acutely pointed as those in the south tower and the openings themselves have a tracery pattern which is subtly different. The arch is of a shallower pitch and the pointed quatrefoil in the head has delicately ogeed tips which, on either side, are drawn downwards. This has something in common with the lowest lucarne windows of the central spire which are authentic 14th-century work. This could be taken to suggest that the northern tower may have been constructed at the same period as the crossing tower and Lady Chapel.

If Langton had a hand in the construction of the south-west tower, it could have been begun either just before his arrest in 1307 or immediately after his final release in 1312. It is perhaps of some interest that Hugh de la Dale was replaced as the bishop's mason after 1310 and perhaps before 1312–13 when Langton's new mason, William Franceys, was employed to direct the digging of the outer ditch of the Close.[42] We have seen that by analogy with the north curtain at Caernarvon and the Lady Chapel, the crossing tower is likely to have been built between c.1315 and c.1320. Thirteen hundred and fifteen was the year in which Langton was finally dismissed from the Council and after which he concentrated increasingly on the administration of his diocese rather than the affairs of state. It followed moreover the completion of his new palace in 1314. Added impetus to finish the west front towers would no doubt have been provided with the burning down of the old free-standing belfry in 1315.[43] So if the early 14th-century work at Lichfield can be divided up into definable phases, we could see the construction of the palace between 1299 and 1314, the first campaign on the upper west front c.1310–14, encompassing the south-west tower and west window. There would then commence a second campaign on the Cathedral in c.1315 which included the construction of the north-west tower, the crossing tower, the choir remodelling, and the building of the Lady Chapel which by Langton's death in 1321 remained unfinished.[44]

If this would seem to compress a great deal of building activity into too small a compass, the well-known account of Simon Simeon could be taken as evidence that the towers and spires were probably complete around the time of Langton's death in 1321. Simon Simeon, with his friend Hugh the Illuminator, passed through Lichfield during a journey from Dublin to the Holy Land in 1323, and described the Cathedral as 'mire pulcritudinis, turribus lapideis sive campanilibus altissimis, picturis, sculpturis, et aliis ecclesiasticis apparatibus excellenter ornata atque decorata'. Simeon was careful to specify that the bell towers which he saw were of stone. Although cathedral towers were invariably built of this material, it was common even in the grandest churches to build spires of timber.[45] Finally Simeon describes the steeples as being very high, whereas without their spires the Lichfield towers are unusually low. So although the Lady Chapel was incomplete in 1321 the famous three-spired silhouette of Lichfield was probably in being by 1323. It is not possible to say when the Lady Chapel was finished, but the appointment of two keepers of its fabric in 1336 is sometimes taken as the *terminus ante quem* for its completion.

Langton's episcopate at Lichfield was one of the busiest building periods in the history of the Cathedral. The great programme of construction through which the building was transformed was bound to be of some significance in the development of a regional style. One can point to other local churches, in addition to Ashbourne, which are probably contemporary with the Lady Chapel build and which share some of its features. In Staffordshire the chancel at Cheddleton and the nave aisles at Clifton Camville both have the same distinctive quatrefoil tracery of the Cathedral's crossing tower, and in the chancel at Blymhill this feature is combined with a gabled external tomb recess which closely resembles those of the Lady Chapel in their original form. Somewhat later, in the 1330s, it is possible to identify the arrival in the diocese of a mason whose distinctive work (Fig. 4), though informed by

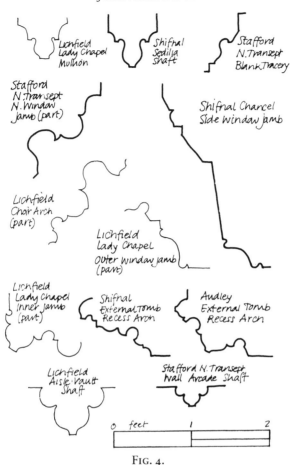

FIG. 4.

other sources, pays close attention to the details of the Cathedral.[46] At St Mary's Stafford this master built a sumptuous north transept with a densely ornamented doorway. Inside the transept there is blank tracery derived from the lower section of Lichfield west front and there are base mouldings that acknowledge those of the Cathedral nave as well as the late 12th-century details of the choir. At Audley chancel moreover, the same mason combined the quatrefoil tracery of the crossing tower with external tomb recesses in imitation of the Lady Chapel (Pl. XIXc). This mason may also have been involved in the rebuilding of the crossing of St Werburgh's Abbey, Chester (now the Cathedral) and in the adjacent bays of the choir clerestory there are windows which may have been derived from the lost west window of Lichfield. Likewise, in the chancel at Shifnal, Salop we once more encounter an external tomb recess, together with fish-scale tracery in the east window that may be derived from the choir aisle windows at Lichfield. Similar windows are found in the late 16th-century remodelling of Old St Chad's Shrewsbury — presumably reclaimed from the earlier church — and as far afield as West Kirby on the Wirral. The planning of the Lichfield east end may also have led, in the 15th century, to the adoption of a polygonal chancel at St Michael's, Coventry and at the large parish church at Northwich in Cheshire.

Langton's real achievement in creating one of the great set pieces of Decorated architecture was of more than regional importance. Had it survived intact it would have long been acknowledged as a key monument of the English court style. It should perhaps be regarded as the forerunner of the remodelling at the east end of Wells which, it has been argued convincingly by Peter Draper, was begun in c. 1323/4.[47] The polygonal Lady Chapel there, with its fish-scale tracery and zigzag parapet, may owe a good deal to Lichfield, as may the window tracery of the choir aisles. Recognition of Langton's work would also have helped to establish that the court style cannot be understood entirely as a question of princely monuments and richly detailed churches. There is also a military vocabulary, used on a monumental scale which, for all its severity and functional imperatives, is an integral part of the architectural movement which Thomas Rickman and later ecclesiologists have called Decorated. At Lichfield, moreover, Langton's works were very much more than architecture and decoration. Design, layout and ornament proclaimed the sanctity of Chad and gave visible witness to the embattled authority of the king's Treasurer.

ACKNOWLEDGEMENT

I am grateful to Dr Richard Morris for allowing me to copy his full-scale drawings of Lichfield profiles. Several of the scale drawings illustrating this paper are derived from them. Dr Jill Hughes kindly provided helpful information on Langton.

REFERENCES

1. J. Bony, *The English Decorated Style* (1979), 12, pls 68–71. P. Draper, 'The Sequence and Dating of the Decorated Work at Wells', *BAA CT*, IV (1978), 18–29.
2. J. Hughes, 'Walter Langton, bishop of Coventry and Lichfield 1296–1321: his family background', *Nottingham Medieval Studies*, XXV (1991), 70–6. See also J. Hughes, *The Episcopate of Walter Langton, Bishop of Coventry and Lichfield, 1296–1321, with a calendar of his register*, unpublished PhD thesis, University of Nottingham, 1992.
3. A. Beardwood, 'The Trial of Walter Langton, bishop of Lichfield, 1307–12', *Transactions of the American Philosophical Society*, new series, LIV (1964).
4. H. E. Savage, 'The Great Register of Lichfield', *WSAS* (1924), 307.
5. PRO, *Calendars of Patent Rolls* 1292–1301, 408–9, 'procinctum domorum suarum et canonicorum infra clausum, Cathedral. Lichfeld. mure lapideo includere et murum illum kernellare'.
6. See p. 92.
7. Thomas Fuller, *The Church History of Britain from the birth of Jesus Christ until the year 1648*, quoted in A. B. Clifton, *The Cathedral Church of Lichfield* (London 1898), 9.
8. The influence of the castle-building programme in North Wales on architecture in western England is discussed in J. M. Maddison, *Decorated Architecture in the North-West Midlands — an investigation of the work of provincial masons and their sources*, unpublished PhD thesis, University of Manchester, 1978, 72–125.
9. A. J. Taylor, *The History of the King's Works* (1963), I, 370. For the walls of Constantinople see C. Foss and D. Winfield, *Byzantine Fortifications* (1986), 41–73 and A. M. Schneider, 'The City Walls of Istanbul', *Antiquity*, XI (1937), 461–8.
10. A. J. Taylor, 'The Castle of St-Georges-d'Esperanche', *Antiquaries Journal*, XXXIII (1953), 32–47.
11. *VCH Staffordshire*, XIV (1990), 60.
12. W. Camden, *Britannia*, II (1695), 38.
13. Bodleian MS Tanner 217.
14. Caverswall castle, Staffs, for which licence to crenellate was obtained by William de Caverswall in 1275 could, if the document dates the existing towers and walls, be considered a local forerunner of Eccleshall. Samson Erdswick's assertion that it was built by another William Caverswall in the reign of Edward II may have been based on evidence which was available in his time or may simply have been a confusion. Samson

Erdswick, *A Survey of Staffordshire* (compiled 1593–1603), revised and collated T. Harwood (1844), 249.

15. A. Beardwood, 'Records of the Trial of Walter Langeton Bishop of Coventry and Lichfield 1307–12', *Camden Society*, 4th series, 6 (1969).

16. H. Rothwell (ed.), 'The Chronicle of Walter of Guisborough', *Camden Society*, 3rd series (1957), 383.

17. Quoted in Beardwood (1964), 40.

18. *VCH Staffordshire*, III, 153.

19. Beardwood (1964), 27 and Beardwood (1969), 185. The Ballardi wrote, 'Et dicit quod ipse et socii sui predicti de debitis predictis habent multas allocaciones ad petendum versus prefatum episcopum tam de quodam feretro sancti Cedde quod ipsi mercatores suis sumptibus et expensis fieri fecerunt Paris' ad opus ipsius episcopi et de expensis nepotum suorum ibidem in scolis existencium etc.' The nephews who were being educated in Paris at Langton's expense were Walter and Robert de Clipston. Walter de Clipston lived in a house which Langton built for him in the south-west corner of the Close until his death in 1310: *VCH Staffordshire*, XIV, 67; Hughes (1991), 74.

20. Ibid., 32.

21. See pp. 22–6.

22. J. H. Harvey, *English Medieval Architects*, 2nd edn (1984), 243; also J. H. Harvey, 'The Origin of the Perpendicular Style', in E. M. Jope (eds), *Studies in Building History. Essays in Recognition of the Work of B. H. St. John O'Neil* (1961), 134–65.

23. *VCH Staffordshire*, XIV (1990), 5.

24. Mackenzie's engravings were published in J. Britton, *History and Antiquities of the See and Cathedral Church of Lichfield* (1820). Buckler's drawings are BM Add. MS 36386, ff. 187–203, and the Buckler watercolours are held in the William Salt Library. Gerald Cobb, *English Cathedrals the forgotten centuries* (1980), 56, pl. 255 illustrates a photograph of 1875 which shows the south side of the Lady Chapel before the major restoration of Scott.

25. *VCH Staffordshire*, III (1970), 150.

26. Lincoln angel choir was built between 1256 and 1280. See Mary Dean, 'The Angel Choir and its Local Influence', *BAA CT*, VIII (1986), 90–101. The bifurcation of the cinquefoils in the spandrels by the rising vault shafts finds a French parallel in the south elevation of the choir of Beauvais which was reconstructed after the collapse of 1284.

27. R. Willis, 'On the Foundations of Early Buildings Recently Discovered in Lichfield Cathedral', *Archaeol. J.*, XVIII (1871), 1–24.

28. See n. 19.

29. J. H. Harvey (1984), 45–7.

30. I am grateful to Dr Paul Crossley for pointing out this relationship.

31. T. Tatton-Brown, 'The Buildings and Topography of St Augustine's Abbey, Canterbury', *JBAA*, CXLIV (1991), 73.

32. P. Frankl, *Gothic Architecture* (1962), 221. Frankl suggested that the bases in the choir of Prague Cathedral of *c.* 1350 are the first that appear to grow out of the floor. The vertical mouldings die into the sloping plinth in a manner similar to both the Bristol piers and the Lichfield wall arcades, which of course predate the Bohemian example by at least a quarter of a century. For discussion of possible English Decorated influence on the architecture of Central Europe see B. P. Crossley, 'Wells, the West Country and Central European Late Gothic', *BAA CT*, IV (1981), 81–109.

33. *VCH Staffordshire*, XIV (1990), 53. Shrewsbury Public Library, MS 2 contains an important description of St Chad's shrine and its ornaments in 1445. For the military career of Thomas de Berkeley Senior, J. E. Morris, *The Welsh Wars of Edward I* (1901), 237, 247, 273, 288.

34. J. Bony, *The English Decorated Style* (1979), 35, pl. 208.

35. A. J. Taylor, *The History of the King's Works* I (1963), 384–95.

36. G. O. Jones, *The Story of St Mary's Church in the Parish of Llanbeblig with Caernarfon* (1970), 3–4. Although the building has been much altered and the window moved from its original position, the tracery design is confirmed in a drawing by J. C. Buckler, BM Add. MS 36396, f.163.

37. For the iconography of the west front sculpture see *VCH Staffordshire*, XIV (1990), 51, and for surviving medieval figures, Richard Morris's article p. 106 and Richard Lockett's article p. 119.

38. R. K. Morris, 'The Local Influence of Hereford Cathedral in the Decorated Period', *Woolhope Naturalists' Field Club*, XLI (1973), 1, 48–65. Dr Morris notes the relationship between the Ledbury windows and others at Tewkesbury and thereby deduces a date for the former of *c.* 1330. The relationship with the west window of Lichfield implies that Ledbury could be earlier. Dr Morris also notes the similarity between the choir clerestory windows of Chester Cathedral and those at Ledbury.

39. R. K. Morris, op. cit., and *Decorated Architecture in Herefordshire, Sources, Workshops, Influence*, unpublished PhD thesis, London University, 1972.

40. H. M. Colvin, *The History of the King's Works*, I (1963), 484.

41. J. T. Irvine, 'The West Front of Lichfield Cathedral', *JBAA*, XXXVIII (1882), 353. I would, however, support Irvine's suggestion that the original west window was the contemporary of the south-west tower.

42. J. Harvey, *English Medieval Architects*, supplement to revised edn (1987), 4.

43. *VCH Staffordshire*, XIV (1990), 55.

44. In 1322 the mason William of Eyton took an oath to aid the Chapter in the defence of the Close. It is conceivable that he was synonymous with Master William Franceys, but he may have been his successor. He is recorded at Lichfield again in 1327 and 1336, and was probably responsible for the completion of the Lady Chapel and the south-east gate. J. Harvey, *English Medieval Architects* (1984), 105.

45. *VCH Staffordshire*, III (1970), 157 n. 78.

46. J. M. Maddison, *Decorated Architecture in the North-West Midlands* (1978), 200–15.

47. See n. 1.

The Palace of Bishop Walter Langton in Lichfield Cathedral Close

By Nigel Tringham

Walter Langton, bishop of Coventry and Lichfield from 1296 until his death in 1321, was a considerable benefactor of his Cathedral at Lichfield. He was also responsible for fortifying the Close with a stone wall and building himself a new palace. The purpose of this article is to attempt an architectural reconstruction of that palace, which was for the most part destroyed during the Civil War sieges of the Close. The article is based chiefly on two sources: a series of early 14th-century account rolls which include details of payments for work done on the palace (see Appendix) and a late 17th-century drawing of the ground-plan of the palace (Fig. 1). Further information is provided by reports of visitors in the late 16th and early 17th century, by a Parliamentary survey of the bishop's property made in 1652, and by a letter of 1671 which describes the ruined palace.

Langton's palace stood in the north-east corner of the Close, evidently the traditional site for the bishop's residence.[1] A description of the Close, probably written in the late 13th century, records that area as the *locus episcopi* and notes that the *locus* was twice the size of the dean's place, which in turn was twice the size of the canons' places.[2] The 'old hall', mentioned in the 14th-century accounts, was evidently part of the residence replaced by Langton. It probably stood in the centre of its plot of ground, in what became the garden and inner courtyard of its successor.[3] Langton's choice of a new site was presumably connected with his plan to fortify the Close with a stone wall. His palace, ranging north–south along the new east wall of the Close and incorporating its north-east tower, was an integral part of that work, begun in or soon after 1299, when the bishop acquired a royal licence to build a wall and to crenellate it.[4] The palace was almost certainly finished by March 1314, when Langton is known to have been at Lichfield.[5] Its predecessor, the 'old hall', which was still standing in 1312–13 (A 109), would then have been demolished.

Visitors to Langton's palace in the late 16th and early 17th century provide details of the architecture and decoration of its great hall. For Sampson Erdeswick, the Staffordshire antiquary, writing in the 1590s, the palace was the fairest of all the houses in the Close:[6]

having in it a goodly large hall, wherein hath been excellently well painted, but now much decayed, the coronation, marriage, wars, and funeral of Edward I; and some writing, which there is also yet remaining, which expresseth the meaning of the history: where is especially mentioned the behaviour of Sir Roger Pewlesdon, and others, against the Welshmen; as also of Almaric de Bailgiol, Burnell, Valence earl of Pembroke, of the lord Badlesmere, and other barons, against the Scots, where the said earls and lords are very lively portrayed, with their banners of arms bravely before them; but it is a great pity that the same is not restored by the lord bishop before it be quite decayed.

Three gentlemen travellers from Norwich in 1634 were also impressed.[7] They described the palace as

built castle like, at the entrance whereof we mounted some dozen stairs into a spacious goodly hall ... all the roof whereof is Irish timber richly and curiously carved and the covering lead, church like; the carving expressing sundry strange forms and a great part thereof gilded.

The hall fell victim to the Civil War sieges of the Close.[8] According to a Parliamentary survey of the bishop's property made in 1652,[9] the palace was a 'large and fair edifice but [i.e. built] all with stone and a great part of it leaded on the roof; it contains not many rooms, but large. It is divided several from the rest of the Close by a wall and out-buildings, but now broken down'. A wall which surrounded a garden in front of the hall had been pulled down and the garden itself had been dug up to create defensive trenches. Much of the lead, iron, glass, and timber had been taken away by both Royalist and Parliamentarian soldiers, and also by the inhabitants of the Close.

By the time Bishop John Hacket arrived in Lichfield in 1662, the building was evidently beyond repair, and he chose instead to occupy a house on the south side of the Close.[10] As a result the palace fell further into decay, not least because Hacket himself used it as a quarry to provide stone for the conversion of his new residence. Hacket died in 1670 and his successor, Thomas Wood, sued his son, Sir Andrew Hacket, for compensation for this additional demolition. It was evidently as a reply to a request from Sir Andrew for information that a letter was sent to him in July 1671 giving details of the physical remains of the palace.[11] Of the letter's authors, H. Archbold and James Alleny, the former is identifiable as Sir Henry Archbold, diocesan chancellor from 1675.[12] They told Sir Andrew that when Bishop Hacket first came to Lichfield he found the

whole building from the south end of the hall of the said palace pulled down to the very grounds; the hall, consisting of 33 yards in length and 13 [apparently an error for 19] yards in breadth and a cellar under it substantially vaulted (saving one or two flaws by granadoes), was left standing as to the stone work but all the timber, lead, iron, glass, and the very plaster floor of the hall were taken away and sold to the best they could make of them; and two fair rooms at the north end of the said hall were left standing as to the stone only.

As noted above, Hacket himself made use of stone from the ruin in order to convert his new residence, 'whereby all the said vault under the hall and some part of the walls of the said hall and some part of the two rooms on the north end of the said hall are become much more ruinated and dilapidated'. Beside the main part of the palace, there were also 'some outer rooms of stone within the circuit of the said palace, wherein the former bishops did lodge their servants, which were left standing as to the stones only'.

The foundations, however, were evidently still substantial. Indeed, the task of demolishing what remained, following the decision in 1685 to build a completely new palace, was not an easy one. Demolition began in the middle of December 1685 and was still going on in February 1686, the cost amounting to £64.[13] Even so, it seems unlikely that the entire fabric was razed. The new palace was constructed on the west side of the medieval range, straddling the former garden and inner courtyard, and it seems probable that the foundations of the medieval palace were simply covered over with earth and still survive, awaiting future archaeological investigation.

Before attempting an architectural reconstruction of Langton's palace, it is necessary to describe and evaluate the principal sources on which this article is based. The early 14th-century financial accounts are those of the reeve of the bishop's manor of Longdon. The manor corresponded to the extensive estate in south-east Staffordshire held by the bishop at the time of Domesday Book. It was then centred on Lichfield, but was later known as the manor of Longdon, a village which lies north of the city, in order to distinguish it from a separate manor which was established for the 'new town' of Lichfield, created in the mid-12th century.[14] The accounts, therefore, concern a large manor, and references to building work on the palace probably only included to the extent that they are only because it was deemed convenient for the purposes of accounting. Separate accounts of the 'new work', now lost, certainly existed in the years 1304–5 and 1305–6, when items originally entered on the Longdon manor rolls were struck through and transferred to them.[15] (The 'new work' presumably referred to the fortification of the Close, as well as the construction of the new palace.) In later years, however, the Longdon manor rolls contained detailed entries under such headings as 'Expenses about the new work', 'Cost of the new work', and 'Cost of the houses', suggesting that separate accounts of the 'new work' were no longer being kept. Although the reeve seems to have concentrated on the provision of raw materials, especially timber and stone, much of which came from within the manor, his accounts also contain payments to workmen engaged by the bishop's steward or other household officers. It may be that some payments were not accounted by the reeve, but the scope and detail of the items that were suggests that a major proportion of the costs of the building of the palace survive in the accounts.

The drawing of the ground-plan of the palace was made in 1685 by Henry Greswold, one of the residentiary canons.[16] It was conceived as part of an attempt to prevent the complete demolition of the ruined medieval palace and its replacement by the present building. Greswold favoured the restoration of the medieval palace, partly on the grounds of reducing expense, but principally because its situation was such a fine one, certainly superior, in his opinion, to that proposed for the new building. The medieval palace stretched north–south along the east wall of the Close and, as a result, enjoyed fine views and plenty of sun. In a letter intended to accompany Greswold's plan, William Walmisley, a lawyer who also lived in the Close, noted that 'the late palace by being placed along the east wall had much more of the east, south, and west sun than it can have anywhere else there, or indeed in all the Close, and had prospect of [i.e. from] every room (except the apartments for servants which stood a little separate from the rest) some way for many miles and several ways for a mile at least and that taking in the views of the greater part of the city to boot'.[17] Greswold drew at least two other plans, intended to indicate how the remains of the medieval palace could be refashioned into a new building.[18] Although he bemoaned his lack of skill as a draughts-man,[19] Greswold's plan may be taken as an accurate record of the surviving fabric: Walmisley noted that Greswold was anxious to produce something that was 'plain and true' rather than 'compt and neat', and that he had relied on the testimony of the older residents of the Close, presumably for the identification of the different parts of the palace complex.[20] There is, of course, no guarantee that the people Greswold consulted provided accurate information, or that he properly understood what he was told. The plan, moreover, suffers from a possible further limitation when used in an attempt to reconstruct the layout of the 14th-century palace: it would naturally reflect any substantial alteration that might have been made to the original fabric. It is known, for instance, that building work, although possibly only repairs, took place in the mid 1520s[21] and in the early 17th century.[22] The fact, however, that the late medieval and post-Reformation bishops rarely lived at Lichfield when they were in residence in the diocese, preferring instead their houses at Beaudesert, Haywood, and Eccleshall, all in Staffordshire, may be some guarantee that no major work of remodelling or improvement was undertaken. Certainly Bishop Robert Wright lamented in 1638 that he was unable to contemplate living in the palace because it was in a ruinous condition, inhabited amongst others by maltsters.[23] The internal arrangements of the 14th century, therefore, may have been left largely unaltered.

The heart of the palace was the great hall, 100 ft long and 56 ft wide, making it perhaps the fifth or sixth largest in the country at its time.[24] Resting on a stone vault, the floor of the hall was probably 9 or 10 ft above ground-level, judging from the flight of 'some dozen stairs' mounted by the visitors of 1634; the stairs themselves were roofed over (A 40). The hall may have been aisled, with pillars supporting the elaborately carved wooden roof so

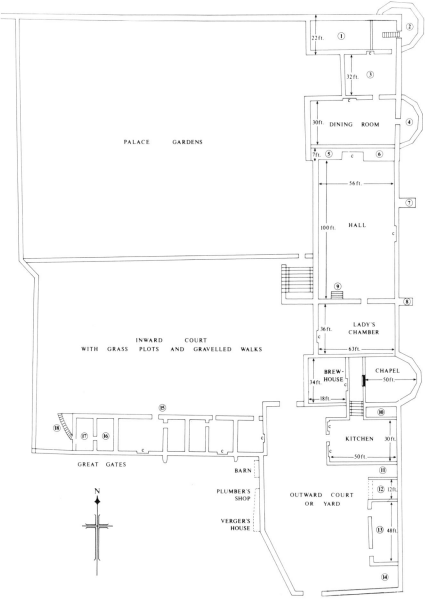

PALACE GARDENS

22 ft. ①
② ②
32 ft. ③
30ft. DINING ROOM ④
7ft. ⑤ c ⑥
56 ft.
⑦
100 ft. HALL c
c
⑨
⑧
LADY'S
36 ft. CHAMBER
c 63ft.
INWARD COURT
WITH GRASS PLOTS AND GRAVELLED WALKS
BREW- CHAPEL
34ft. HOUSE c 50ft.
18ft. ⑩
KITCHEN 30 ft.
c 50 ft.
⑮ ⑪
⑱ ⑫ 12ft.
⑰ ⑯ c
GREAT GATES c ⑬ 48ft.
BARN
PLUMBER'S OUTWARD COURT
SHOP OR YARD ⑭
VERGER'S
HOUSE

N

KEY TO FIGURES
1 Lodging or other room
2 Tower, 52 ft high, each edge 13 ft on the outside
3 Bishop's lodging room
4 Second tower, each edge 10ft
5 and 6 Pantry
7 and 8 Buttery [i.e. buttress] made out into the Dimples
9 Stairs into the passage under the Lady's chamber
10 Open ground for a sough for the rainwater from the roofs of the chapel and kitchen

11 Open ground for pens for poultry etc.
12 Coach-house with folding doors
13 Stables
14 Where [there] was the dunghill
15 Lodging rooms for the bishop's gentlemen, 20 ft high
16 Porter's chamber
17 Gatehouse chamber
18 Stairs up side of buttress
c chimney

FIG. 1. Tringham, Bishop Langton's Palace

admired by the same visitors in 1634. (It must remain a possibility, however, that the carvings noted in 1634 were done after Langton's time.) The roof, evidently pitched and rising to a central ridge, was covered with lead. There may have been windows in the gables at the north and south ends: masons made windows at the 'ends of the hall' (A 55), for which William the glazier provided 97 ft of glass (A 79). If 'ends' (*capita*) does indeed refer to the gables, as seems most likely,[25] then the hall roof apparently rose above the level of the adjoining chambers. This may well have been the case, as those chambers were constructed transverse the hall, their length (63 ft) being greater than the hall's width.[26] The chambers, moreover, were not an integral part of the hall range, resting on timberwork rather than a stone vault. The hall, in addition, presumably had windows on the west side, looking over the garden and inner courtyard. In contrast, there were probably only small openings on the east side, where the wall also formed part of the defensive wall of the Close. The high table presumably stood at the north end of the hall, furthest away from the entrance. At that point Greswold marks a chimney, with a 'pantry' on either side. A chimney may indeed have been inserted there in the 15th or 16th centuries, but is unlikely to have been an original feature. The chimney set into the east wall, however, may have been contemporary with Langton.

The arrangement of chambers on the north side of the hall as the bishop's private quarters seems unexceptional. What Greswold terms the 'dining room' may have been the bishop's 'great chamber' recorded in the 14th-century accounts (A 1, 120), while the chamber beyond, called the 'bishop's lodging room' by Greswold, may be the 'small chamber' (A 31). They correspond to the 'two fair rooms' mentioned in the letter of 1671. The chamber along the north wall, called by Greswold the 'lodging or other room', may have been used by the bishop's most senior manorial official, his steward: the office, under Bishop Langton, was held by John de Hotton, whose chamber may well have been near the bishop's (A 66).[27] Greswold's plan shows no doorway between the hall and the adjoining north chamber, but there must have been some means of access. There may also have been some means by which the bishop could enter the palace garden without having to go through the hall and down the main entrance stairs.

The function of the chamber on the south side of the hall is problematical. Greswold records it as the 'Lady's chamber', a name possibly derived from some aspect of decoration, perhaps of the Virgin Mary: Langton evidently had a special devotion to her in view of his inauguration of work on the Cathedral's Lady Chapel.[28] The chamber was a private room, undisturbed by the traffic of servants. Probably it was a lesser hall, used in the Middle Ages as a reception or conversation room, in which visitors could be entertained more comfortably than in the great hall. Otherwise, it may have been the chapel, whose position on Greswold's plan presents its own problems of interpretation.

According to Greswold the chapel stood at almost groundlevel and was entered from a passage which led, from the hall, underneath the 'Lady's chamber' (where the pantry and

NOTE TO FIGURE 1 (Opposite)
The names for the various parts of the palace are those given in the original plan (Bodleian Library, Oxford, MS Tanner 217, f. 42). The spelling has been modernised. The measurements have been translated into diagrammatic form. In addition to those shown it should be noted that the inner wall of the palace range from 1 (the Lodging or other room) to the brew-house is marked as being 6 ft thick.

The plan provides additional information relating to the cellars and roofs: Hall 'roof leaded, cellar[e]d under all with stone arches'; Dining room, chambers 1 and 3, and Lady's chamber 'roof leaded, cellar[e]d under with timber (*or* wood) work'; Chapel 'roof leaded'; Brew-house 'roof[e]d shorewise only [i.e. a lean-to roof] and tiled'; Kitchen 'roof tiled, not cellar[e]d under but as low as least as the cellars'; Coach-house and Stables 'roof tiled'; Lodging rooms for the bishop's gentlemen 'all chamber[e]d over, but the chamber floors were all lay[e]d with plaster'.

buttery may have been situated), and on to the kitchen. Such access hardly seems fitting for a bishop, and it is possible that Greswold and his informants were mistaken in their designation. The only topographical reference to the chapel in the 14th-century accounts places it at the 'end of the great hall' (A 54), which may suggest that it occupied the position of Greswold's 'Lady's chamber'. Elsewhere in the accounts, however, 'hall' is used generally for the whole palace range (A 103), and Greswold's 'chapel' could therefore still be its 'end'. It may also be supposed that the temporary use of the chapel as a grainstore at one time during the construction of the palace (A 94) makes Greswold's identification, given its proximity to the outer courtyard, more likely than the 'Lady's chamber'. Possibly there were two chapels, a lower one (approached from the kitchen passage) for the use of servants, and over it another for the bishop's use. An upper chapel may have extended the full length of the cross-wing, matching in its proportions the 'Lady's chamber', from which there would have been access. Otherwise, the chapel may have been a single-storey building, but tall enough to allow a view down on to the altar from a window or balcony in the 'Lady's chamber'. (For private devotions there may have been an oratory in one of the chambers at the north end of the hall.) The only architectural detail about the chapel recorded in the accounts is the laying of the floor (A 54).

A treasury is recorded on a single occasion in the accounts (A 120), but is not shown on Greswold's plan. It probably lay somewhere near the chapel.

The brew-house is mentioned several times, but no topographical details are given (A 74, 113–14, 117–18). It may well have stood where Greswold places it, with a large chimney. No doorway is marked on the plan; presumably there was one into the outer courtyard. The kitchen was a free-standing building, connected to the main range of the palace by steps with a roof over them (A 32, 103, 111). Greswold marks two chimneys in the kitchen; they evidently served two ovens (A 112). The kitchen opened out into a service courtyard, which contained the stables (A 59, 71, 100–1) and presumably the other outbuildings recorded in the accounts: bakery, near the kitchen (A 32, 39–41, 43–4, 68, 74, 76, 95, 102, 105–6, 110, 111, 117–18); granary (A 5, 19, 56, 77, 123); hay barn (A 5, 17, 36, 64, 69, 71, 115, 117–18, 129); saucery (A 61); 'dressours', a food cupboard or a place for dressing meat (A 39, 41, 45–8, 53); dovecot (A 107, 118); and pinfold, or pound for animals (A 12, 62). The various buildings in the courtyard may have been separated from each other by small fences (e.g. A 95).

At the southern end of the courtyard, there was a gateway which faced the south-east entrance of the Close, itself giving access to the city of Lichfield. The gateway was evidently the 'great gate' recorded in the accounts (A 123), and should be distinguished from a smaller gateway which gave access into the inner courtyard (see below).

The range of 'lodging rooms for the bishop's gentlemen' is probably identifiable in the accounts as the 'long chamber' (A 28). Greswold's plans shows it lying on a straight east–west alignment. His other plans, however, show it at an angle, the western end some feet further north than the eastern end.[29] That was probably its true alignment, coinciding with the direction of the wall of the present Bishop's Palace, built in 1686–7. The front of the range, in fact, probably lay along the outer edge of that wall. Although two-storeyed, the range was only twenty feet high and would not have impeded the view of the Cathedral from the palace windows. At its western end, opposite the Chapter House of the Cathedral, was a gateway with a chamber (divided into two) over it for the porter or palace gate-keeper (A 35, 75, 109, 116–18). The chamber incorporated an oriel (A 16), and was approached by an external staircase against the west end of the range. Presumably only light traffic would have been admitted into the inner courtyard: on one of Greswold's other plans,[30] he makes provision for a gateway there fourteen feet wide.

On the north side of the inner courtyard was a garden (A 15, 110). The accounts record the creation of a *herbarium*, possibly an enclosed area separate from the rest of the garden (A 93), and payment over a period of months to a gardener (A 121). Water for the garden came from a pond (A 96–7), evidently in one of the palace courtyards (A 17, 88–92).

The Close had its own water supply, and there was a conduit at the west end of the Cathedral.[31] A lead pipe brought water to the palace (A 13, 99, 110, 128), and probably fed the pond, making it a kind of cistern. At one time during construction work, the supply was cut off and water had to be brought in by cart (A 73).

On the north and south sides of the palace grounds, security was provided by the Close wall, which faced out over a deep ditch. The north wall, however, may have been pierced from the garden side by a gate which apparently gave access to a 'quarry' (A 65): the ditch was certainly used as a quarry during building work (see below). The east wall may also have been pierced: the accounts record a postern by the kitchen (A 107). The enclosure of the palace grounds was completed, on the west side, by a wall which separated it from the deanery; there was apparently a postern along that wall and windows set into it (A 82–7).

Information on the cost of building materials and of labour and on the techniques of construction can be gleaned from the accounts presented in the Appendix. It is not proposed here to go into any detail on these matters, but attention may be drawn to particular items of interest: the use of timber for 'soldering the lead', presumably for casting and jointing the lead roof of the hall and adjoining chambers (A 3, 7, 21); the acquisition and deployment of lead and tin for roofing (A 58, 119, 124); the use of various types of thatch for the roofs of the outbuildings (A 39, 106, 111); the construction of centres, probably for use in erecting the hall roof (A 22); the 'beam-filling' of the walls of the hall and of other chambers (A 120); the charges of the painters responsible for the wall-paintings in the hall and perhaps elsewhere in the palace (A 81 (where there is mention of a movable scaffold), 104, 109, 122); and the purchase and manufacture of a variety of pieces of ironwork (A 25, 27, 31, 80, 86, 98, 125).

Timber used for building work evidently came from land in the bishop's manor of Longdon, and possibly also from his adjoining manor of Cannock to the north, where there was an extensive area of woodland.[32] Some stone may also have come from the Cannock area; the accounts, however, make specific reference only to a quarry at Freeford, on the south-east outskirts of Lichfield (A 84, 91), and to the extraction of stone from the Close ditch (A 82).

The two principal craftsmen responsible for the new palace are recorded in the accounts, albeit briefly: Master Walter the carpenter, who was one time also engaged on work at Langton's house at Thorpe Waterville in Northamptonshire (A 4, 23), and Master Hugh the mason (A 10), who is more precisely identifiable as Master Hugh de la Dale.[33]

APPENDIX

Extracts relating to the construction of the palace of Bishop Walter Langton in Lichfield Cathedral Close from the rolls of the reeve of the manor of Longdon (Staffordshire).

Source

Staffordshire Record Office, D (W) 1734/J 2057, mm 1–9. The accounts run from Michaelmas to Michaelmas. The present order of membranes is chronologically incorrect: mm 7–9 cover the years 1304–5 to 1306–7, mm 1–6 the years 1308–14. A further two membranes included in the bundle (mm 10–11) date from 1365–7 and have no information relating to the palace, whilst a third membrane (m. 12), dating from 1384–5, contains the accounts of the reeves of manors other than Longdon.

Note

Only extracts which can definitely or almost certainly be associated with the palace at Lichfield have been included. Imprecise references to building work have been excluded on the grounds that they might relate to contemporary work on a new bridge at Lichfield and on the bishop's house at Beaudesert, in Longdon, both of which occur in their own right in the accounts. The order of sections is that in the original accounts. Within sections the individual entries have been abbreviated and standardised. Figures have been translated from Roman to Arabic numerals. The original form of place and personal names has been retained, except in the case of the variants of Lichfield which have been standardised.

1304–5 (m. 7)

'Cost of the houses' — the section includes cancelled entries for transference to the account of the 'new work':

1   to a man cutting rushes for the bishop's great chamber at Lichfield and for the houses at Beaudesert — 2s. ¼d.
2   to a carpenter making a new *fabrica* [smithy, forge, or workshop] in the court of Lichfield, and plastering and roofing it — 3s. 6d.

'Forinsec expenses' — most of the section is cancelled for transference to the account of the 'new work':

3   to 2 men for 2 days felling wood for soldering the lead (*circa plumbum consolidand'*) at Lichfield for 2 days — 8d.
4   to a man taking a letter to Master Walter the carpenter at Thorp Waterville [Northants.] — 10d.

1305–6 (m. 8)

'Minute things':

5   (struck through: for 3 locks for the door of the hay barn (*grangia feni*) — 3d.; for one key for the granary — 1d.)

'Wages and fees':

6   to Ralph the clerk staying at Lichfield in order to keep the court and supervise the workers from the feast of St Fabian and St Sebastian [20 January] up to Michaelmas, at 10½d. a week — 31s.; also his robe — 13s. 4d.

'Forinsec expenses' — the whole section is cancelled for transference to the account of the 'new work':

7   to 4 men for one day finding and felling an oak in the wood for soldering the lead at Lichfield about [the feast of] Purification [2 February] — 8d.; to 3 men for one day doing the same about the feast of St Peter in cathedra [22 February] — 6d.; to one man cutting and preparing brush-wood (*busca*) for soldering the lead — 5d.
8   to one man for 2 days cutting rushes for roofing the *fabrica* in the court of Lichfield — 5d.
9   for 8 hurdles for making a scaffold (*steyr'*) for whitewashing the bishop's chamber (*ad cameram episcopi dealband'*) — 4d.

1306–7 (m. 9)

'Forinsec expenses':

10   for 31 [cart-loads] of charcoal (*carbon'*) for the *fabrica* in the court of Lichfield by view of Master Hugh the mason — 9s. ½d.; and its carriage to Lichfield on several occasions — 35s.

11 for one cord bought for measuring land — 3*d.*
12 to 3 men for cutting down fencing [materials] (*claustr'*) in order to make 2 enclosures (*haiis*) around the old hall (*circa veteram aulam*) and around the pinfold (*punfald*) at Lichfield . . . (and other work) — 6*s.* 2½*d.*
13 to 2 men digging in the bishop's court at Lichfield in order to inspect the conduit pipe (*pro pipa conducti scrutand'*) — 3*s.* 7½*d.*
14 for cleaning the bishop's garderobe — 12*d.*

'Expenses about the new work' — the section repeats the items in the cancelled 'Forinsec expenses' section of the 1305–6 account.

1307–8

No surviving account. Langton was imprisoned in August 1307, and the accounts of his episcopal and personal estates were evidently taken to the Exchequer, which drew up an account for them during their forfeiture: PRO, E 358/13. No allowance was noted in that account for building work on the Lichfield palace.

1308–9 (m. 1)

'Minute expenses':

15 for the carriage of 4 cart-loads of fencing (*claustr'*) for enclosing the garden of Lichfield (*pro gardino de Lich' claudend'*) — 16*d.*; making an enclosure there around the garden — 3*d.*; making 140 planks of the palisade (*plank' palicii*) and placing them around the garden — 18*d.*; to 3 men for 2 days repairing the palisade around the garden — 6*d.*
16 for repairing the oriel (*oriell'*) at the gate of the court of Lichfield — 15*d.*
17 to 2 men cleaning the hay barn and a certain gutter for one day — 4*d.*; to one man cleaning the pond (*stagnum*) in the court of Lichfield — 9*d.*
18 for a pole-gate (*porta de baculis*) for the new enclosure in the court — 3*d.*; to one man cutting down fencing in the wood for making an enclosure in the court of Lichfield for 3½ days — 7*d.*; to 2 men making an enclosure for 2 days — 8*d.*
19 for a key for the granary door (*pro hostio granar'*) in the court — 1*d.*
20 to a man roofing over the hall (*super aulam*) for 4 days — 6*d.*; to 2 women helping him — 6*d.*

'Cost of the new work':

21 for 3 cart-loads of wood for soldering the lead — 12*d.*; tallow (*cepum*) for the lead — 1*d.*; to 2 carpenters for 1½ days felling wood for soldering the lead — 9*d.*; for tin bought at Coventry — 4*s.*; for tin [bought on another occasion] — 4*s.* 6*d.*; to William de Slindon making gutters from the lead — 3*s.* 2*d.*; for 260 lednails — 7½*d.*; 100 spikings — 4*d.*; 100 nails (*clav'*) for the lead of the great hall — 2½*d.*
22 to William le knave for felling 620 alder trees in the park for making centres (*pro cintris fac'*) — 29*d.*
23 to Master Walter the carpenter at Pentecost for paying several workers — 21*s.* 4*d.*; and a similar payment in the week after Pentecost — 21*s.* 4*d.*; to carpenter(s) for 5 weeks — 45*s.*
24 for the carriage of 4,500 laths for stone slates (*stonlaths*) to Lichfield — 3*s.* 9*d.*

'Minute expenses for the new work':

25 for 29 pieces of iron bought after Easter — 4*s.* 11*d.*
26 to William le knave and John de Halsey for 2 days making moulds (*formulis*) and ridge-tiles (*crestell'*) and repairing defects — 8*d.*
27 for 29 pieces of iron for the new work — 5*s.* 7*d.*; bars and bolts for the same — 20*d.*; 7 hasps with 24 staples for the windows of the bishop's chamber — 5*d.*; one bar for the door (*hostium*) of the same — 2*d.*; one latch for the windows [*sic* plural] of the kitchen and 2 staples for the door of the same and of the chamber — 2*d.*; 4 iron bars for the doors of the chambers — 9*d.*; 16 iron candleholders (*candelabr'*) — 20*d.*; one iron door-handle for the door at the end of the hall (*ad*

capud aule) — 1*d*.; 5 locks with keys for the doors of the hall and of the chambers — 5*d*.; 21 iron pegs with chains (*chathen'*) for the windows of the hall — 2*s*. 6*d*.; 14 dozen and four pieces of iron for the new work — 20*s*. 9*d*.; to Adam Walrand for his work — 20*s*. 9*d*.

1309–10 (m. 2)

'Expenses about the new work':

28 to William de Slindon and a man for making a gutter for the long chamber — 2*s*. 6*d*.

29 for one hemp cord — 7*d*.

30 to one mason placing glass in the window(s) of the hall — 12*d*.

31 for 2 iron bars for the door of the garderobe and of the lord's small chamber and for mending a lock with an iron door-handle — 4*d*.; for making two latches (*lacchis*) with two iron pegs, one iron door-handle with one staple, and one key for the door of the garderobe of the bishop's chamber — 8*d*.; for 20 pieces of iron bought for the new work after Easter — 4*s*. 4*d*.; for 3 pieces of iron for the new forge — 10*d*.; for bars, bolts and chains (*cathenis*), iron clips, and other iron goods for the window(s) of the new work — 20*d*.; payment to Adam Walrand for the work of the said iron — 4*s*. 4*d*.; for 4 dozen [pieces] of iron for the new work ('new work' struck through and 'anndirings' [andirons, for hearths] written over in the same hand) — 6*s*.; payment to Adam Walrand for his work — 6*s*.

'Expenses against the coming of the lord':

32 for 100 thack boards (*thachbord'*) for the louvers (*pro lodiis*) in the bakery (*pistrina*) and other minute things in the kitchen and the bakery — 3*s*.

'Cost of the houses in the court':

33 to one man for 1½ days for cutting down wattling (*clamstod'*) for chambers by order of John de Langeton — 3*d*.; for cutting down 6 oak sills (*silles de quercu*) in the wood and preparing them for the chamber of the same John — 4*d*.

34 for the carriage of 2 cart-loads of timber for stairs (*pro steyres*) in the bishop's chamber about the feast of the Ascension [28 May] — 8*d*.; for rushes for the chamber about the same time — 1*d*.

35 for 100 board-nailes (*claverbord'*) for the chamber over the gate (*ultra portam*) — 3½*d*.

'Forinsec expenses':

36 for 140 lednails for making a gutter between the hay barn and the great wall — 4*d*.

37 for 4 locks with keys for doors in the court once of Master Thomas de Abberbury — 3*s*. 5*d*.

1310–11 (m. 3)

'Cost of the houses':

38 to carpenters working in the court of Lichfield and to other workers between the feast of St Matthew [21 September] and the feast of St Andrew [30 November] — £6 6*s*. 6¾*d*. (struck through and 110*s*. 10½*d*. written over); to carpenters and other workers — 26*s*. ½*d*.

39 for 7 thraves of oat straw for roofing the bakery (*pistrina*) and the *dressurs* before the Nativity [25 December] — 14*d*.; for 6 thraves of corn straw for the same — 15*d*.; for 10 thraves of barley straw for the same — 10*d*.; for 47 thraves of rye straw for the same — 9*s*. 9½*d*.; for 20 thraves of oat straw — 2*s*. 6*d*.

40 to a roofer (*coopertor'*) roofing the end (*capud*) of the bakery next to the kitchen for 3 days — 6*d*.; to John le clerk helping him — 4½*d*.; to a woman helping him — 3*d*.; to a roofer roofing for two days over the stairs (*ultra gressus*) against the hall (*v[ersus] aulam*) — 3*d*.; to 2 helpers — 3*d*.

41 to John le clerk for 9 days helping the carpenters about the *dressours* and raising and plastering the new end of the bakery — 13½*d*.; to William Prick for plastering the new end of the bakery next to the kitchen and doing other things — 3*s*.; to the same man and his mate for 4 days plastering the end of the same [i.e. the bakery] and helping the carpenters to raise it again and

enlarge it (*pro eodem iterum levand' and elargand'*) — 12*d*.; to William Pilard for the same there — 9*d*.

42 entries for purchase of 2,000 lath-nails, 800 board-nails, 400 shingle-nails (*clav' cindularum*) and 120 spikings totalling 4*s*. 8*d*.

43 for 4 boards for the bakery with hurdles and other things — 8*s*. 7*d*.

44 for 400 laths for the janitor's chamber and for the porch (*porticam*) of the bakery in the week after Michaelmas — 10*d*.; 2,700 lath-nails for the same — 19¾*d*.; for plastering the janitor's chamber and the porch of the bakery and in the bishop's chamber — 3*s*.

45 to a roofer roofing the house over (*domum ultra*) the *dressurs* — 12*d*.; and roofing the janitor's chamber and the porch — 8*d*.

46 entries for 900 board-nails, 2,600 lath-nails, 1,000 laths and 30 thack boards for the *dressurs* and the gutter of the bakery totalling 6*s*.

47 to Richard de Russale for one week making the walls of the *dressurs* — 8*d*.; to Adam de Asshel' for the same — 8*d*.; to the same men for half a day — 2*d*.

48 to a roofer for 2 days roofing *super le dressur'* blown down (*raptum*) by wind about the feast of St Gregory [12 March] — 6*d*.; to a man helping — 3*d*.

49 to Thomas the plasterer for whitewashing (*dealbacione*) the hall — 24*s*.

'Stipends of the carpenters for minute things in the court, with the stipends of the masons':

50 to one carpenter repairing the tables in the hall of the bishop and other necessities for 2 weeks after Epiphany — 3*s*.

51 to Robert Spaynel for making 10 hurdles for the scaffold of the wall in the court — 10*d*.

'Expenses of the house(s) and other things in the court':

52 payment by Henry the chaplain against the hire of masons and other workers in the court by the hand of Adam de Rugg' — £13 3*s*. 10*d*.

53 to William Prick for plastering the walls of the *dressours* and their rafters (*cheveroun'*) by agreement about the feast of St Mark the evangelist [25 April] — 2*s*. 8*d*.

54 to the same man for making out of clay (*ex argillo*) the floor (*area*) of the chapel at the end of the great hall — 3*s*.

55 for 4 carts carrying poles for making scaffolds in the hall for whitewashing the same, and for placing over the lead of the hall for protection when the masons made the windows at the ends of the hall, and other things — 16*d*.

56 for repairing the granary with shingles and repairing the walls — 4*d*; for felling 7 alders for making stairs for the same [i.e. the granary] — 1*d*.

57 for making 3 stairs (*scalis*) for the hall — 7*d*.

58 to William de Slindon engaged for 2 days buying lead — 6*d*.; for tin bought at the same time — 3*d*.

59 to one man for binding staves for the stalls of the horses in the stable (*ad colligend' bacul' pro presepiis equorum in stabulo*) — 1½*d*.

60 for binding rods for making hurdles for the scaffold — 1*d*.; for making 10 hurdles — 15*d*.

61 for board-nails and shingle-nails for the saucery (*pro domo salsar'*) about the feast of St Denis [9 October] — 6*d*.

62 to John Mile cutting down fencing for 3½ days for enclosing the lord's garden — 5½*d*.; to William de Linton for making an enclosure about the garden and pinfold (*punfald*) for 3 days — 4½*d*.

63 to one man binding staves for hanging meat in the old hall (*pro carn' pend' in veteri aula*) — 1½*d*.

'Cost of the hay barn':

64 for 200 shingle-nails bought for repairing the hay barn about the feast of the exaltation of the Holy Cross [14 September] — 4*d*.; for 60 spikings for the gutter of the same and for fastening boards (*bord' firmand'*) — 2*d*.; for 4,000 shingles for the same about Michaelmas — 8*d*.; for one key for the door of the hay barn and for repairing its lock — 1*d*.

65 for one key for the gate of the garden by the quarry (v[*ersus*] *quarr'*) — 1*d*.

1311–12 (m. 4)

'Cost of the houses':

66 to one man for making walls in the chamber of the lord bishop and the chamber of John de Hottot — 20*d.*

67 for 300 shingle-nails for the hay barn — 6*d.*; and spik-nails for the same — 3*d.*

68 for felling 12 alders for repairing the bakery after the fire — 1*d.*; to one carpenter for repairing the bakery — 2*s.* 7*d.*; for plastering and whitewashing the bakery — 18*d.*; for board-nails and spik[-nails] for the same — 6*d.*

69 for 4 thack boards for roofing the porch (*portica*) of the hay barn — 2*d.*

70 for felling 9 alders for making a wall in the bishop's chamber — 1*d.*

71 for one board bought for the louver (*lodium*) of the stable — 6*d.*; to one carpenter for preparing and setting the louver — 2*d.*

72 to one carpenter laying shingles over the hay barn and repairing all defects for 4½ days — 9¼*d.*; for 6 boards for making the gutter there — 3*d.*; for shingle-nails, board-nails, and spiking for the same — 7*d.*

'Expenses about making provision against the coming of the lord':

73 for the carriage of one cart-load of water for brewing and baking (*pro brac' et furn'*) against the coming of the lord because no water came to the court by pipe (*per pipam*) at that time — 3*s.* 4*d.*

74 to one carpenter repairing the walls of the bakery and the brew-house and laying shingles in diverse places for one week and 4 days — 2*s.* 6*d.*

75 to carpenter(s) repairing and laying shingles over the chambers over the gate (*ultra portam*) — 10*d.*; for 300 shingles — 6*d.*

76 for plastering a wall of the bakery — 2*d.*

77 for repairing the door of the granary — ½*d.*

'Cost of the great hall'

78 to one carpenter stopping up the openings in the top of the hall (*ad obstupand' foramina in summitate aule*) for 5 weeks — 8*s.* 4*d.*

79 to William le verrer for making 97 feet of glass for the windows at the ends of the great hall — 24*s.* 3*d.*, per foot 3*d.*

80 for 3 pieces of iron bought for making bars and fastenings (*takett'*) for the same windows, with the hire of a smith — 3*s.* 2*d.*

81 for making the painters' 'belfry' [movable scaffold] (*berefrid' pictorum*) — 11*s.*; for making 60 hurdles for the scaffold, and collecting rods in the wood — 6*s.*; collecting rods for the scaffold, and binding and carrying them — 4*d.*; felling 20 alders for the same — 2*d.*; buying 12 great alders for the same — 3*s.*; for felling 33 alders in the park for the painters' 'belfry' — 2*d.*; sawing a great alder for the same — 4*d.*; help of 3 boys raising the 'belfry' in the hall — 2*d.*; grease bought for the wheels of the 'belfry' — 1*d.*; felling 30 alders for the painters and 33 small alders for the nests of the swans — 2*d* [The swans were those which nested on the edge of the bishop's pools, which separated the Cathedral Close from the town of Lichfield]; (struck through 'because in the account of Lichfield': to John le Blound chaplain for the work of the painters this year — £28)

'Cost of the new wall':

82 for cleaning 3 perches and one quarter of a plot of land in the ditch next to the garden for breaking stone (*pro petr' frang'*) — £4 4*s.* 6*d.*, per perch 26*s.*; for breaking stone, namely one perch one quarter — 66*s.* 8*d.*, per perch 53*s.* 4*d.*; for stone breaking, [namely] 2 perches — £6 13*s.* 4*d.*, per perch 5 marks

83 for all costs of one postern of the new wall — 5*s.* 7*d.*

84 for a cart carrying stone from the quarry of Freford for 6 days — 3*s.* 6*d.*

85 for lime (*calce*) bought for the stone — 33*s.* ¼*d.*

86 for 4 pieces of iron bought for the bars and hooks (*uncis*) for the windows of the wall behind the old hall, with the hire of a smith — 2*s.*

87 to Ralph de Kelbi for making 3½ perches and 3 feet of new wall between the court of the bishop behind the old hall and the court of the dean — 43s. 6d., per perch 12s.; to the same for 11¼ perches of new wall in the court extending from the new hall up to the great wall of the close — 15s., per perch as above

'Cost with regard to making the pond':

88 to Thomas le ovenemaker for repairing the pond in the court (*pro stagno … reparand'*) in work done with earth (*ex opere terrestr'*) [e.g. ? puddling clay] and drawing off the water from it — 25s.
89 for 100 stones called *tablos* bought for the foundations of the pond — 18d.
90 to one *Tersus* (*in stip' .I. Tersi* [personal name or occupation name]) for enlarging the pond in the court by 5 feet and filling in the old pond (*adimplend' vetus stagnum*) — 13s. 4d.
91 for 840 large stones bought from the quarry of Freford — 50s., per 100 6s.; for carving the stones — £4 3s. 6d. by tally against Ralph the mason, per 100 10s.
92 to mason(s) placing the stone in the pond — £4 13s. 3d.

'Forinsec expenses':

93 to 2 men making an *herbarium* next to the new hall for 6 days — 18d.; digging clods there — 6d.; to 6 men cleaning and repairing the ditch around the bishop's garden (*gardinum*) at Lichfield for one week — 5s. 3d.; digging up 200 hawthorns (*alb' spinet' assartand'*) and planting them in the bishop's garden — 3d.; in carrying them — 3d.
94 for 8 ells of hemp bought for the window(s) of the new chapel lest the corn there be destroyed by birds (*destruantur per volucres*) — 18d.

1312–13 (m. 5)

'Necessary expenses':

95 for cutting down fencing for an enclosure made in the court opposite the kitchen and the bakery — 6d.
96 for iron for one bucket (*bokett'*) for drawing water from the pond to the garden — 2d.
97 for 4 clouts with nails (*clut' cum clav'*) and 2 iron cart-shafts (*limeis*) for a small wagon taking water from the pond to the garden — 2d.
98 for 17 candleholders for the great hall and the chambers — 2s. 1½d.; for repairing 6 iron candleholders — 1d.
99 to William le plomer for repairing the lead conduit for taking water from the conduit of the Close (*de conducto in claust'*) up to the court of the bishop — 33s. 4d.

'Cost of the houses':

100 for one lock bought for the stable door — 2½d.
101 for rods collected for the kitchen in the court — 2d.
102 for 18 thack boards for the bakery — 9d.; for roofing the porch of the bakery — 2s. 6d.; to one carpenter roofing with boards the defects of the bakery and of the gutter for 3 days — 7d.
103 to a roofer roofing the stairs (*grossus*) between the hall and the kitchen for one day, together with 2 women helping him — 4d.
104 to William Prick roofing the defects over the chamber of the painters for 4 days — 8d.
105 for 9 thack boards for the windows [*or* shutters] of the bakery — 7d.; to one carpenter roofing the defects over the bakery with 1,000 shingles, and repairing the trestles and making a new ladder, [for] 5 days — 12½d., per day 2½d.
106 for 300 shingle-nails bought for the bakery — 6d.; 16 thraves of straw bought for roofing the bakery — 2s. 8d.
107 for one key and for repairing a lock of the lord's garderobe — 2d.; for one key for the postern next to the kitchen — 2d.; for one key for the door of the dovecot — 1d.; for one iron bar for the door of the chamber next to the door of the great hall with 10 long-nails for the same — 3d.; for one key for the stable — 1d.

108   to Thomas le ovenemaker for repairing the oven (*furnum*) against the feast of the Nativity of Our Lord — 16*d*.

109   to Richard the carpenter for roofing defects over the old hall in the court with shingles and over the chamber over the gate, and also for making one gable at the chamber of the painters and repairing the walls of the house once of Thomas le Nevyle and the barn, and for making 2 rat-traps (*truncos ratonum*), for 11 working days — 2*s*. 11*d*., per day 3*d*.; for nails, shingles, laths, boards, and spik' for the same — 14½*d*.

110   to a carpenter for making a gutter for the pipe of the lead conduit (*ad pipam plumbi conducti*), and for making wheelbarrows and windows and louvers in the bakery, for one week — 16*d*.; for nails, boards, and spik' for the same — 2½*d*.; for 2 hoops, 2 ? hooks, and 2 plates of iron for the wheelbarrow for the garden — 3*d*.

111   for 8 thraves of straw bought for roofing the stairs (*grossus*) between the hall and kitchen — 16*d*.; for roofing the bakery with straw — 2*s*. 6*d*.

112   to William le hors for making 2 hearths for 2 ovens (*furnos*) — 12*d*.

113   for 100 thack boards for the brew-house — 3*s*. 6*d*.; for nails, boards, and shingles for the same — 17*d*.

114   for 100 shingle-nails and 50 lead-nails for the hay barn — 3*d*.; to one carpenter for roofing the defects over the brew-house and kitchen for one week — 18*d*.

115   to the same man for repairing the gutters of the hay barn for 2 days — 6*d*.

116   for a quarter-board for the chamber over (*ultra*) the gate — 12*d*.

117   for 100 board-nails for the bakery — 3*d*.; for 1,000 shingle-nails for the chamber over (*ultra*) the gate, the kitchen, the brew-house, and the hay barn — 2*s*. 6*d*.; for spik' for the chamber — ¾*d*.; for 200 board-nails and lead-nails for the same — 6*d*.; for 100 board-nails for the dovecot — 3*d*.

118   to Richard the capenter for roofing and repairing defects over the bakery, brew-house, chamber over (*ultra*) the gate, hay barn, and dovecot for 5 weeks — 6*s*. 3*d*., per week 15*d*.

'Cost of the great hall':

119   for 100 nails for the lead gutter — 6*d*.; for 300 lbs. of tin for roofing the hall and adjoining chambers — 5*s*. 7½*d*., per lb. 2¼*d*.; for 12½ lbs. of tin for the same — 2*s*. 7¼*d*., per lb. 2½*d*.; for 10 feet of lead for the same — 18*s*. 9*d*., per foot 22½*d*.; for a cart and two horses going to Derby and coming back with the lead — 6*d*.; for a third horse for the same for 2 days — 4*d*.; to William le Plumer for soldering the tin and lead and for repairing the defects of the roofs and the gutter of the great hall and of the adjoining chambers for 9 weeks — 13*s*. 6*d*., per week 18*d*.; to a boy helping him for the same time — 4*s*. 7*d*., per day 1*d*.

120   to William Prik for wattling (*le bemfulling*) the great hall *per latera* and at one end outside — 8*s*.; [similarly] the great chamber — 10*d*.; for 2 other chambers — 12*d*.; the chamber against the kitchen — 8*d*.; the chapel — 8*d*.; the treasury — 8*d*.; and the openings (*foraminibus*) outside the hall — 3*d*.

'Wages and fees':

121   to Walter the gardener from Friday after Christmas with the wages of that day up to Michaelmas with the wages of that day — 45*s*. 8*d*., per day 2*d*.

'Livery of pence':

122   to John Blound for the work of the painters — £12 10*s*.

1313–14 (m. 6)

'Necessaries':

123   to 2 men making a hedge between the great gate and the granary for one day — 3*d*.

'Cost of the house(s)':

124   for 2 lbs. of tin for the repair of the hall and chambers of the lord — 6¼*d*.; spik-nails for the same — 1½*d*.

125 to William the plummer setting candleholders in the hall and in the lord's chamber and chapel about the feast of All Saints [1 November] for 5 days — 15*d*.; to his boy for the same time — 7½*d*., per day 1½*d*.

126 to the same man for repairing the hall and chambers for 11 days about the feast of the invention of the Holy Cross [3 May] — 2*s*. 9*d*., per day 3*d*.; to his boy for the same time — 16½*d*.

127 to William de Chesterfield cooper for repairing brewing vats against the coming of the lord for 15 days — 3*s*. 9*d*., per day 3*d*.; to the same for repairing wine casks about Epiphany [6 January] for one day — 2*d*.

128 for 3 lbs. of tin bought after the feast of St Gregory [12 March] for the pipe of the lead conduit — 9*d*.; to William the plummer for repairing the same — 6*s*.

129 for 200 shingle-nails for the hay barn — 4*d*.; to a man repairing the same with shingles for 2 days — 5*d*.

ACKNOWLEDGEMENTS

I am most grateful to Dr John Harvey for reading through the article in draft and making most helpful suggestions for its improvement. Figure 1 prepared for volume 14 of the *Victoria County History of Staffordshire* and is reproduced here by kind permission of the General Editor of the *Victoria County History*.

REFERENCES

1. The term 'palace' is not contemporary. It is recorded as a description for the bishop's house at Lichfield in 1447–8: LJRO, B/A/21, CC 124078, m. 1 (fee of *custos palacii domini*). The early 14th-century usage was *curia*, translated as 'court' in the accounts reproduced in the Appendix.
2. W. Dugdale, *Monasticon Anglicanum* (1673), iii. 219. The ratio is confirmed by modern measurements, based on a frontage of some 60 ft for the sites occupied by canonical houses.
3. See Appendix nos 12, 86–7, 109. Future references to entries in the Appendix will appear in the text of the article, in the form of A plus relevant number, enclosed in parentheses.
4. *Calendar of Patent Rolls*, 1292–1301, 409.
5. LJRO, B/A/1/1, f. 117.
6. S. Erdeswick, *A Survey of Staffordshire*, ed. T. Harwood (1844), 281–2.
7. L. G. Wickham Legg (ed.), *A Relation of a Short Survey of 26 Counties, 1634* (1904), 58. The reference to 'Irish' timber is almost certainly misleading.
8. For a brief account of the sieges see N. J. Tringham, 'Two Seventeenth-Century Surveys of Lichfield Cathedral Close', *TSSAHS*, xxv (1985 for 1983–4), 39.
9. SRO, 547/1/106–108 (the spelling has been modernised).
10. For this paragraph see, unless otherwise stated, *VCH Staffordshire*, iii, 175, 177, and N. J. Tringham, 'Bishop's Palace, Lichfield Cathedral Close: its construction, 1686–7', *TSSAHS*, xxvii (1987 for 1985–6), 57–63.
11. LJRO, D. 30 (unlisted).
12. C. H. Josten (ed.), *Elias Ashmole*, iv (1966), 1512, n. 4.
13. LJRO, B/A/21, CC 123828, item 1; Tringham, 'Bishop's Palace', text on n. 16.
14. *VCH Staffordshire*, xiv, 67.
15. See Appendix.
16. Bodleian Library, Oxford, MS Tanner 217, f. 42. Redrawn, it was printed in an article on Lichfield Cathedral Close by William Beresford: *The Reliquary*, vii (1867), figure facing p. 249.
17. Bodleian Library, MS Tanner 131, f. 185 (the spelling has been modernised). Also see Tringham, 'Bishop's Palace'.
18. One is Bodleian Library, MS Tanner 217, f. 43; the other is in the possession of Lichfield Cathedral School, which currently occupies the present palace.
19. Bodleian Library, MS Tanner 131, f. 170.
20. Ibid., f. 185.
21. SRO, D (W) 1734/3/2/12, m. 16.
22. LJRO, B/A/21, early 17th-century book of accounts; T. Harwood, *The History and Antiquities of the Church and City of Lichfield* (Gloucester 1806), 385.

23. *Calendar of State Papers Domestic*, 1638–9, p. 119.
24. For a list of other great halls (with dimensions) see Margaret Wood, *The English Medieval House* (1965), 45–6, 62–6.
25. For the use of the word *capud/capita* meaning 'end' see e.g. A 27, 40, 54; *latera* is used for 'sides' — A 120.
26. In drawing his plan Greswold misplaced the line of the west wall of the 'Lady's chamber', showing it aligned with that of the hall, although his annotated measurement shows that it was as long as the 'Dining room' on the north side of the hall.
27. For a description of Hotton as steward see SRO, D (W) 1734/J 2057, m. 1, 'Liveries'.
28. *VCH Staffordshire*, III, 157.
29. The plans are those recorded in n. 18.
30. That in possession of Lichfield Cathedral School.
31. J. Gould, 'The Twelfth-Century Water-Supply to Lichfield Close', *Antiquaries Journal*, LVI (1), 73–9; William Salt Library, Stafford, Staffordshire Views, VI, 37.
32. *VCH Staffordshire*, II, 338–43; V, 53.
33. Bishop Langton gave Hugh de la Dale, mason, and his wife Agnes a tenement in Lichfield on 4 August 1307: Bodleian Library, MS Ashmole 1527, f. 39ᵛ; land in the fields of Lichfield which had been held by Master Hugh de la Dale, mason, was mentioned in 1319: SRO, D 948/3/34.

The Lapidary Collections of Lichfield Cathedral

By Richard K. Morris

In 1982 the author was invited by Canon Graham Smallwood (then the Custos) to examine the lapidary collection in the upper chamber of the Cathedral's north-west tower, in advance of a scheme to convert it to a schools project room. Nothing came of this proposal, and in 1985 all the contents were removed when the chamber became a choral practice room instead. In the meantime, the catalogue was compiled by Carol Lovelock in 1983 under the author's guidance, and has subsequently been extended to include loose, worked stones and related artefacts in other parts of the Cathedral. A copy of the catalogue is deposited in the Cathedral library, with a record of the location of each piece.[1]

At the time of writing, some of the more interesting stones are on permanent display in the new Visitor and Study Centre created in Bishop Hacket's former stable block at the south-east corner of the Close. These include all the carved stones of the Romanesque period formerly loose on the north side of the retrochoir, where they were inspected by members of the Association in 1987. Most other items of importance lie in temporary storage in the basement of No. 24 The Close, with a few very large sculptures such as the Roman cement statues from the Cathedral west front, in the garage used by No. 23. They are not accessible to the public, and a better arrangement for their display and long-term conservation is badly needed. Just a few pieces remain around the Cathedral church, notably the roof bosses from the nave vault (currently in the south choir aisle) and the Roman cement statues from the south transept (in the crossing tower). Other pieces are stored in the north gallery of the nave, and in buildings called the 'stoneyard' on the east side of Dam Street.

Overall the lapidary collections are one of the most interesting in any great church in the country. The majority of items in the catalogue are of considerable significance for the history of the Cathedral, and a number of pieces are of national importance, such as the group of Romanesque stones and the unique survival of the Roman cement statues of the Regency period. To facilitate discussion and identification, the collections have been divided here into seven provisional categories based on stylistic periods or on the type of material. A full list of items placed in each category is given in the Appendix at the end. Reference to an individual piece in the text is by its catalogue number (e.g. 'L(ichfield) C(athedral) 57') which is also marked on the object. All items are sandstone unless stated otherwise.

1. ROMANESQUE AND TRANSITIONAL

This category consists almost entirely of items from the 12th century.[2] Most of these stones must be associated with the lost Romanesque Cathedral church, and constitute the only evidence for its style. A few may be late enough to belong possibly with the Transitional phase of c. 1170 sqq. for the east end postulated by Warwick Rodwell.[3] The majority appear to derive from the extensive works attributed to Bishop Roger de Clinton (1129–48) and perhaps also from the remodelled eastern axial chapel of c. 1150–60.[4] They may be compared with contemporary works in the north Midlands, such as Stafford St Chad, Tutbury Priory (west front) and Southwell Minster, especially in their use of varieties of chevron and carved ornaments clasping roll mouldings (Fig. 1, J, L). One capital from a nook shaft takes the form of a head with foliate tendrils issuing from the mouth (LC 125,

Pl. XXa); the whole composition generally reminiscent of the right capital in the south portal of Kilpeck church, Herefordshire, c. 1150.[5] Several corbels survive, mostly carved with human heads and apparently from the eaves stringcourse of a roof (e.g. Fig. 1, E; and cf. Southwell Minster, south-west tower), and the finest example depicts a bird, perhaps a pelican pecking its breast (LC 26, Pl. XXb). Two lengths of stringcourse carved with a band of lozenges (LC 19A–B) find an exact parallel inside the west front of Tutbury church, but comparisons for some of the other patterns are less easy to find (e.g. Fig. 1, B, G, L, N, P). Also worthy of note is a fragmentary stone carved with a haloed, bearded head, apparently from a panel and later Romanesque, but possibly early Gothic (LC 103, height of head 9 cm).

Most of the stones seem to have survived because they had been reused in the fabric of the Gothic Cathedral and discovered in subsequent restorations. A drawing of 1856 by the wife of Charles Gresley, Chapter Clerk from 1847 to 1900, records the general locations where a number of them were found, which may provide a rough guide in some instances to their original position in the Romanesque church (Fig. 1). A multi-scalloped capital came from the 'old foundations' of the choir (Fig. 1, A), and other pieces from the north choir aisle (Fig. 1, K, N, P), the nave south aisle (Fig. 1, B, F), the west doors (Fig. 1, D, L) and the Consistory Court — probably St Chad's Head Chapel (Fig. 1, E, R).

2. EARLY ENGLISH AND GEOMETRICAL

These are pieces similar in period to the existing fabric of the Early English Gothic Cathedral, begun c. 1200, and of the nave of c. 1260–90. A number of the worked stones are similar to ones still extant in the church, indicating that they come from areas which have been remodelled, perhaps as early as the 14th or 15th centuries (e.g. the presbytery and the upper parts of the transepts), or have been removed during later restorations. They are thus a valuable check on the archaeological accuracy of such restorations. For example, a foliage capital with a broad serrated leaf (LC 2) may be compared with specimens in the west bays of the choir, and spandrel LC 50 with the Chapter House dado. Capital LC 3 has incised on the underside the outline of a fluted shaft, an unusual feature in early Gothic but found in the triforium of the south transept in the shafts adjoining the crossing piers.[6] Two large foliate roof bosses LC 147A and 147B, can be firmly identified with the nave high vault because of the profiles of their rib mouldings, which also indicate that each boss fitted at a tri-radial junction of a transverse rib with two tierceron ribs. In addition, there are two lengths of ridge rib (LC 53A–B), one of which still retains traces of decoration in red, green and gold. Presumably they were all removed when the centre bays of the nave vault were rebuilt in lath and plaster under Wyatt, 1788 sqq.,[7] and thus constitute an invaluable record of the lost parts of the 13th-century vault.[8] Another interesting survival is two fragments carved with volutes (LC 46A–B) which may originate from the lost 13th-century rose window in the gable of the south transept.[9] A label tied to LC 46A reads: 'Found buried in the wall above the South Transept Window September 3rd 1894. Probably a fragment of the original Rose Window. C. Bodington'.[10]

Evidence that earlier stones were recut to construct the Early English Cathedral is provided by an early Gothic base carved on the back of a Romanesque capital decorated with trellis pattern (LC 11). The base is comparable to some still surviving in the 13th-century dado of the choir aisles. Moulded stones from the Early English Cathedral were also reused, as wall filling, when the east end was rebuilt in the 14th century, e.g. LC 136, a piece of early Gothic dado arch exposed during modern restoration in the recessed wall of the south choir aisle (third bay from the east).

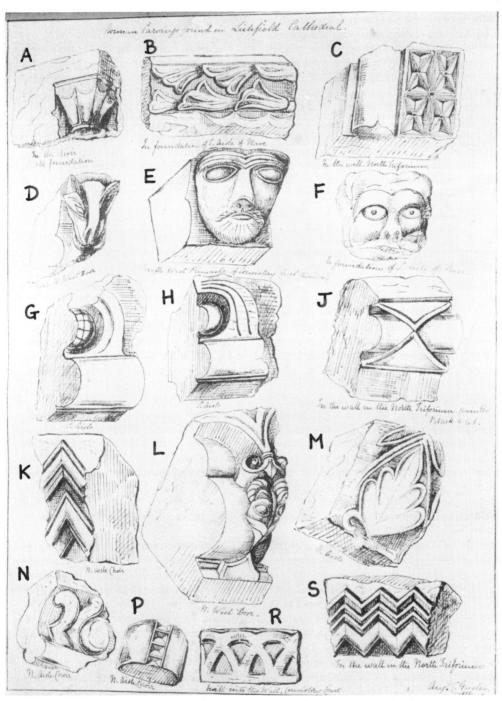

FIG. 1.   Fragments discovered during restorations, drawn by Mrs C. Gresley, 1856
(*Anastatic Drawing Society* (1856), pl. XXXV). Identifying letters added by R. K. Morris.
All these pieces exist today except D and R

Of the several pieces of figure sculpture in this category, a piece of outstanding quality is a roof boss carved with two (mutilated) figures in an elegant, swaying composition (LC 55, Pl. XXIA): the foliage between them is stiff-leaf. The boss formed the centrepiece of a quadripartite vault, and its style and the plain chamfer profiles of the rib ends suggest that its most likely location was in St Chad's Head Chapel, the vault of which was apparently seriously damaged during the 1646 siege and eventually completely renewed in 1897.[11] The date of the boss would thus seem to be *c.* 1250–60: Dean Mancetter (1222–54) is buried in the ground-floor wall of the two-storey structure. Two other sculptured stones represent the lower half of a figure seated on a throne, *c.* 1250–75 (LC 101, height of figure when complete, about 45 cm), and a crucifixion in a very abraded condition (LC 104, Pl. XXC). The latter may well belong with other carved stone panels mounted in the walls inside St Chad's Head Chapel.

3. DECORATED

These belong to the period *c.* 1290–1350, and the majority are essentially architectural. As with Category 2, a number of these stones seem to have been replaced at restorations, and relate to existing fabric in the Decorated work of the east end. The mouldings of LC 40A–C and 41A–B prove that they derive from the tracery and mullions respectively of the Lady Chapel windows, and LC 47A–G are sections of the ornamental interior parapet from the same chapel. They are most likely to have been removed during Oldrid Scott's restoration of 1895. A fragment of an arch carved with two rows of small ballflower (LC 87) might be a sole survival from the external tomb recesses on the south side of the Lady Chapel, restored out of recognition under the same architect in 1879. LC 133 is a length of respond from the Decorated dado of the east bays of the choir aisles (*c.* 1320–30), reused shortly afterwards as wall filling when the recess in the third bay of the south aisle was created, apparently as an afterthought.

Within this category there is also a small group of stones mostly to be associated with work in the style of the royal master mason, Master William Ramsey, who was supervising the completion and fitting out the eastern arm of the Cathedral from 1337. In particular LC 28 is a moulded jamb stone incorporating a band of openwork quatrefoils, similar to the interior frames which Ramsey designed for the choir clerestory windows; but on a smaller scale, and the exact provenance of this stone is unresolved. Another moulded jamb stone, LC 82, includes a small bowtell set in a hollow casement between two three-quarter roll mouldings, a distinctive combination first appearing in early Perpendicular work at Gloucester and Windsor.[12]

Exceptional in their quality are several panels which must derive from elaborate monuments or fittings of Ramsey's period, some perhaps from St Chad's shrine base. One alludes to the royal arms with lion's heads and fleur-de-lis set in vertical bands of quatrefoils (LC 66A, Pl. XXD), which John Maddison has proposed is part of an unidentified episcopal tomb illustrated in a drawing preserved in the College of Arms. Another stone, LC 69, is carved on one side with the arms of France Ancient and England quartered (adopted by Edward III in 1340), but the block has been recut on the other surfaces apparently to create a foliate roof boss of about the same date. LC 67A–C includes multi-petalled roses set in a band of delicate quatrefoils with a miniature vault, and LC 51 seems to be a piece of small-scale vault decorated with foiled shapes, reminiscent in style of the vault under the viewing platform of St Chad's Head Chapel.[13] LC 68A–G are seven pieces from a Gothic stone screen, probably to be dated to this period because the ornamentation includes sparse tufts of foliage particularly associated with Ramsey's style, as in the interior stringcourses of the choir clerestory. LC 66B is a panel which exudes the restraint and elegance of the court style of the early 14th century, and may actually pre-date Ramsey's time at Lichfield: its likely provenance is the side of a tomb-chest (Pl. XXE). Another piece to note is LC 27, a small pinnacle carved with some figures; the material appears to be Purbeck marble and this has led to the suggestion that it derives from St Chad's shrine, but the quality is poor.

4. LATER GOTHIC

This category covers stones from the Perpendicular period, but also others for which it is difficult to give a more precise designation than Decorated or Perpendicular. More of them derive from fittings than from architecture, and overall this is the least interesting category (though note that Category 5 also covers this period). LC 93 is the mutilated stump of a corbel apparently showing the wing and hand of an angel, which may be 'the portion of the sculptured wing of an angel' discovered by Sir George Gilbert Scott above the dean's stall, and which supplied the idea for his own angelic supports for the choir vault shafts.[14] Judging by the crude quality of the carving, the stone might not be Gothic but a 17th-century replacement after the Civil War damage.

5. THE REREDOS

The rationale underlying this category is that all the items seem to derive from the late medieval high altar screen, substantial parts of which survived *in situ* until 1788, when they were moved and reused by Wyatt for his new altarpiece in the Lady Chapel and the organ screen at the entrance to the choir.[15] During the 19th-century restorations, both these works were demolished — the organ screen in Smirke's time before 1856. Some of the pieces such as canopies were incorporated during Bishop Lonsdale's episcopacy (1843–67) into Scott's new south sedilia and the monuments to Dean Howard and Lonsdale himself, where they may still be seen.[16] A considerable number of other pieces survive in the lapidary collection.

The most distinctive feature is that all the stones are an even-grained oolitic limestone of a 'Bath' type, indicating that the reredos was imported to the Cathedral during the Middle Ages, probably already carved. A more precise geological attribution could be helpful in determining its likely place of fabrication, such as Bristol or Oxford. The majority of stones constitute such features as bases (e.g. LC 62), pinnacles (e.g. LC 63), canopies (e.g. LC 126), brackets carved with vines (LC 130), and particularly a series of angels holding shields (LC 18, Pl. XXF). These obviously belong to the late 15th or early 16th centuries on the basis of stylistic comparison with surviving screens at the Cathedrals of Winchester (c. 1475) St Albans (1476–92) and Southwark (c. 1520).[17] The frieze of heraldic angels relates to the usage of similar friezes at St George's Chapel, Windsor, and Henry VII's Chapel, Westminster. However, a smaller group of oolitic stones (LC 57A–H) are carved with a variety of miniature lierne and panelled vaults which could belong as well to the transitional phase between Decorated and Perpendicular around the third-quarter of the 14th century. For example, LC 57F combines a form of fan vault with a curvilinear mouchette wheel (Pl. XXG). Thus there is a hint that an earlier reredos, perhaps commissioned for the sanctuary of the new east end remodelled by William Ramsey, was heightened or partly reused in a grander screen of c. 1500.[18] However, the main difficulty with this interpretation is that apparently the same imported oolite has been used for the work of both periods. Altogether, these stones deserve much closer study, not only because they represent the rare remains of at least one great medieval altar screen, but also because through their reuse they embody the history of the Cathedral at several later periods.

6. MONUMENTAL STATUARY

This very important group consists of original sandstone statues of *c.* 1300, which were cut back and coated in Roman cement by Armstrong and Harris (*c.* 1820–30) — seemingly a unique survival of a common Regency treatment for medieval carvings.[19] When they were finally removed and replaced in the late 19th century (west front restored, 1878–84), selected specimens were placed in the chambers of the north-west tower and the crossing tower, suggesting that certain Victorians appreciated their significance as the remnants of a great medieval scheme of monumental statuary rare in this country. The main survivals today are five figures from the central porch of the west façade, all of them originally column statues, apparently monolithic (LC 95A–E, Pl. XXIb). Also two impressive seated figures from the gallery of kings, one without Roman cement coating (LC 97A–B), and two other standing statues, possibly from the north-west tower (LC 96A–B). In the central tower are six of the seven figures from the south transept façade, possibly dating originally from *c.* 1240 (LC 140–6). All these statues are damaged or broken. In addition numerous loose pieces survive such as heads, drapery and canopy work, most showing traces of Roman cement; and also a small piece of sandstone sideshaft with 'Found in front West Door 1878' written in ink on its surface (LC 56).

7. MISCELLANEOUS

The pieces in this category are almost entirely post-medieval, except for three floor tiles with green glaze (LC 113, 114A–B). It includes the top four stone courses of the central spire, rebuilt after the Civil War and taken down in 1949 (LC 132); five small marble pieces apparently from Sir George Gilbert Scott's reredos (LC 112A–E); and a large number of pieces of late 18th-century and early 19th-century monuments in various stones which need to be recorded properly (LC 139 in the 'stoneyard' building, at least 100 pieces; and more in the nave north gallery, uncatalogued). Of considerable interest is LC 149, about twenty-five pieces of what appear to be moulds resembling the foliage frieze along the eaves of the nave north aisle. The most likely explanation of their use is that they were made as models for the sculptors to follow, probably during Scott's restoration (1856–78); apparently Scott recommended the making of plaster copies in the 1860s.[20]

APPENDIX

ITEMS IN EACH CATEGORY

(identified by 'LC' catalogue number)

1. *Romanesque and Transitional:* 1, 5, 10, (11), 16, 19, 20–2, 24–6, 30–9, 90–2, 103, 122–5, 131?, 150
2. *Early English and Geometrical:* 2–4, 6, 11–15, 17, 18, 46, 50, 52–5, 101, 104, 134, 136, 137, 147
3. *Decorated:* 7–9, 27–9, 40–3, 47, 51, 65–9, 82, 87, 88, 133
4. *Later Gothic:* 44, 45, 48, 49, 71–80, 83, 93, 105, 111, 135

5. *The Reredos:* 57–64, 70, 81, 116–18, 121, 126–30
6. *Monumental Statuary:* 56, 84, 85, 89, 94–100, 102, 105–8, 119, 120, 140–6, + uncatalogued canopies in nave north gallery
7. *Miscellaneous:* 86, 109, 112–15, 132, 138, 139, 148, 149, + numerous uncatalogued items in nave north gallery

Items with traces of paint: 35, 43, 53, 55, 57ABCG, 65, 66, 70, 74E, 75, 82, 86, 102, 104
Items with mason's marks (post-medieval): 51, 62ABC

ACKNOWLEDGEMENTS

My warmest thanks are due to Carol Lovelock BA for the excellent inventory of the contents of the north-west tower chamber, and to countless Warwick University students who have helped me continue the catalogue since then. I should like to thank the Dean and Chapter for the grant which enabled Carol Lovelock to carry out the work, and to Jean and Graham Smallwood for their generous hospitality. Many people at the Cathedral have provided valuable assistance and information, including Tony Barnard, Godfrey Hives, John Howe, Richard Ninis and Graham Smallwood. I have also benefited from the good advice of Thomas Cocke, Phillip Lindley, Richard Lockett, Warwick Rodwell and Pamela Lady Wedgwood.

REFERENCES

SHORTENED TITLES USED

COBB (1980) — G. Cobb, *English Cathedrals, the Forgotten Centuries* (London 1980)
RODWELL (1989) — W. Rodwell, 'Archaeology and the standing fabric; recent studies at Lichfield Cathedral', *Antiquity*, 63 (1989), 281–94.

1. Photographs of all the items are also to be found in the History of Art Photograph Library, Warwick University, Coventry, which holds the negatives.
2. Except possibly the simple shaft bases LC 10A–B, which might equally be later 11th century.
3. Rodwell (1989), 283–5.
4. For the dating, see ibid.; and A. R. Dufty, 'Lichfield Cathedral', *Archaeol.J.*, CXX (1963), 293–4.
5. Illustrated in G. Zarnecki, *Later English Romanesque Sculpture 1140–1210* (London 1953), pl. 19. This is not to imply that the Lichfield carving is a product of the 'Herefordshire school'.
6. Found also at Lincoln Cathedral (St Hugh's choir, 'Trondheim piers') and the former priory church of St Mary, Nuneaton (crossing).
7. See further J. M. Frew, 'Cathedral Improvements: James Wyatt at Lichfield Cathedral 1787–92', *TSSAHS*, XIX for 1977/8 (1979), 33–40.
8. There seems to be no foundation for the idea that stone bosses were kept *in situ*, as stated in Cobb (1980), 151, n. 45.
9. See Rodwell (1989), 291, for the history of this window.
10. The author was presumably Canon Bodington, who wrote a guidebook to the Cathedral in 1899.
11. Rodwell (1989), 286–8. I am grateful to Warwick Rodwell and Pamela Lady Wedgwood for suggesting this location.
12. See further R. K. Morris, 'The development of later Gothic mouldings in England c.1250–1400', *Architectural History* XXII (1979), 5–7, n. 162 and fig. 12C.
13. J. M. Maddison, 'Master Masons in the Diocese of Lichfield: a study of 14th-century architecture at the time of the Black Death', *Lancashire and Cheshire Antiq. Soc. Trans*, 85 (1988), 139 and n. 46. The tomb is illustrated in Cobb (1980), 156, Fig. 242. Maddison dates the ballustrade of the viewing platform to St Chad's head chapel at c.1380–90.
14. A. B. Clifton, *The Cathedral Church at Lichfield* (Bell's Cathedral Series, London 1898), 76.
15. See further Cobb (1980), 144–6.
16. See R. B. Lockett, 'Sydney Smirke, George Gilbert Scott and "The Rearrangement of Lichfield Cathedral for Divine Worship" 1854–1861', *Institute for the Study of Worship & Religious Architecture, Research*

Bulletin (1980), 28; where it is also noted that Nicholson reused further pieces from this group in 1913/14 for the matching north sedilia.

17.   For the Winchester screen, see P. G. Lindley, 'The Great Screen of Winchester Cathedral I', *Burlington Magazine* CXXXI/1038 (Sept. 1989), 604–15; and J. Hardacre, *Winchester Cathedral Triforium Gallery: Catalogue* (Winchester 1989), 21–33.

18.   It is interesting that in the 18th century, when the screen was still *in situ*, Stukeley commented upon the variety of its decoration, and Pennant thought it to be a work of Bishop Langton; cited in Cobb (1980), 142.

19.   For this notorious 19th-century restoration, see further R. B. Lockett, 'Joseph Potter: Cathedral Architect at Lichfield 1794–1842', *TSSAHS*, XXI (1981), 39; and Cobb (1980), 148.

20.   I am grateful to Christopher Wilson and Richard Lockett for advice on this matter.

Ruin and Restoration: Lichfield Cathedral in the Seventeenth Century

By Thomas Cocke

The history of Lichfield Cathedral in the mid-17th century is not only eventful, indeed highly dramatic, in itself but it also illuminates aspects of church history and architecture insufficiently appreciated. The story has been ably told by several authors, most recently in the carefully documented account in the *Victoria County History* and in the current archaeological investigations by Warwick Rodwell.[1] This article seeks to explore the issues raised by it.

Lichfield has the sad distinction of being the most hotly disputed of all the English cathedrals during the Civil Wars. It was besieged and then stormed no fewer than three times between 1643 and 1646. Unfortunately the Close was an easily defensible site and lay in a strategic position in the north-west Midlands, commanding communications with Lancashire and with Wales, both areas of great importance to the king as centres of support. The whole area was also one of disputed loyalties, unlike largely Roundhead East Anglia or Royalist Lancashire, and both sides had their turn of occupying the Cathedral as a stronghold. In this respect the Royalists were no more respectful of the religious nature of the site than the Parliamentarians.

The first act was the most famous, although it had little effect on the fabric. The details are worth rehearsing again as they illustrate contemporary attitudes to church buildings. On 2 March 1643, the patronal festival of St Chad, the Cathedral and Close, which had already been occupied by a Royalist garrison, were assaulted by Lord Brooke. Brooke was not only an active Parliamentarian and Lord Lieutenant of 'the Associated Counties of Staffordshire and Warwickshire', but a prominent anti-clerical. Dugdale described him as 'strangely tainted with fanatic principles by the influence of one of his near Relations ... though in his own nature a very civil and well humor'd man. ... [He] became ... so great a zealot against the establish'd Discipline of the Church that no less than the utter extirpation of Episcopacy and abolishing all decent Order in the service of God would satisfy him'.[2] According to Dugdale, Brooke directed his forces against the Cathedral because of these religious principles, though he also of course had good strategic motives. Brooke was then killed by a chance shot from a marksman on the spire, according to legend the deaf and dumb son of the Royalist Commander, Sir Richard Dyott. This ironic disposition of providence was not lost on Archbishop Laud, by then a prisoner in the Tower.[3] Legend usually glosses over the sequel; the Royalists were forced to evacuate only three days later and the Roundheads took over the Cathedral, whence they were in turn dislodged a month later by Prince Rupert.

The iconoclasm and vandalism of the occupying Roundheads, with their mock baptisms and hunting parties, even if not invented by Royalist propaganda, can have done little damage to the building.[4] As elsewhere, the chief victims were service books, vestments, communion plate and manuscripts. Precentor Higgins rescued St Chad's Gospels and Ashmole secured others. Damage to tombs was also extensive, but much of this could have occurred in the three years after Prince Rupert's successful assault, during which the Close formed a Royalist garrison. As John Evelyn noted after the similar sack at Lincoln Cathedral, tombs attracted the attention of the soldiery for motives of profit, rather than any religious reason.[5] Dugdale, who had recorded the tombs and glass of the Cathedral in his famous anticipation of the 'impending storm' of the Civil War, reckoned that 67 gravestones were robbed of their brass inscriptions, 100 coats-of-arms destroyed, five 'raised tombs' of bishops and the tombs of great lords, such as Lord Bassett and Lord Paget were wrecked.[6] The finding of a chalice and crosier in the tomb of Bishop Scrope confirmed the soldiers' suspicion that riches were hidden beneath.

The third and final siege of the Close lasted for four months, from March to July 1646, and was the most severe. It was apparently at this stage that bombardment not only damaged the roofs and vaults but also the upper part of the central spire. There is a crude representation of its fallen state by Dugdale in the Ashmole manuscripts.[7] The extent of the damage was catalogued by the Parliamentary Commissioners surveying former Dean and Chapter lands, who were indignant at the degree of damage and thus loss to the Exchequer. The Cathedral was 'exceedingly ruinated', having been the target of allegedly 'two thousand shot of great ordnance and one thousand five hundred grenadoes'.[8] Much lead and ironwork, especially from the roof, had been stolen by the garrison, and more had been removed later. A similar story happened at Worcester where over £8,000 worth of lead was taken. Colonel Henry Danvers, Governor of Stafford, stripped the rest of the roof in October 1651 and sold it together with other materials for £1,200. The bells also went shortly afterwards.

The whole structure was condemned to disappear. A Parliamentary Order of 4 April 1651 resolved that 'the Cathedral of Lichfield be disposed of for the Use of the Poor, to set them on Work'.[9] Parliament was anxious, here as elsewhere, that the potential value of the building materials and those of other chapter buildings should be realised, being superfluous now bishops and chapters had been abolished, provided there were 'other Churches or Chapels sufficient for the people to meet in for the worship of God'.[10]

It is not clear (to what degree) any parts of the Cathedral could be used by a congregation. A head lecturer was appointed at the Cathedral on 22 July 1646, as at Canterbury, Winchester and elsewhere, and there were still payments for him seven or eight years later. Services were apparently held in the Chapter House.

Thus by May 1660 the fate of Lichfield Cathedral must have appeared to be sealed. Yet although the restoration of the monarchy did not necessarily involve the restoration of the traditional hierarchy, within a few weeks there was sufficient confidence at Lichfield for the round of services to be resumed. What sort of building remained to house them?

In 1600 Erdeswick had described the building as 'a goodly Cathedral Church, if I should say one of the Fairest and best Repaired in England, being thoroughly Builded and Finished, which few are'.[11] He singled out for praise

three Pyramids or Steeples of a good convenient and seemly height, all very well wrought with Freestone and especially the two Gemetts that stand Westwards, very well cut and curiously wrought. The which West Part is at the end also exceeding finely and cunningly set forth, with a great number of Tabernacles, and in the same, the images, or pictures of the Prophets, Apostles, Kings of Judah and diverse other Kings of this Land, so well Embossed, and so lively Cut, that it is a great pleasure for any Man that takes delight to see Rarities, to behold them.[12]

In 1634 the Norwich visitors had been impressed both by the building and its furnishings. 'As the outward part of this building is fair, so the inward part thereof is neat, and glorious, with fair Pillars, rich windows, and the Quire beautified with six fair gilt statues.' In the vestry were three 'old rich copes, a communion Cloth of cloth of gold for the High Altar and the Plate belonged thereunto, rich and fair, answerable for such a sacred place'.[13]

Of these splendours only the shell was left by 1660. The engraving published by Daniel King in 1656 bears the cartouche: '*Quod Petra conservare non potuit ut aeri incisum sempiterne maneat.*' Fuller, writing at the same time, described the Cathedral as 'a very carcase'.[14]

Only the Chapter House and the vestry were protected from the elements. Being two-storey buildings, it was the vaults of the upper chambers which had borne the brunt when the roofs collapsed. However, the Chapter House soon proved to need urgent repair. Urgent discussions must have been held as to the future of the building but there is no record either of a debate as to the style in which any rebuilding should take place or even whether a rebuilding of the medieval shell was sensible or practicable. Probably there was no one moment when such fundamental matters came up.

Luckily Lichfield had influential friends at Court, William Dugdale from nearby Warwick-shire and, a Lichfield man by birth, Elias Ashmole. Already in the summer of 1660 Dugdale was canvassing the restoration of the Cathedral with Dr (later Archbishop) Sheldon, and Ashmole pressed the matter on the king himself.[15] A crucial local figure seems to have been the Precentor, William Higgins, a survivor from the pre-war Chapter who carried out first-aid repairs as soon as it became apparent that the authority and estates of Cathedral Chapters were to be revived. These, which were supplemented by more permanent works once William Paul arrived as Dean in February 1661, were probably as important as the later energy of Bishop Hacket in ensuring the Cathedral was rebuilt to its former scale and in its former style. Bishop Frewen, consecrated bishop in 1644 in Oxford, was translated to York soon after the Restoration and Hacket did not receive the bishopric till December 1661 and did not arrive in Lichfield till August 1662. Presumably the bishop could have migrated to the 'twin' Cathedral city of the diocese at Coventry or he could have erected a smaller replacement at Lichfield. The medieval remains would surely have become a quarry for the citizens and any reduced building would have rejected the Gothic for a classical style.

Because of the rescue and reuse of much collapsed medieval stonework and the subsequent restorations by Wyatt, Potter and Gilbert Scott, it is hard to judge from the present fabric how much craftsmen still understood of Gothic detail. Warwick Rodwell considers that the 17th-century work can be distinguished by its cruder, bolder style. The foliage on the vaulting ribs was copied but the new bosses necessary were carved in a contemporary interpretation of the originals amongst which they were placed. Stone vaults were repaired, not replaced by wooden roofs and ceilings: all windows seem to have been given Perpendicular tracery.[16] The speed of rebuilding argues that the masons were still familiar with medieval construction. Already in 1663 consideration was being given to reglazing and repaving the choir and transepts.[17] By September 1665 the Lady Chapel, choir, chancel, transepts and nave were roofed and leaded; by the end of the next year a great part of the external stonework, including the central spire and the west window, was complete (Pl. XXIIA). By 1668 Bishop Hacket could turn his attention to the floor and the furnishings, and on Christmas Eve the next year he rededicated the Cathedral. Hacket died, his work completed, in October 1670. The bishop's desire to press ahead — he will have been aware of his own advancing years — may have led to skimped craftsmanship. The topmost courses of the central spire needed to be taken down and rebuilt in Wyatt's restoration, and the peal of six bells, which were the bishop's last benefaction, had to be recast within twenty years.

It is hard to discern who, if anyone, was the guiding artistic spirit behind the Lichfield work. A 'Mr. Fisher' was engaged in April 1661 as 'surveyor', but nothing is known of his background or other activities. Bishop Hacket himself was a historian and controversialist rather than a connoisseur.[18] His tomb, now to the south of the choir (Pl. XXIIB), followed medieval precedent in portraying him as a recumbent effigy clad in episcopal robes but contains no specific Gothic detail. His background as a close follower of John Williams, Bishop of Lincoln and patron of the library at St John's College, Cambridge, 'a very early case of Gothic Revival' would suggest at least a tolerance of medieval architecture.[19] His second Dean, the 'phrenetick' and mean Dr Wood, who 'sided altogether with the Puritans', told Hacket to his face that he 'did more harm than good in re-edifying this church'.[20] This antipathy to the building is reminiscent of Lord Brooke and the Puritan hostility to the rebuilding of Old St Paul's.

Hacket seems, like his patron's great enemy, Archbishop Laud, not to have cared particularly about artistic detail but simply to have desired the best possible for the Church from the funds available. The major piece of 'Gothic revival' was the idiosyncratic tracery of the west window which can have borne little relation to its predecessor; other windows received conventional panel tracery. The fittings installed in time for the consecration in 1669 were in an old-fashioned taste. The stalls with their canopies (three of which survive reset in the Consistory Court) were reminiscent of the kind of woodwork found in church furnishings of the 1630s, for instance in the 'Cosin' churches of County Durham, with the basically Gothic idea of canopies translated into a variety of classical details. It was not until 1678 that Dean Smalwood presented a sumptuous classical reredos, a replica of that recently erected in Whitehall Chapel to the designs of Christopher Wren, and executed by the same London craftsmen.[21]

The financing of the work at Lichfield was enough to daunt a lesser man than Hacket. The immediate work in 1660 was financed by accumulated fines and improved rents from Chapter property. A subscription list was opened in April 1661 and had, by July 1663, raised £2,729 of which Hacket contributed £1,160 and the Chapter £965. The next two years produced only £800, of which more than half came from the bishop, so stimulating him into taking over the fund-raising. A month before his death in 1670, he responded to Archbishop Sheldon's enquiry to all dioceses about their spending since the Restoration, claiming to have raised £15,000 in donations, of which he himself had given £3,500 for the fabric and half as much again for the bells and fittings.

Lichfield was never rich. At the Restoration the lands belonging to the fabric fund yielded only £25 and the common fund revenues just over £300, which paid for basic overheads such as salaries and royal dues; real income had risen to £450 by 1664–5.[22] The surplus each year was minimal, so all extraordinary fabric costs had to be met by contributions from entry fines or by special donations. Hacket was extremely ingenious in his methods of fund-raising.[23] He prevailed on the local gentry, such as Sir Edward Bagot of Blithfield, to 'sponsor' one of the fifty-two choir stalls for £8 a piece. The donor's arms were displayed in an escutcheon on the stall. The ladies of the diocese were invited to contribute to the 'ladies' organ'. Genteel visitors to the Cathedral city were liable to the honour of an episcopal visit, directed to fund-raising or, as a contemporary phrased it, 'bare-faced begging'.[24]

What conclusions can be drawn from this story of ruin and restoration? The first and most obvious is that the rebuilding of Lichfield Cathedral in traditional style was an affirmation of the continuity of the historic Church of England. Both the Cathedral and the Church itself had been brought to apparent ruin by the Civil War; both now needed to be re-established as if that catastrophe had never occurred. It was particularly important to proclaim the return of bishops and chapters, so vilified by their enemies as over-endowed and under-employed. Can it be coincidence that Hacket, the zealous champion of Lichfield's rebuilding, had been the clergy's advocate to the Long Parliament in defence of cathedral chapters and the value of their ministry?

To rebuild in a classical style would be to admit that there had been a change, to remain with Gothic denied it, just as the regnal years of Charles II were reckoned from the day of his father's execution, not from his effective coming to the throne in 1660. The link between restored Church and restored King was spelt out by the crowning of the west gable by the statue of Charles II, carved by William Wilson, literally at the apex of the structure (Pl. XXIIc). It was not just the gift of 100 oaks from the Royal Forest of Needwood which earned him this right. The experiences of the Civil War and Interregnum had taught Englishmen the dangers of No Bishop, No King. The stability of both Church and State depended on their close interrelationship, an understanding not questioned until the Tractarians. The placing of the king where traditionally a figure of Christ belonged would not have seemed sacrilegious. As Erdeswick's description shows, any understanding of the detailed iconography of the west front sculpture had been replaced by a general historical appreciation of it as a heroic stone tapestry, depicting saints and kings, somewhat like the statues of the Nine Worthies adorning Montacute House in Somerset.[25]

The involvement of Hacket with the restoration demonstrates yet again how wrong it is to connect the promotion of church restoration and the 'beauty of holiness' too exclusively with Archbishop Laud. A close dependence on Laud would have been anathema for a disciple of John Williams, who had been relentlessly persecuted by Laud. Hacket recognised, like Lord Clarendon, that much of the opposition to the ecclesiastical pro-gramme of Charles I was provoked by the manner, rather than the matter of its reforms. He urged that Church discipline should be tempered to lambs, as well as sheep, and souls gained to Christ by all means that were lawful, without excessive rigidity.

Hacket's uncomplicated acceptance of Gothic did not outlast his death. Like other prominent figures concerned with rebuilding past monuments in the 1660s, such as Bishop Cosin of Durham and Lady Anne Clifford, he belonged to a generation grown to maturity long before the true lessons of classical architecture had been absorbed into the English tradition. For younger men like John Evelyn and Christopher Wren, good churchmen though they were, classical architecture was a matter of course, to be adopted for churches and houses alike. The new St Paul's and the City churches provided classical models that were acceptably Anglican.

Finally, the vicissitudes of the fabric hint at a continuing opposition to the preservation of ancient churches. For Lord Brooke and others who shared his views, ancient architecture implied Popery and the power of prelates to direct worship. 'It was more agreeable to the rules of piety of demolish such old monuments of superstitition and idolatory than to keep them standing.'[26] The mere existence of such relics incited counter-Reformation. Mary Tudor's reign showed how these 'old idolatrous shapes, with their ancient appurtenances ... may be replenished and garnished with all their idols again'.[27] There was also a strong Puritan distaste for the ceremony of consecration and the 'superstitious' idea that there was some sanctity in the stones of the building. When the Recorder of Winchester during the Interregnum pleaded for the preservation of the Cathedral, he was careful to stress that he was moved by 'zeal for the propagation of the Gospel and not out of any conceit of holiness in the walls'.[28] It is not surprising to find Dean Wood echoing this suspicion even after the trauma of the Civil War. The maintenance of medieval buildings inevitably implied a respect for the rites and ceremonies of worship. Those who preferred more freedom and spontaneity required more utilitarian structures in which to worship. It was only the particular Anglican compromise between Reformed doctrine and traditional practices which could ensure the survival, let alone the rebuilding, of the great churches of the past.

REFERENCES

1. The *VCH* article, in the third of the Staffordshire volumes, published in 1970, was prepared by Ann J. Kettle and D. A. Johnson. Warwick Rodwell has generously shared his researches with me. They are yet to be concluded and published, but a summary has appeared in *Antiquity*: 'Archaeology and the standing fabric: recent studies at Lichfield Cathedral', LXIII (1989), no. 239, 281–94.

2. William Dugdale, *A Short View of the Late Troubles in England* (Oxford 1681), 117.

3. Brooke, when viewing the restoration of Old St Paul's Cathedral, inspired by Archbishop Laud in the 1630s, was reported to have hoped that 'he would live to see not one stone of the building left upon another'; W. Laud, *The Works of Archbishop Laud*, ed. J. Bliss and W. Scott, III (Oxford 1847–60), 249.

4. Dugdale, op. cit., 559–60.

5. J. Evelyn, *Diaries*, ed. E. S. de Beer, III (Oxford 1955), 132.

6. B. Willis, *A Survey of the Cathedrals*, II (London 1727–30), 373–7.

7. Bodleian Library MS Ashmole 1521, p. 147. It is represented in stained glass in the former Hacket 'chapel' in the south choir aisle. Warwick Rodwell has discovered that only the first two metres of the three western faces are medieval (unpublished Progress Note on the recording of the central tower, kindly shown me by Dr Rodwell), but presumably much that had survived the Civil War was so ruinous that it had to be demolished prior to rebuilding.

8. T. Plume, *An Account of the Life and Death of ... John Hacket*, ed. M. E. C. Walcott (London and Lichfield 1865), 79.

9. Commons Journal, VI, 556.

10. Commons Journal, VI, 450.

11. S. Erdeswick, *A Short View of Staffordshire* (London 1717), 100.

12. Erdeswick, op. cit., 101.

13. L. G. Wickham Legg (ed.), *A Relation of a Short Survey of the 26 Counties, Observed in ... 1634* (London 1904), 58.

14. T. Fuller, *The History of the Worthies of England* (London 1662), 39.

15. E. Ashmole, *Works*, ed. C. H. Josten, II (Oxford 1966), 783.

16. It would have been easy to alter earlier tracery since all the windows needed to be replaced: Lichfield Cathedral Archives MS 06.

17. Lichfield Cathedral Archives MS 06.

18. His major architectural commission, apart from his work at Lichfield, was the rebuilding of Garret Hostel as the Bishop's Hostel for Trinity College, Cambridge, in a classical style. He seems to have taken no interest in the details of the design; R. Willis and J. W. Clark, *The Architectural History of the University of Cambridge*, II (Cambridge 1886), 552–60.

19. N. Pevsner, *B/E Cambridgeshire* (Harmondsworth 1970), 148. Hacket was in Williams' service for 30 years as well as writing his biography. He makes no stylistic comment in his account of the various building operations undertaken by Williams at Westminster, Buckden, Cambridge, Oxford and elsewhere.

20. Hacket recounted this in a letter to Archbishop Sheldon of 12 December 1668: Bodleian Library MS Tanner 44, f. 66, quoted in *VCH*, op. cit., 177.

21. Lichfield Cathedral Archives MS 08: H. M. Colvin (ed.), *History of the King's Works*, v (London 1976), 275.

22. For Hackett's fund-raising, see T. Plume, op. cit., 80–1, 122–30; T. Harwood, *History and Antiquities of the Church and City of Lichfield* (Gloucester 1806), 57–67.

23. Lichfield Cathedral Archives MS 20; *VCH*, op. cit., 179.

24. The impressive figure of Christ at Swynnerton is most unlikely to have been brought there from the west gable of the Cathedral. In utilitarian terms it would be virtually impossible to lower such a weight of stone undamaged without scaffolding or equipment enough to attract notice, let alone transport it over 20 miles across country. There was also no moment during the period when such an action would have been called for; there is no sign of deliberate iconoclasm of the west front's statues to stimulate such an extraordinary initiative. Preservation for 17th- and 18th-century antiquaries meant recording on paper, not rescuing the object.

25. R. North, *Lives of the Norths*, ed. A. Jessopp, I (London 1890), 185.

26. H. R. Trevor-Roper, *Archbishop Laud, 1573–1645* (London 1962), 124.

27. H. Barrow, *A Brief Discoverie of the False Church* (Dort (?) 1590), 132.

28. W. R. W. Stephens and F. T. Madge (eds), *Documents relating to the History of the Cathedral Church of Winchester A.D. 1636–1683*, Hampshire Record Society, II (Winchester 1897), 97.

The Restoration of Lichfield Cathedral:
James Wyatt to John Oldrid Scott[1]

By Richard Lockett

JAMES WYATT

During the 18th century, maintenance work was done on the Cathedral as and when required; roofs and windows are the items most frequently mentioned. Architects were consulted for special problems but no one architect held a post equivalent to that of the modern Cathedral architect. There was a small permanent force of masons and the head mason no doubt exercised a measure of technical independence, although supervision of the 'several workmen that are employed about the church', to quote a line from the Chapter Act Book in 1748, was the responsibility of the superior verger who also held the office of sub-sacrist.[2] This was still the arrangement apparently a century later when Sydney Smirke held the, by then, established office of Cathedral architect. John Carter, one of Wyatt's most vehement critics who included 'common house slating' in his indictment,[3] was presumably unaware of the major works programme of 1774–8 for which Mr Storer was paid £547 for timber and 'on account of the roof'; £525 more was required for 205 tons of slates. Johnson and Kettle, in their comprehensive history of the care of the Cathedral fabric over the centuries, notice that James Wyatt was instructed almost immediately afterwards, in 1781, to make 'a survey of the intended alterations in the body of the church, the great choir and lady choir'.[4]

Wyatt was brought in not to take up a permanent and continuous responsibility but for a specific commission. Frew, in his detailed discussion of Wyatt's activity at Lichfield, explains that this commission took the form of two distinct contracts, one relating to the nave where the vaults were causing particular concern, and the other relating to the choir where the existing arrangements were inconvenient and uncomfortable. These two contracts, or rather the estimates relating to them, are dated March 1787 and March 1788, six and seven years, that is, after the original commission noticed by Johnson and Kettle.[5]

The works carried out by James Wyatt at Lichfield Cathedral were widely reported at the time, for instance in the correspondence pages of the *Gentleman's Magazine*,[6] and by the local historian the Revd Stebbing Shaw.[7] The 1782 and 1811 editions of Thomas Pennant's *Journey from London to Chester*, for which Moses Griffith made illustrations in 1780, gives something of a before-and-after view (Pl. XXIII).[8] In recent years Johnson and Kettle and Cobb have discussed the history of the fabric of the Cathedral from the beginning up to the present day, while Frew has brought together contemporary published accounts and manuscript evidence for the Wyatt years.[9] Frew has also placed the Lichfield works within the wider context of Wyatt's other Cathedral restorations, as well as his collegiate and secular architectural practice.[10] I have attempted to detail the work of Joseph Potter, originally Wyatt's agent at Lichfield in the years 1788–93, who thereafter grew into the post of Cathedral architect which he held until 1842.[11] Here, therefore, I shall concentrate on unpublished drawings and other material showing what Wyatt might have done at Lichfield rather than what he actually did.

Wyatt, as part of the campaign to convert Lichfield Cathedral to late 18th-century needs, produced plans for the improvement of the Consistory Courts; both the bishop and the dean had Court rooms in the transepts in the earlier 18th century. John Harris's 1727 ground plan shows the north transept eastern aisle as divided between the bishop's Consistory Court and the St Stephen's Chapel, and the south transept similarly providing a space divided between vicars' vestry and the dean's Consistory Court.[12] This was still the arrangement when Thomas Pennant visited Lichfield in 1780. Among the surviving drawings from the Wyatt Office are four which illustrate a particular proposal for improving the bishop's Court (Pl. XXIVA).[13] Seating for the bishop and his officers is placed at the north end; St Stephen's Chapel serves as a waiting room and has 'the great Eagle' inserted at the expense of the two central column-shafts to the triple lancet window on the south wall. The west side of the transept aisle as seen from the east is blocked off, with dado panelling and neo-Gothic doorways. These drawings evidently relate to a proposal that received the support of the Dean and Chapter:

In consideration of the great important work now carrying on at the Cathedral Church of Lichfield for its support and improvement, whereby it will be in every part greatly beautified and ornamented; according to the plans given in by Mr. Wyatt, the Architect, save in the part of the Church where the Bishop's Consistory Court is held, and the same being in a very ruinous and decayed state, the walls in many parts bulging and giving way, and letting in the damp air so as to render it very uncomfortable and hazardous to the Officers of the said Court, and the Suitors, as well as being insufficient for the accommodation of the clergy etc. at an Episcopal Visitation, and on various other occasions, it was signified to Mr. Wyatt, on his late attendance at Lichfield, by the parties immediately concerned as well for their own accommodation and conveniency, as for the completeness of the laudable plan of Reparation in which he was engaged, were anxious to promote it, by their subscriptions ... he was desired to take it into contemplation, and make a survey and estimates. The proposition had been previously made to the Lord Bishop of the Diocese and to the Dean and Chapter, who expressed their highest approbation of the intended alteration and improvement, and their consent that the adjoining chancel should be laid into the Consistory. Mr. Wyatt accordingly made a survey and report with plan and estimates, as annexed, which have been much admired, and give the greatest satisfaction, and it is obvious, that by the execution of the design that noble structure, the ancient Cathedral, will in every way be compleat and uniform.[14]

(The drawings do not indicate how the Consistory was to be opened into the Chancel).
   An undated estimate (£180) gives further detail:

To restore all the decayed parts of the stone work, put new steps to the two doorways and enclose the arches with stone, to wainscot the walls 4 feet above the floor, put a seat where marked in the drawing against the wainscot and to put a new oak floor to the whole, to raise the Proctor's seat 6 inches above the other floor and lower the top, and remove the whole of it about a foot or 18 inches further from the north window, to leave room within the seat behind the Registrar's chair and line the whole of it above the seat within and side with green cloth the same as the pews in the Choir — To put 3 seats according to the drawing under the north window — and a stove where the present fire place is — to paint the whole of the wood work of a wainscot colour and varnish it — to new glaze the windows with white glass, place the great Eagle at the south end, colour all the walls like the choir.[15]

The improvement of the bishop's Consistory Court was considered in the context of the other works, presumably work on the choir, and therefore should be dated to 1787. However, it was almost immediately superseded by a second idea to combine both courts in the south transept and to further use this space as a chapel. This idea and some Wyatt drawings for the south transept should date from May 1788 when Samuel Pegge, by open letter, appealed for £5,950, which would seem to be a simplification of the £5,955 10s. estimate for finishing the choir and undertaking the nave.[16] This estimate, otherwise published by Frew, also contained the following relative to the south transept:

To fit up the Dean's Court for a Morning Chapel, reinstate all the columns and other decayed parts, enclose the arches, plaster the walls and colour them, new glaze the windows and point the same, to lay down an oak boarded floor and put up three old stalls from the Choir for the Bishop, Dean and Residentiary Prebend, make a reading desk and pews out of the best of the old wainscot.[17]

Yet another plan, the one eventually executed by Potter in 1796/7 and recorded in watercolours by J. C. Buckler dated 1806 and 1833 (Pl. XXIVB),[18] owed its origin to Wyatt. An undated memorandum reads:

It has been thought proper to delay taking any steps towards carrying into execution the plan which Mr. Wyatt has given for the improvement of the Consistory Court, in consideration of another plan which has lately been suggested, and which Mr. Wyatt will explain when he comes to Lichfield.

If the early prayers may be read in the Consistory Court and, considering how very few persons attend them, the Bishop thinks they may, without giving any offence, it will save a great deal of expense, and can be the means of adding to the beauty of the Cathedral. Mr. Wyatt thinks the old vestry in the south aisle may be rendered very commodious for the intended new Consistory Court, and by opening the spaces into the Cathedral now occupied by the present Court, the Vicars' Vestry room, and the Dean's Court, a fine effect will be produced by widening those parts of the Cathedral, and it will likewise afford very eligible places for the erecting of monuments.

At any rate, should the old vestry and its adjoining part be found too small for the purpose, it will certainly be advisable, and will save expense, to remove the Consistory Court to the place now intended for early prayers and to make it servicable for both.[19]

Wyatt's 'Lady Choir', his own apt description for his rearrangement of the east end of the Cathedral which consisted of a conflation of choir and Lady Chapel, was a long, narrow corridor, unkindly described as the grandest drawing room in Europe. With its glazed finale, a painted glass window made by Francis Eginton of Handsworth, Birmingham after a design by Sir Joshua Reynolds (Pl. XXVA),[20] this space did have affinities with the long gallery and oratory that Wyatt concocted for William Beckford at Fonthill Abbey a few years later. Beckford's theatrical control of light was paralleled at Lichfield by curtaining the windows flanking the Reynolds-Eginton *Resurrection*.[21] The plan to fill the two immediately flanking windows with similar painted glass, anticipated by Stebbing Shaw in 1798, came to nothing. Indeed, within a decade, the *Resurrection* itself had been replaced by the 16th-century Flemish glass purchased by Sir Brooke Boothby and sold to the Dean and Chapter, one reason why Wyatt's Lichfield Cathedral is imperfectly known through 19th-century prints and drawings (Pl. XXVB).[22] The collaboration of Eginton and Wyatt has proved rather ephemeral, but they did much business together. The Reynolds *Resurrection* was repeated at Salisbury Cathedral. Eginton also supplied stained glass to St Paul's, Birmingham for a high altar arrangement designed by Wyatt. It was probably through Wyatt that Eginton was commissioned to supply glass for two Oxford colleges as well as for Brocklesby Park and Wilton House.[23]

The Wyatt Lady Choir as a whole has vanished and since early 19th-century publications were illustrated in black and white the general colouristic effect is gone also. It is therefore worth noticing an original watercolour drawing of the choir by Charles Wild, the drawings used for one of the black and white plates in his 1813 publication on the Cathedral. This drawing shows the walls as the colour of Bath stone, lightening towards the vaults under the influence of the light streaming through the clerestory windows. This colour was achieved after scraping, cleaning, making good with Roman cement and then painting this composite surface.[24]

Several drawings exist that were made for the refurnishing of the new choir, including a coloured drawing of the new pulpit (Pl. XXVC).[25] There are finished and unfinished drawings for the elevation of the choir east of the organ screen, for the organ screen itself (Pl. XXVD)[26] and for the reredos at the end of the Lady Chapel. Most of them support the idea that Wyatt's general strategy, like that of Sydney Smirke in the 1850s, was to follow a stylistic mode based upon the remains of the medieval high altar reredos. There are, perhaps significantly, no extant drawings of the medieval reredos, although there is a Wyatt drawing of the 'Grecian' or classical reredos that was erected on its west face. The latter has been published by Cobb.[27] Wyatt incorporated fragments from the medieval reredos into his new reredos and organ screen, and intended to follow the same clues for the stalls promised in 1787 to replace Bishop Hacket's 17th-century stalls. Canopied stalls, only drawn out for one bay, are shown in a Wyatt elevation of the south side of the choir between the organ screen and the doorway linking choir and aisle (Pl. XXVIA).[28] A very similar drawing for this doorway is signed and dated: 'James Wyatt Augᵗ 1787'.[29] As far as I know, Wyatt never realised the six-foil oculus with Gothic wall panelling above and around a Perpendicular-style doorway. This doorway, and that opposite into the north choir aisle, retained their traditional position in the fifth bay from the crossing. This bay made the transition between the western 'Hacket' bays and the remaining Wyatt bays brought together by the removal of the high altar to the end of the Lady Chapel. Uniformity was strengthened by blocking the arcade of the Wyatt bays to match the already blocked Hacket bays. Wyatt's proposed replacement stalls were eventually realised by Potter when he widened the choir for Dean Woodhouse c.1813. This is the choir as illustrated by John Britton and others.[30] There is even a photograph of the Wyatt/Potter stalls taken at the moment of destruction of the Wyatt choir in 1856/7.

Wyatt fell foul of some antiquarian contemporaries as well as later critics because he destroyed the medieval arrangement of the Cathedral which had survived in principle up to that moment. The new arrangements were not, however, decided overnight and surviving drawings show that Wyatt arrived at the executed plan only after considering a number of alternatives between 1781, when he was first called to Lichfield, and 1787 when the choir works began. Variations to the final solution are implied by the 1787 estimate which refers to galleries in the side aisles.[31] The mention of galleried aisles conjures up a picture of an 18th-century parish church quite different from the long corridor. In one elevation and one plan, Wyatt adapts the Lady Chapel and the two bays east of the high altar (in its traditional and present position) into a serviceable space for 'divine worship'.[32] Had this idea been followed up, then existing arrangements could have continued, although it would have produced a curious duplication.

Other plans represent more radical solutions. One of these fills the fourth bay east of the crossing with the organ screen, with pews and aisle galleries to the east. This too is a parish church solution.[33] In another plan, Wyatt places a narrow screen across the centre and side aisles of the choir at the third pier east of the crossing. Pews occupy the next three bays with an unspecified chancel arrangement beyond leading into the Lady Chapel.[34] Yet another plan adds six bays of the choir to the Lady Chapel, with or without galleries, leaving one or two bays between the screen and the crossing.[35] Thus Wyatt anticipated the great debate about the dimensions and arrangement of the Lichfield choir that took place in the 1850s. As well as his final solution of a Lady Choir stretching from the organ screen (occupying the whole of the first bay) to the extreme east end of the Cathedral, that is the Lady Chapel plus seven bays, Wyatt also experimented with shorter versions of Lady Chapel plus two, four, five or six bays!

Nearly all the drawings from the Wyatt Office are undated, but there is a notable exception signed and dated: 'James Wyatt 1783'. This is labelled: 'Design for altering the Chapel of our Lady in Lichfield Cathedral with four different Designs for the front of the Gallery' (Pl. XXVIB).[36] This elevation offering the Dean and Chapter four alternatives is an important document for understanding Wyatt's appreciation of or respect for English

Gothic with a 'c'. He evidently intended to simplify the window tracery so that the Lady Chapel became uniform with the Perpendicular traceried windows in the choir. But he also scouts the possibility that the single-storey elevation of the Lichfield Lady Chapel might be improved by the introduction of a triforium or gallery as he misleadingly, in this context, calls it. Wyatt offers Decorated and/or Perpendicular solutions as from a catalogue, although Thomas Rickman's terminology may be too precise to be applied to these drawings.[37] On this evidence one would have to characterise Wyatt's appreciation of medieval architecture as aesthetic rather than antiquarian. Fortunately Richard Gough, John Milner and John Carter were all unaware of the à la carte gothick menu that James Wyatt placed before the Dean and Chapter of Lichfield Cathedral in 1783.

The idea of introducing a triforium into the Lichfield Lady Chapel elevation is echoed in an undated Wyatt drawing for the reredos (Pl. XXVIIA).[38] This places a free-standing screen in front of the lower section of the east window and so is analogous to the drawing of the *Resurrection* window published here which has a (?) painted *Glory* triptych in a similar position below it (Pl. XXVA). The screen is only lightly sketched; the reredos below is more firmly outlined and is in the Perpendicular style, and implies that Wyatt was already intent on using fragments from the medieval high altar reredos for his Lady Chapel reredos. In the event, this did take on another storey and obscured the lower part of the glazed window above, without which the reredos would have been visually ineffectual from the distant west boundary of the Lady Choir (Pl. XXVB). One last reredos thought makes the same point. This 'Altarpiece for the Lady Choir of Lichfield' (Pl. XXVIIB) has a raised, gabled centre to break the horizontal line.[39]

JOSEPH POTTER

I will sketch over the activities of Joseph Potter since I have described these elsewhere, but there was considerable restoration activity from the mid-1790s until 1842, the years when he was effectively the Cathedral architect without ever being formally appointed as such. Some £41,000 was spent from the fabric account between 1800 and 1842.[40] These sums were not reserved to the Cathedral itself, and a significant percentage was taken up by payments for stained glass introduced into the Lady Chapel and transepts and for the composition statuary provided for the west front and south transept façade. I have not managed to break down all the expenditure figures, and amounts totalling £1,500, for instance, might relate to carpentry, plumbing or masonry. However the overall impression is that decorative work took precedence over structural; £240 was spent on stonework, £648 on cementwork and £1,616 on stained glass. Structural work certainly included windows, buttresses and plinths, and was additional to special contracts such as Joseph Johnson's restoration of the south-west spire (£162). The top 41 ft of the north-west spire was also rebuilt by Johnson in Potter's time. Most of Potter's structural work was replaced by later work by Sydney Smirke, G. G. Scott senior and his heirs.

Potter put forward three ideas for the south transept which failed to find any support and hence were unrealised. The first of these was to raise the buttress in the centre of the west side to match Wyatt's buttresses to the south façade, and the second was to lower the clerestory windows towards the stringcourses between them and the lancets below. Thirdly, Potter wanted to restore the external tomb on the south transept front on the analogy of a traceried window with the cusps falling on to column shafts. This idea could be contrasted with John Oldrid Scott's more erudite restoration and elaboration of the external monuments on the south side of the Lady Chapel. Scott had the Westminster tombs firmly in his sights for these and he would have regarded Potter's project as a gross solecism.

SYDNEY SMIRKE

Sydney Smirke succeeded Joseph Potter senior as the Cathedral architect at Lichfield in 1842 and was immediately allowed to carry out extensive structural restorations to the south side of the nave which had been the subject of Potter's later annual reports to the Dean and Chapter.[41] Smirke was chosen by the Chapter 'as an architect of sound judgement and experience in ecclesiastical architecture'.[42] He was authorised to spend £1,000 in his first year and for the years 1846–52, when expenditure on the church fabric as distinct from all capitular property, is recorded, expenditure averaged £500 per annum. This suggests that about a third of the annual expenditure during Smirke's time was spent upon the church alone and two-thirds on other buildings.

Smirke wanted to confine his south nave works to the south transept, but the Chapter drew back from the restorations he advised and in the years mentioned Smirke was principally active in the north transept. Ewan Christian in 1872 describes Smirke's north transept campaign of 1847–52 as having included most of the façade: 'the whole of the masonry has been restored, excepting only the very highly enriched doorway'.[43] But Smirke's own letters and reports suggest a final result much more interesting than Christian's blanket description implies. We cannot judge because the transept was restored again by J. O. Scott in the 1890s. Similarly Smirke's work on the south side of the nave carried out in the mid-1840s was undone thirty or forty years later.

Smirke's other major structural achievement at Lichfield was the demolition of Wyatt's choir boundaries in 1856/7 in preparation for the great reordering which, after a complicated struggle of variant ideas between 1853 and 1857, was carried out not by Smirke, who then resigned as Cathedral architect, but by G. G. Scott senior. Since I have published an account of the 1850s argument about how to rearrange Lichfield Cathedral, I will only mention here the implications of this argument for the structural restoration.[44]

From Smirke's reports and letters (Appendix) quite a lot can be learnt of his attitude towards restoration, his philosophy of restoration, if that is not too grand a word. Smirke began on the south nave in 1844, worried by the splaying outwards of the walls — a problem tackled by Wyatt sixty years before. The aisle wall was four inches out of line at the top and the clerestory wall was six inches out. There was a longitudinal fissure through this clerestory wall. Smirke details his approach to the decorative detail:

In finishing the exterior I have continued to restore scrupulously to the best of my belief the original forms of the building, but in the clerestory parapet and in the buttress heads I have been compelled to exercise some freedom. I have no direct proof to adduce of the panelled parapet having appeared as I have now built it but there is good presumptive proof of it in the panelled parapet now remaining on the east side of the south transept. As to the larger buttress heads, the meagre aspect they now wear is so manifestly modern and incongruous . . . I have introduced no part that cannot be paralleled either in the cathedral or in other buildings of the same date.

The grounds of his proceeding were thus clearly set before the Chapter and he made no claim to infallibility.

Some restoration was also done to the nave interior at this time but this work was restricted to cleaning operations. In 1854 Smirke writes:

I observed that since my last visit the whole of the canopied arches under the windows in North and South aisles of the nave have had their surface cleared from the old plastering and coloring; this has certainly had the effect of bringing out the beautiful carving that ornaments this arcade, but it was not one of the works recommended in my report . . . The Columns with their capitals and bases are in sufficiently good condition; are of stone, and chiefly original work: but the space above the capitals up to the string course under the windows (the greater part thereof being in Plaster) should be cut out and restored in masonry; of course leaving untouched *every* portion of old work that is in moderately good condition.

Further cleaning was undertaken in 1860/1 by Scott and the wall arcades were restored *c.* 1868–72. One would have to say that relatively little old work got by the Scotts.

Smirke's work on the north transept was also significant and his 1851 Report shows this to have been unusually undoctrinaire:

Careful moulds are now being formed of zinc of all the moulded parts previously to their removal & these moulds will be compared with corresponding details in other parts of the fabric. Stones from the Tixall Quarries are also now being worked ready for use so that there may be no standing still for want of materials when the restoration is commenced. The course which I propose to take is to remove all the decayed stones, both moulded & plain & substitute new, worked, stone for stone, exactly as before in all those parts that are of mediaeval date, without attempting by alterations or deviations of any kind to bring the design of the whole to the style of any one particular period. There is at present visible evidence of at least three distinct dates in the mediaeval work (i.e. exclusive of the recent or post-mediaeval parts) & these parts are so intimately blended that to attempt to bring the façade to any one homogenous, consistent style would involve the obliteration of two thirds of the old work, & it appears to me that it would be greatly exceeding the duties of a restorer to make any such attempt. My intention therefore is to reinstate the building as nearly as possible into the condition in which our ancestors were satisfied to leave it prior to the great destruction & consequent renovation in the 17th century; thus the incomplete portions of early pointed work will be retained & restored which were left undisturbed when the subsequent alterations were made that so materially modified the architecture of the North Transept, to obliterate these would be to destroy a record of great interest to the archaeologist, shewing clearly the existence of a North transept in the 13th century.

I beg leave to submit herewith an Elevation of the Front shewing the work as proposed to be restored, which will I trust fully explain my suggestions, but any further explanations that the Dean & Chapter may consider desirable I shall be happy to furnish.

Smirke's catholicity of taste was revealed again by the argument over the style of the furnishings for the new choir. Smirke belonged to an earlier generation of taste than Scott, one closer to our modern conception of Cathedral buildings as the product of many generations rather than as peaks and troughs in the history of architectural style. Smirke expressed his ideas to the Lichfield Chapter in a Memorandum in 1855:

The style of Architecture adopted for the proposed fittings, is that which prevailed at the commencement of the Fifteenth Century, when screen and tabernacle work reached the extreme point of lightness and beauty. The Original Stone Screen that was removed by Wyatt, was of this date, as appears from remaining portions of the East End of the Lady Chapel, and under the Organ Gallery.

The Altar Screen, is proposed to be of stone; in the design submitted, authorities for every portion, exist either in the above mentioned remaining portions of original work, or in the Stone [Neville] Screen at Durham Cathedral, an example of singular beauty and in many respects closely resembling the original screen at Lichfield. Its graceful and slender spiral forms, seem to harmonize happily with the general character of the building.

This adherence to early 19th-century taste flew in the face of Camdenian opinion which was firmly established by the 1850s and which, through Scott, Ferrey and Beresford-Hope, predictably dominated a committee appointed to advise the Chapter on the rearrangement of the choir in 1856. Scott's designs for the new Lichfield choir were published in the *Ecclesiologist* in 1859. In 1861, when the choir was reopened, Beresford-Hope published his *The English Cathedral of the Nineteenth Century*. This selects Middle Pointed as 'the golden mien, the practical and practicable style for our wants.'[45] Although the committee 'after anxious and careful consideration' did decide to place the high altar in its ancient position, it could not bring itself to accept the logic of the argument by advising that the style of the altar reredos should be *c.* 1400, the date that Smirke and others gave to the fragments of the Lichfield reredos spared by Wyatt.[46]

When the competition was drawing to a close and the issue was clearly between two sets of designs by Smirke and Scott, Smirke was not prepared to abandon his preference for later medieval style in order to make certain of the victory. He struck to his guns and enlarged the argument by relating the reredos to its architectural setting:

a capricious departure from the date of the surrounding structure would not be justifiable . . . there are in this case two reasons for adopting a style somewhat later than the Choir.

1st. because the screen work of this later date is undeniably lighter, more delicate & graceful, than the early screen work.

2ndly. because the mediaeval architects, themselves who erected the Altar Screen, (subsequently removed by Wyatt) thought proper to adopt this later style, and I am content to abide by their judgement.

The design now submitted is in all its essential details similar to the Screen then put up: the central pinnacles etc. being adapted from the screen at Durham of like date.

Although the committee did not specify a style, they did tip the scales in Scott's direction by suggesting that 'marbles, alabasters, and flour spars', which could be found within the diocese, would be 'peculiarly appropriate'. It was but a short step to the reredos that Scott designed and that John Birnie Philip made *c.* 1864.[47]

Ironically (as far as Smirke was concerned) Scott was to design the sedilia on the south side of the high altar and the Dean Howard tomb behind it in the Perpendicular style using fragments from the medieval screen reused and thus preserved by Wyatt. However, on the north side, for the monument to Bishop Lonsdale, the other co-founder of Scott's Lichfield, the architect took Edmund Crouchback's tomb in Westminster Abbey as his model (Pl. XXVIIc).[48] This was perhaps too flamboyant for the Lichfield Chapter and was not executed; uniformity was introduced in 1913 when Charles Nicholson designed Perpendicular-style sedilia for the north side of the high altar also.

Smirke had therefore given considerable thought to the style of the architecture of the Lichfield choir before his clerk of works and the team of masons were faced with the damaged structure lying beneath post-medieval alterations. Smirke refers to the 'arches lately unblocked' in July 1856; Wyatt's organ screen was demolished in May 1857. A debate was carried on from May to September 1857 about the precise manner in which the fabric of the choir should be restored. A series of letters from Sydney Smirke to Charles Gresley, the Chapter Clerk, record the architect's hesitancy in the face of heavy pressure to carry out a thorough and doctrinaire restoration such as G. G. Scott shortly thereafter undertook and which he justified in his *Sketch of the Restorations*, published in 1861. Smirke was instructed to cease his works in the choir in September 1857.

Smirke first refers to the problem of restoring the structure of the choir in June 1856 when he advised repair, whatever that might mean. In April 1857 the demolition of the organ screen was under way and in June Mr Allen, Smirke's clerk of works, called in from a house job in Warwickshire, was replaced by Mr Ridley, the chief clerk from Smirke's London office. Both were preferred as overseers to John Hamlet junior, the head mason of the Chapter's permanent workforce: 'Hamlet junior is an excellent . . . workman but he is too young to trust to; the *others* on the spot have *hands* and not *heads* . . . The builders of the new Screen seem to have been ruthless destroyers & have done serious mischief.' In June he adds that the surrounding structure was in a somewhat dangerous state: 'The difficulty arises from the 13th century work & that of the 14th century not being very carefully united.' In July Smirke advocates a remarkably conservative strategy:

I propose to confine the Restorations now in hand exclusively to the removal of the most modern work, partly brickwork and partly stone, substituting new masonry.

I do not purpose disturbing any of the old stones that are at all sound, and fit to remain, — I by no means propose to attempt any assimilation of the later work to the earlier portion ... I am much obliged by your letter of yesterday with tracings etc.

Smirke found that the 14th-century masons had not bothered to disguise their alterations to the 13th-century choir, using different stone inadequately tied in:

the change is frequently made very abruptly and inartfully, yet I purpose making no amendments of this, rather preferring to leave the work in its mutilated state (provided it is sound and fit to stand) to attempting any speculative restorations for the sake of producing an harmonious whole.

He even proposed using different coloured stones for any replacements that he had to make for safety reasons. The radical party, however, had enlisted the support of the head mason and Smirke was put on the defensive:

If the pencil sketch by Hamlet junior is right I quite concur with you in thinking that the restoration would be more exact if the earlier capitals were substituted for the later as shewn on my sketch. But you will be so good as to understand that the drawing I sent you was not for the guidance or the use of the Masons: more exact instructions would be given to them, and before doing so it was my intention that I, or Ridley, should still farther examine the work ... In the mean time Hamlet shall have instructions to insert stones of such scantling as shall admit of either form of capital being worked on them.

Five days later Smirke is still puzzled:

I have spent the whole day here pondering over the arches & piers ... so much was cut away in Wyatt's time that it is impossible now to trace the exact original treatment otherwise than by conjecture. I *believe* I see what that treatment was but as long as there is uncertainty I feel uneasy in proceeding, because the one arch we are now engaged on will necessarily be the guide for the 7 other arches, or half the Choir ...

His remarkable solution (in the context of 1857) was to restore the choir arcade in plaster: 'The effect of the whole would then be realised and a final decision safely arrived at. I shall be happy to hear that this measure of precaution meets the approval of the Dean and Chapter.' It did not. Scott got the vote for the new choir furnishings and, following Smirke's resignation, undertook the structural restoration also.

Scott's 1861 *Sketch* resounds with self-confidence:

It would be difficult here to particularise the evidence on which these facts have been ascertained; suffice it to say, that it has been most minutely traced out and proved beyond doubt, and the work restored to its ancient form, — that is to say, to the form which it attained in the fourteenth century, and which it must have, in the main retained, till nearly the end of the eighteenth. The design of the angels was really almost the only point left to conjecture.[49]

GEORGE GILBERT SCOTT

This account of the structural restoration of the choir was issued at the completion of the choir project and on the occasion of the formal reopening in 1861. Further campaigns of restoration for the nave and the nave aisles followed; the interior of the transepts and crossing had been restored in 1860–1. Scott's clerk of works, George Clark, continued to provide the Dean and Chapter with Reports and advised that work should be done on the external walls of the west towers, the nave, the transepts and the choir aisles. A new philosophy (the Smirkeian) appears in Clark's Report of 1862: 'The great principle in external restorations should be to preserve the greatest possible amount of old work — in fact never to mark over or smarten up old work for the sake of making it look new.'[50] Clark left the Lichfield works not long after.

Restoration of the medieval fabric in the 1860s included the unblocking of windows in the south transept and in the Chapter House vestibule, the rebuilding of the south-west pinnacle of the central tower, the restoration of the nave aisle wall-arcading and the installation of Scott's new west window. Surviving drawings show that he had more than one idea for the detailing of the tracery of this window (Pl. XXVIID).[51] The major task of restoring the west front itself was put forward by the architect but proved too daunting to the client for the moment, and in the 1870s the Scotts (father and sons) turned to the interior of the Lady Chapel; Wyatt's reredos was removed in 1876. No doubt as a result of Scott senior's death in 1878, his design for the new reredos 'guided by the ancient retabulatum in Westminster Abbey' (Pl. XXVIIE)[52] was never installed and was supplanted by one designed by C. E. Kempe in the 1890s.[53] External works to buttresses, windows and parapets were deferred until the 1880s and 1890s.

JOHN OLDRID SCOTT

Scott senior left two specific legacies to his sons George Gilbert (1839–97) and John Oldrid (1841–1913) — the restoration of the external tombs and the making of the Selwyn Chapel on the south side of the Lady Chapel, and the restoration of the west front. An appeal for the latter was launched in 1876. Even earlier, in 1875, it had been suggested that the south-west tower and façade should be undertaken first, since surviving medieval details on the north-west tower 'must furnish the key-note to the whole restoration' and 'most careful study must be made of every evidence of the ancient design and details' (Pl. XXVIII).[54] Scott senior had made the same point ten years earlier.[55] The work on the west front was begun in 1878 and continued until 1884 under six successive contracts.

According to the *Staffordshire Advertiser* in 1884, the Gallery of Kings was re-created by Bridgeman 'mainly from sepia sketches in the possession of the Dean, which were taken from the old dilapidated figures existing prior to the application of the cement'. These sketches, which I take to be those now in the Birmingham University Library, are very similar to Charles Wild's illustrations of the west front and the south transept published in 1813 and may even be by him (Pls XXIXA, B, XXXA, B).[56] Their subject matter does of course recur in other antiquarian illustrations by or after John Carter or John Britton, for example. Comparisons between sketches and surviving cement figures argue that the Roman cementers of the 1820s occasionally got closer to the Middle Ages than Bridgeman's masons who started from scratch. Substantial medieval cores were preserved by the early 19th-century envelopers. These were abandoned in the 1880s and one has to say that the stylistic message conveyed by the wash drawings was not apparently understood at that time.

The façade of the north transept as left by Smirke evidently proved an irritant to his successors (Pl. XXXIA).[57] By implication Smirke is blamed for allowing the north window to escape improvement. Ewan Christian commented in 1872: 'This window, both in respect of tracery and glass, is a poor and unhappy substitute for the more ancient work. The glass was inserted in the present century.' Smirke's views about the opposite window in the south transept (Pl. XXIII) are not recorded but Christian's are predictably the same: 'There is nothing beautiful in the 15th century window either in respect of tracery or of glass, and it is much to be desired that the original forms may some day be restored.'[58]

Canon Lonsdale, recollecting the course of the restorations in 1895, was evidently of the same opinion, although by then the tide of Gothic taste or at least restoration taste had perhaps turned and the Perpendicular south window was safe. Lonsdale, however, supplies the interesting information that 'the few traces discovered lead to the supposition that possibly a three light lancet window stood in the place of the later design'.[59] This is interesting because, in 1883, J. O. Scott recommended that the south transept window should be restored as four lancets.[60]

That the Cathedral received neither three nor four lancets in exchange for its 15th-century window is perhaps due to J. L. Pearson, who wrote a Report for the Dean and Chapter in 1892 just at the time that Scott's Early English restoration of the north transept was nearing completion. Pearson said of the latter: 'under the circumstances [?archaeological] I entirely approve of this restoration'. However, of the great window in the south transept he said: 'I should be disposed to leave it as it now is, and I should also recommend that no alteration be made in the curious tracery in the circular window in the gable'.[61] Christian had described this curious tracery as 'grotesque'.[62] Scott's guns were spiked and he had the galling experience of carrying out a comprehensive structural restoration of the south wall of the transept in 1893/5 which included the entire removal of the wall above the great window; he had to put everything back 'as before' but in new stone.

J. O. Scott was asked to prepare a design for the restoration of the north window in 1882,[63] that is, four years after his father's death, and hence it would be dangerous to assume that the son was merely carrying out the wishes of the father. However, it is fair to notice that J. O. Scott did become Cathedral architect at Lichfield as his father's son and at his father's express wish contained in a printed letter sent out posthumously to clients of current work. The father asked that G. G. Scott junior and J. O. Scott should be appointed jointly: 'My younger son has for some years past been in the position of a quasi-partner in my practice, and is acquainted with my various engagements.' John Oldrid added in a covering letter: 'I can confidently state that our views in works of restoration are identical with those held and impressed on us by my father. It will be a very high pleasure to us to be accepted as his successors...'.[64] By 1882, J. O. Scott was half-way through the great restoration of the west front, a project prepared and perhaps drawn out in the office before Sir Gilbert's death.

John Oldrid's designs for the new north façade of the transept were completed in 1883 and he wrote anxiously in March: 'I hope that the work may be approved and ordered by the Chapter so as not to give anti-restorationists any opportunity of interfering.'[65] He had to wait ten years for his designs to be executed and then one suspects that Pearson's interference might have frustrated him had it been requested a month or two earlier.

Lonsdale defended the north transept alterations in 1895 as:

in every sense a restoration: for on taking out the Perpendicular window, and removing such of the stonework as was defective on either side, the headings of the five Early English lights, which had unquestionably composed the original windows, were discovered, hidden away by the later workmen. The cusps, or headings, of the lights, as they are now seen from the inside, are, with the exception of six stones, the very identical material which the Early English builders carved, and placed in that spot.[66]

Scott had of course made his lancet design before the later window was removed and therefore before the evidence which Lonsdale cites had come to light. Lonsdale is no doubt quoting from the text of a lecture given by Scott at the dedication in 1893.

There are two justifications given by Scott himself. One of these was published in *The Architect* in 1900:

the most interesting antiquarian fact, which in my opinion infinitely surpasses the historical value which the old window had [was] that the lovely design of the ancient lancets could be recovered with absolute certainty ... out of the hundreds of stones forming the five beautiful arches above us, only twelve new ones were required. We have removed a feature which was architecturally a serious blot on the beauty of the cathedral, and while doing this we have recovered a lost beauty.[67]

Both these published accounts suggest that Scott used his considerable knowledge of Gothic architecture to deduce the original design of the Lichfield north transept windows and that his deductions, to which the Dean and Chapter were then committed, were fortunately, and perhaps unexpectedly, justified by the discovery of fragments of Early English ashlar during the course of restoration. The absolute certainty of which Scott later spoke was not his, however, at the crucial design stage, as we shall see. There is a subtle difference of tone between the published statements and a letter written by Scott in February 1883 to accompany drawings upon which the Chapter would make their decision. 'I have carefully adhered to every piece of evidence which remained of their [the lancets] original design, supplying some of the missing features from corresponding work in the other transept.' (Evidence that the depressed arches of the 'present large window' had been formed out of older arch stones was to follow). 'The drawing shows the present gable, etc, retained, while another, which is made to fit into it, shows a design for returning to the ancient higher gable in which I have designed a circular window founded on that which still remains in the South Transept. This drawing also shows a suggestion for finishing the buttresses in a more suitable manner.'[68] There was evidently room for manœuvre when it came to the level of the gable, and here archaeology quite definitely gave way to taste. The gable was to receive three windows to light the roof space above the level of the transept vault. However, there is an undated drawing by J. O. Scott that proves that at one stage he planned only to glaze the centre lancet and to have those flanking it blind (Pl. XXXIB).[69]

This drawing is more significant for what it tells us of the proposed design of the great north window below. This is of four lancets, an arrangement confirmed by a section with plan. If these drawings were dated, one could be sure of the sequence of events; I would guess the date to be c. 1883, when Scott certainly proposed to remake the south transept window in the form of four lancets. His letter of 1883 implies that he was seeking to establish some symmetry between the two arms of the transept, and the north and south windows are of course the two most style-asserting features. However, the drawings may date to any moment between 1883 and 1891 when the Chapter accepted an offer from a private donor to restore and glaze the north transept window 'according to a design and plans of Mr J. O. Scott the architect, to its original design of lancet or Early English lights'.[70] The works which produced a north window of five-light lancets must have got under way shortly thereafter.

The most probable explanation on the available evidence is therefore that Scott's absolute certainty came from real archaeology, from 'digging', from the demolition of the Perpendicular window in early 1892. The superficial archaeology that he undertook c. 1882, and upon which authority the demolition of the existing window was undertaken, proved erroneous. Scott's knowledge of Gothic architecture in general, and his assumptions, aesthetic and otherwise about how the Early English architect had designed the fenestration in this part of the Cathedral, proved inadequate. Had he not discovered proof of a five-lancet window, he would have been perfectly content with a four-light window and, but for the drawings, we should be none the wiser. But for his letter of February 1883, we should not know how much of the archaeological evidence later used in evidence was actually hidden from Scott at the time that he argued his case with the Chapter of Lichfield Cathedral. Luckily for Scott and for us, Sydney Smirke had not decided upon a doctrinaire restoration of the north transept in the 1840s, and if he had, it might well have been in the Perpendicular style.

APPENDIX

LETTERS AND REPORTS BY SYDNEY SMIRKE RELATING TO
THE RESTORATION OF LICHFIELD CATHEDRAL: 1842–57

Excluded from the correspondence etc. given here in paraphrase or verbatim, are papers relating to the refurnishing of the Lichfield choir, a question with which the structural restoration became interconnected in 1854. In September 1854, Sydney Smirke and George Gilbert Scott presented a joint report on *The Rearrangement of the Choir of Lichfield Cathedral* to the Dean and Chapter. Most of the documentation relevant to Smirke's views on the plan and style of the rearrangement are given in my 'Sydney Smirke, George Gilbert Scott and "The Rearrangement of Lichfield Cathedral for Divine Worship": 1854–1861', Research Bulletin, *Institute for the Study of Worship and Religious Architecture* (University of Birmingham 1980).

Chapter Act Book for 1842:

Resolved that:

Members of the Chapter make enquiries after an architect of sound judgement and experience in ecclesiastical architecture.

Workmen engaged on the restoration of some windows under Mr Potter to complete them.

Mr Smirke be authorised to spend £1,000.

LJRO, Muniments of the Dean and Chapter, D30, 8/1

Letter of Sydney Smirke to Archdeacon Hamilton, 12 November 1842:

Smirke questions the exclusion of red and related colours from the coloured glass proposed for the choir windows, and suggests some variety of colour and patterns within and between these windows.

He proposes to acquire stone from Mr Ward's Tixall quarry at 13*d.* per foot cubic to the nearest wharf; Plows to go and select the blocks.

Chapter Act Book for 1843:

Resolved that:

Mr Smirke continue on the same plan and to a similar extent as he has already proceeded upon, but that the clearstory of the nave be restored to the same extent as the south aisle before progress be made towards the rest east of the same aisle.

Chapter Act Book for 1844

Mr Smirke's Report and Resolution with regard to the South Transept:

Smirke comments on the condition of the old masonry, the urgent necessity of these repairs, the substantial defects arising chiefly from the original want of a proper balance between the thrust of the roof and the ceiling, and the power provided to receive that thrust.

The aisle wall is reported to be 4 in. out of its proper upright position; the buttresses also are pushed over and the back of a flying buttress broken; the clearstory wall is overhung upwards of 6 in. in the short space between the aisle roof and the parapet.

There is a longitudinal fissure through the middle of the clerestory wall by which the outside and the inside faces had been separated due to the roof rather than to the ceiling and which had pulled the walls outward.

Smirke reports the entire removal of one of the flying buttresses and that the work had now been rebuilt upright.

... in finishing the exterior I have continued to restore scrupulously to the best of my belief the original forms of the building, but in the clerestory parapet and in the buttress heads I have been compelled to exercise some freedom. I have had no direct proof to adduce of the panelled parapet having appeared as I have now built it but there is good presumptive proof of it in the panelled parapet now remaining on the east side of the south transept. As to the larger buttress heads, the (? poor) meagre aspect they now wear is so manifestly modern and incongruous ... I have introduced no part that cannot be paralleled either in the cathedral or in other buildings of the same date.

Smirke reported that it would be advantageous to carry on the south side of the nave to completion which would require a further £2,000 over two years; the single most important object would be the restoration of the nave.

Chapter Act Book for 1845

Smirke reported that:
the external masonry of two bays on the south side of the nave had been restored, but that the upper part of the clerestory of one of these bays had not been completed because of the loss of two masons;
an external channel of stone had been laid along the feet of the whole of the north and part of the south side of the nave, and an old drain across the centre of the nave had been restored;
the ground had been lowered on the south side between the Cathedral and the wall;
two bays and the buttress between them and repairs to the south aisle roof and gutter remained to be done;
the nave walls were drier following the new drainage.

Smirke had inspected the west side of the south transept as requested and noted that two clerestory windows had had their tracery renewed. He disliked the large buttress built of late years and this would have to be considered in the event of a restoration. He suggests ornamenting its surface somewhat in the manner of the new nave buttress; the arcading at ground level should of course be restored and might be continued round the base of the buttress, and this arcade could then form a very beautiful feature in the design of the transept.
The west side of the south transept could be restored for £12/13000.

Ordered:
That work on the south nave aisle be continued to the end, but further work be suspended for lack of funds.

Chapter Act Book for 1846

Smirke reported that:
the restoration should be taken as far as the south-west angle buttress of the south transept so as to suggest completeness; the present termination of the work was disagreeably abrupt;
the south transept clerestory windows, although obviously not of the same early date as the lower part, should be left, and it would be hazardous to make any alteration or to reduce the bulk of the buttress;
'I have therefore merely relieved it by canopied arches and pillars etc. similar to those used in the lower part of the western towers.'

Repairs as recommended to be suspended.

Repairs absolutely required:
1.   Mullion of the east window of the north-west tower.
2.   Pinnacle of the small spire above the Consistory Court to be taken down 13 courses and be leaded.
3.   Parapets to be examined and pointed.
4.   General pointing.
5.   Stone channel along the south side to be completed.
6.   Hamlet and Davis (masons) to be retained.

Chapter Act Book for 1847

Resolved:
Buttresses on the north end of the north transept to be begun.

Chapter Act Book for 1848

Resolved:
   The restoration of the outside of the north transept to be commenced.

Chapter Act Book for 1849

Resolved:
   Memorial tablets in niches are to be plain slabs of white marble and are not to interfere with the niches.

LJRO, D30, 8/1

Letter from Sydney Smirke to Charles Gresley (Chapter Clerk), 17 December 1850:

Dear Sir,
   I have to request that you will inform the Dean and Chapter that in compliance with their desire I have examined the present state of the fabric of the Cathedral with a view to report what repairs or restorations appear to me to demand earliest attention and I beg leave to make the following statement as the results of my survey.
   It is now four years since I closely examined the building and I do not perceive that its fundamental defects have assumed any worse aspect than formerly. I allude to the failure in the South Transept the spreading of the walls of the clerestory and the cracks in the walls of the towers. I have no reason to believe that these evils have at all extended. There are however several minor defects now very visible, which either did not exist in 1846 or were so slight as to escape my notice viz.
   1st. The masonry of the pinnacle on the north side of the south west tower, as the base of the spire is so far disturbed that it is in part fallen inwards and the stones will probably before long separate and fall down.
   2nd. The stone head of the pinnacle at the North East angle of the centre tower, as the base of the spire, has lost its true perpendicular position and will probably soon fall over. As far as I can ascertain without a scaffold, this is owing not so much to the decay of the masonry as to its disruption by the rusting of some iron cramps.
   3rd. The slender panelled buttresses at the South West angle of the centre tower have crumbled away so as to present a very dilapidated appearance when viewed near: These buttresses were at my last survey in a bad state but their decay has visibly increased. These are works which I think it would be expedient to attend to during the ensuing year: the 2 first are, perhaps, the more urgent and certainly the least expensive in their nature. With regard to more important restorations I beg to repeat the opinion expressed in my report of 1846 that it is very desirable to restore the west side of the South Transept, pannelling the parapet so as to make it correspond with the parapet of the nave and relieving the heavy and clumsy appearance of the great buttress by giving it such architectural features as will assimilate it to the other buttresses of earlier date. The restorations that have been recently made at the North End of North Transept certainly render it necessary, or at least very desirable, to extend the restoration to the North end of the aisle east of this transept. The mode of doing this will require very careful consideration: In the elevation of this small part there are traces of no less than three distinct periods: the earliest work has been nearly effaced by the subsequent introduction of a wider window, and the symmetry of this window has been disturbed in its turn by the erection of the buttress at the North east angle of the transept: the satisfactory restoration of this part is rendered the more difficult by the absolute necessity which exists of keeping the centre of the window where it now is, so that it may coincide with the centre of the vaulting of the interior. The octagonal buttresses that have been recently restored at the North transept have now an unsatisfactory appearance, chiefly from the want of any horizontal bands or annulets to the angle shafts which there can be no doubt whatever originally existed, although the workmen assure me that they could find no traces of any. The pediment-heads of these buttresses are not, I think what they originally were although no traces actually exist of them now. I have little doubt but that these gablets were moulded like the gablets of the buttresses of the nave and elsewhere.
   I will not extend my report by adverting to the objectionable state of the fabric between the north transept and the Chapter House: nor to the Consistory court: nor to the West Front of the Cathedral; believing it to be the desire of the Dean and Chapter, not so much to have a general report of the whole building, as to have their attention directed to such defects as it may be within their means shortly to rectify.
   There is one other matter which I cannot refrain from recommending to their consideration. The rain water from the roof of the Choir is led by pipes down to the ground: these pipes now discharge themselves on the surface and the water soaks into the earth: hence have arisen those stains inside, on the North side of the Choir towards the east end, which not only greatly disfigure the building but convey the idea of damp and decay. This might, at no great expense, be remedied by conveying the rainwater from the roofs, through underground drains, away from the foundations, and forming at the level of the ground a stone channel for surface drainage similar to that which was placed in 1846 (with obvious benefit to the building) on the North side of the Nave:
      I am, Dear Sir,
         Very faithfully yours
         Sydney Smirke

Chapter Act Book for 1850

Ordered that the repairs of the North Transept be continued.

8/1

Letter of Sydney Smirke to Charles Gresley, 15 July 1851

Dear Sir,

It will, I doubt not, be satisfactory to the Dean & Chapter that I should report to you for their information the steps that I propose to take in carrying on their instructions for the restoration of the North East end of the Transept of the Cathedral.

Careful moulds are now being formed of zinc of all the moulded parts previously to their removal & these moulds will be compared with corresponding details in other parts of the fabric. Stones from the Tixall Quarries are also being worked ready for use so that there may be no standing still for want of materials when the restoration is commenced. The course which I propose to take is to remove all the decayed stones, both moulded & plain & substitute new, worked, stone for stone, exactly as before in all those parts that are of mediaeval date, without attempting by alterations or deviations of any kind to bring the design of the whole to the style of any one particular period. There is at present visible evidence of at least three distinct dates in the mediaeval work (i.e. exclusive of the recent or post-mediaeval parts) & these parts are so intimately blended that to attempt to bring the façade to any one homogeneous, consistent style would involve the obliteration of two thirds of the old work, & it appears to me that it would be greatly exceeding the duties of a restorer to make any such attempt. My intention therefore is to reinstate the building as nearly as possible into the condition in which our ancestors were satisfied to leave it prior to the great destruction & consequent renovation in the 17th century; thus the incomplete portions of early pointed work will be retained & restored which were left undisturbed when the subsequent alterations were made that so materially modified the architecture of the North Transept, to obliterate these would be to destroy a record of great interest to the archaeologist, shewing clearly the existence of a North transept in the 13th century.

I beg leave herewith to submit an Elevation of the Front shewing the work as proposed to be restored, which will I trust fully explain my suggestions, but any further explanations that the Dean & Chapter may consider desirable I shall be happy to furnish.

I remain, Dear Sir, ...

Chapter Act Book for 1851

Ordered that the north end of the aisle of the north transept be restored.

8/1

Letter of Sydney Smirke to Charles Gresley, 28 October 1851:

Smirke reports that work had been slow due to the taking off of hands for cleaning.

He proposes to restrict the work in the masons' yard and to do all the setting after the winter.

He suggests cutting a channel from the transept east to help dry out the walls which in their present condition do not take white or colour.

12 May 1852:

Smirke reports to Gresley that the scaffolding will be 50 ft above the nave; the south-west buttress pinnacle is very bad.

I propose to prepare a drawing for the leadwork (for a window in the north transept) which may as well be a little more ornamental than mere diamond quarries like a cottage window ... I suppose that we must not contemplate any *coloured* glass?

Smirke advises against employing 'some Birmingham carver' on the north transept corbels and carved work. 'White, the carver who executed all the ornamental work to the Nave, is thoroughly versed in such work.' (White was a London carver.)

5 July 1852:

Smirke promises an accurate drawing of the whole of the angle turret and buttresses etc. about to be restored at the south-west corner of the great tower. The upper pinnacle has been taken down and the turret should be taken down to the lower range of buttresses, which were too thin to admit of being cased as from that level down to the roof of the nave.

He wishes to increase the workforce from five to eight masons and from three to five labourers.

3 October 1852:

Smirke asks that the workforce should not be reduced to the three masons regularly employed until the restoration of the turret has reached the base of the spiral staircase above the level of the first tier of pinnacles.

He recommends three new mullions in the northermost of the two north transept windows ('much repaired and pointed, probably many years ago') prior to reglazing and painting, work that had already been done on the other window.

Chapter Act Book for 1852

Ordered that the buttress of the south-west angle of the Great Tower be restored and that the windows on the west side of the north transept be reglazed under the direction of Mr Willement.

Chapter Act Book for 1853

Ordered that the turret at the south-west angle of the Consistory Court be restored.

8/1

Letter of Sydney Smirke to Charles Gresley, 15 July 1854:

Smirke reports that White would be coming to Lichfield together with another carver, but that White had had great difficulty in selecting a carver competent to undertake work of that nature without perpetual control and direction. 'I am having a rough model made in clay for the statue; the original was *painted in bright colours*: but that would not suit our modern notion of propriety in out door masonry.'

3 August 1854:

Dear Sir,

On Tuesday last I visited the works at the Cathedral. The West tower of the Consistory Court has been carried up to the height of about 21 feet, and so far the masonry is executed quite to my satisfaction, but owing to the deficiency in the supply of the stone, and to a difficulty in obtaining the services of a competent carver, the progress has been slower than one would wish.

These causes of delay are however now removed, and I see no reason why, with the assistance of the two additional masons just taken on, this restoration may not be completed before the winter.

I observed that since my last visit the whole of the canopied arches under the windows in North and South aisles of the nave had had their surface cleared from the old plastering and colouring; this has certainly had the effect of bringing out the beautiful carving that ornaments this arcade, but it was not one of the works recommended in my report because of the following difficulty that it now occasions: By far the larger portion of this work above the caps of the pillars is of white Plaster of Paris: some portions I believe are of Roman cement, and the remainder is the old stone work which is of a deep red colour.

The consequence is that the appearance has become very patchy, and unsatisfactory, and I think can hardly be allowed to remain permanently in its present state. It appears to me that the only course now is by degrees to renew the whole with solid masonry. The Columns with their capitals and bases are in sufficiently good condition; are of stone, and chiefly original work: but the space above the capitals up to the string course under the windows (the greater part thereof being in Plaster) should be cut out and restored in masonry; of course leaving untouched *every* portion of old work that is in moderately good condition. This would be attended no doubt with a heavy expense but admits of being done by degrees; one compartment, or bay, being taken in hand at a time, successively. The plain wall within the arch, which has been stripped of the old plastering, appears to be in a much better state than was supposed, and by sinking the surface of the masonry about ¾ of an inch, on an average (as has been done experimentally in one Arch) a fair face can be given to the wall without cementing it — which of course is very desirable. The cement that has been recently laid on has not apparently been done with a proper material, and it gives the wall as stained an appearance as it had before. Allow me to add that the two laborers who are now employed, I find, in hacking off the plaster, and coloring, from other parts of the carved work inside, should be required to exercise more care and caution than they have done: indeed I am bound to say that some parts have been seriously injured by them. I do not think that they are quite the class of workmen who should be allowed to use the hammer and chisel on carved works of such surprising delicacy as many of these bosses and capitals exhibit.

       I remain, Dear Sir . . .

8/1

Joint Report of the Rearrangement by Sydney Smirke and G. G. Scott, September 1854:

. . . the central church of a diocese, practically, reduced to the dimensions of a small parish church by cutting out a portion in the middle and leaving all the rest useless.

    In Lichfield Cathedral this principle has been carried to an extent almost without parallel — for not content with cutting off the choir from the nave by the ordinary stone screen and from its aisles by the backs of the stallwork the barricading has in this case been extended up to the vaulting of the church all parts external to it being entirely ignored . . . In remedying this anomalous state of things we must first suppose these extraordinary enclosures wholly removed.

    The Report recommended substituting an open for a closed screen and bringing back the choir to its original length.

Letter from Sydney Smirke to Charles Gresley, 30 October 1854:

Proposes that felt hung from horizontal rods round the lobbies would counter the draughts complained of.

                                           8 November 1854:

Smirke opposes the idea of a wooden frame for the west door lobby.

Chapter Act Book for 1854

Mr Smirke to take measures to exclude cold air from the nave.

8/1

Letter of Sydney Smirke to Charles Gresley, 18 April 1855:

Smirke writes about the details of the double glazing that Chance & Co. are to install in the clerestory windows of the choir, e.g. the need to have a groove or rebate in the mullions.

    The mullions and tracery should not be materially mutilated and their artistic effect of light and shade should be carefully preserved.

    Whatever is done should be of a strictly ecclesiastical character.

    It would be best, from a visual point of view, to have the glazing on the inside. Smirke suggests a light neutral tint of two tones forming a lozenge within a border.

    The mullions on the north side need repair, but does not think that a total replacement will be necessary.

Letter from Charles Gresley to Sydney Smirke, 1 May 1855:

Gresley reports with regard to the rearrangement that the ground plan is pretty much settled except for the position of the communion table.

    He requests Smirke to supply a ground plan (assisted by the advice of Mr Scott) together with sketches of the principal features and estimates by Whit Sunday if possible.

Letter from Sydney Smirke to Charles Gresley, 9 May 1855:

Having proposed to submit his plan to Scott for his revision and correction where necessary, Scott does not clearly understand in what position he stands nor exactly what is expected of him.

                                         16 May 1855:

Smirke requests the return of the drawing that was approved of the choir fittings.

    The plans will not be ready by Whitsun.

Letter with Report from Sydney Smirke to Charles Gresley, 30 May 1855:

Smirke encloses a ground plan showing the alterations of the choir 'as I believe the Dean and Chapter last decided — subject of course still to the reconsideration of the position of the Organ and Communion table'.

Has not had time to give due consideration to the subject of the choir but sends a plan as approved; if this approval is confirmed he will proceed to make sections and views.

The plan is in conformity with Scott's views except as to the position of the reredos and organ. On the latter he has received a note from Scott in which he says: 'I confess I am half inclined to keep the Organ on the Screen, as first proposed, thereby enabling the Choir to be kept to only six arches in length.'

(The above are but samples of the correspondence during 1855/7 passing between Smirke and Gresley, Scott and Gresley, and others. Both Smirke and Scott were now making drawings and plans relevant to the rearrangement of the Lichfield choir. Quotations here are restricted to Smirke's views relevant to the style of fittings recommended, since his views on style were to some extent related to his understanding of the architectural history of the Cathedral.)

11 June 1855:

Smirke suggests making a longitudinal section of the choir; a transverse section of the choir looking eastward; another looking westward; a perspective view looking eastward.

26 June 1855:

Haden has not yet advised as to whether or not the Trentham heating system is relevant to the Cathedral.

8/1

Memorandum (from Sydney Smirke) to accompany the designs for alterations to the choir, Lichfield Cathedral, July 1855:

The style of Architecture adopted for the proposed fittings, is that which prevailed at the commencement of the Fifteenth Century, when screen and tabernacle work reached the extreme point of lightness and beauty. The Original Stone Screen that was removed by Wyatt, was of this date, as appears from the remaining portions of the East End of the Lady Chapel, and under the Organ Gallery.

The Altar Screen, is proposed to be of stone; in the design submitted, authorities for every portion, exist either in the above mentioned remaining portions of original work, or in the Stone Screen at Durham Cathedral, an example of singular beauty and in many respects closely resembling the original screen at Lichfield. Its graceful and slender spiral forms, seem to harmonize happily with the general character of the building.

The Side Screens, including the canopied work over the stalls, are proposed to be of wainscot. In the present design the details of the old canopied work, have been as closely adhered to as the difference of material would allow.

The backs of these screens towards the side aisles are proposed to be comparatively plain, with simple panelling and a suitable cornice.

The Organ Front as indicated on the accompanying drawings, is only to be regarded as a first sketch, open to material correction, when more detailed information has been afforded by the organ builder.

The Western Screen is not yet indicated on these drawings. It is proposed that it should consist of three open arches of light masonry, resting on slender marble pillars; in each arch would be provided a pair of folding gates, of light ornamental hammered iron or brass work. The centre gate alone to be usually opened; the two side gates only to be opened, when the Cathedral is crowded, and a portion of the congregation is seated in the Transept.

In the sketches, now submitted, although every part has been well considered, I would wish it to be clearly understood, that there is no portion that will not receive a still more detailed consideration previously to the work being erected; many drawings, full size will be needed, & probably some models of separate parts before the design can be considered as fully matured.

24 July 1855:

The drawings for the Choir fittings are to be sent tonight except for the Western Screen as I have not yet satisfied myself with it — but it is quite independent of the other works.

I have drawn two different modes of carrying the canopies over the stalls. The old stalls had buttresses, but they are of stone — and I think that, being of wood, they had better be pillar shafts — being light in appearance & obstructing the view less.

Estimates to follow.

28 August 1855:

Smirke promises to take steps about the ceilings of the triforium (plastering) and doorways.

He is dissatisfied with the double glazing by Chance & Co. in the Choir. The borders of the glass are much too wide, the leading is not clearly managed and the green tint is too decided.

With respect to the Western enclosure of the Choir, I had hoped to have an opportunity of looking at one or two examples in the Netherlands before finally designing that proposed for Lichfield.

1 September 1855:

I quite agree with you and Canon Hutchinson that the more ecclesiastical treatment of the ceilings of the clerestory would be to plaster in between the rafters as in fact Barns usually are and I will proceed accordingly.

13 September 1855:

... the aisles of the transept need no plastering ... about half the nave aisle roofs plastered in the common way & half *Paine work* i.e. plastered in between the rafters.

25 September 1855:

Sends estimates for the new choir fittings (£12,000) 'including the Chancel Screen for which you have not yet received a detailed drawing'.

2 October 1855:

Chance & Co. to remove the double glazing.

6 November 1855:

Chance & Co. send estimates for quarry lights of Cathedral tinted rolled plate glass and plain white rolled plate glass.

27 November 1855:

Agreed that the choir glazing should be clear except for a slight tinge opposite the pulpit.

Smirke is in favour of double glazing all the choir windows the same — with clear glass.

Chapter Act Book for 1855

Ordered:
      Double glazing of the Choir windows on the south side.
      The central heating scheme designed by Smirke and Haden's.
      G. E. Street's Monument to Archdeacon Hodson.

8/1

Letter of Sydney Smirke to Charles Gresley, 26 July 1856:

Smirke strongly advises the repair of the choir arches 'from whence the partitions have lately been removed ... Wyatt's men seem to have ruthlessly ill treated the old piers & arches.'

'Our report on the subject of the Choir is at length drawn up.'

Report upon the re-arrangement of Lichfield Cathedral for Divine Worship,[1] August 1856

Committee members: Benjamin Ferrey, A. J. Beresford Hope, the Revd J. L. Petit, George Gilbert Scott, Sydney Smirke.

1.   This Report is printed in full in my paper, referenced above.

Petit submitted a minority report to the Dean and Chapter.

The Committee responded to a brief drawn up by the Chapter in March 1856. The Committee broadly followed the ideas of G. G. Scott which dominated the joint report produced by Smirke and Scott in 1854, i.e. for an open screen at the crossing (the organ had now been moved off it) and added a recommendation for a reredos of open design making use of local marbles such as Scott was to provide.

Chapter Act Book for 1856:

The organ to be removed from the present position on the screen at the west end of the choir, and that it be placed for the present in the second arch westward of the Lady Chapel on the north side.

8/1

Letter of Sydney Smirke to Charles Gresley, 24 January 1857:

'My sketches for the Choir have been made some while ... awaiting an appointment with my two professional colleagues.' (Ferrey and Scott whom the Chapter wished to comment on Smirke's designs.)

Letter of Benjamin Ferrey to Sydney Smirke, 30 January 1857:

Ferrey confesses to a feeling of considerable delicacy and declines to make particular criticisms upon Smirke's drawings.

Up to the present time our opinions have been given upon points of general arrangement whereon it did not seem obtrusive to offer some suggestions, & you have very kindly acquiesced and permitted our remarks but I think our interference should end.

Resolution of the Dean and Chapter sent to Sydney Smirke, 9 March 1857:

Having received Mr Smirke's elevations etc., the Chapter decides to seek further and similar drawings from the other professional members of the Committee, i.e. Ferrey and Scott.

Letters of Sydney Smirke to Charles Gresley, 21 April 1857:

He has directed his clerk of works, employed on a house at Hampton-in-Arden, to superintend the removal of the organ screen.

22 May 1857:

Hamlet junr. is an excellent & intelligent workman but he is too young to trust to; the *others* on the spot have *hands* not *heads* ... The builders of the new Screen seem to have been ruthless destroyers & have done serious mischief.

4 June 1857:

the matter (of demolition) is a very ticklish one: there are parts in a somewhat dangerous state ... The difficulty arises from the 13th century work & that of the 14th century not being very carefully united.

16 July 1857:

Dear Sir,
    I send herewith an Elevation of the North West Arch of the Choir of Lichfield Cathedral shewing the masonry (that was very seriously mutilated at the time the alterations were made in the Choir under Wyatt) restored as nearly as possible to its condition previously to those alterations.
    The Dean and Chapter are well aware that masonry of two very different dates occurs in the Choir; and these two dates are singularly intermixed in the three westernmost arches on both sides.
    In the drawing herewith submitted the masonry of these two dates is distinguished by two different tints, viz. the brownish yellow tint being the earlier work, the purplish neutral tint, the later work. It appears that at the later date (14th Century) the thickness of the spandrels was increased by a casing of stone applied in front of the older work with stones only occasionally let into it. The consequence is that the work of restoration becomes a matter of much niceness and some danger, there being a risk of some parts of the later masonry falling when the brick pinning-in,

and making good, done in Wyatt's time, is removed for the purpose of substitution stonework, in order to match exactly the old work.

I propose to confine the Restorations now in hand exclusively to the removal of the most modern work, partly brickwork and partly stone, substituting new masonry.

I do not propose disturbing any of the old stones that are at all sound, and fit to remain, — I by no means propose to attempt any assimilation of the later work to the earlier portion. The masons of the 14th century took but little pains to accomodate their work to the previously existing work, and the change is frequently made very abrupt and inartfully, yet I purpose making no amendments of this, rather preferring to leave the work in its mutilated state (provided it is sound and fit to stand) to attempting any speculative restorations for the sake of producing an harmonious whole. With this view I purpose leaving in their places those fragments of the later carved work which are somewhat unintelligible at present, but which no doubt formed a part of the Roodloft in the 14th century.

I should add that the earlier masonry (13th century) was executed with stone of a somewhat different colour (although of like quality) from that used at the later date: the latter being more red than the former. I think it will be expedient, in effecting these restorations, to use for the two works stones of the two different colours, so that the same difference which the masons of the 14th century thought proper to observe, whether by accident or intentionally, I now propose also to retain.

I am not aware of any further explanation being requisite. With respect to the execution of these works, I think that it will shortly be necessary to add one or two masons to the present number of hands employed, otherwise I see little probability of the 2 arches being finished by the time specified.

I remain, dear Sir . . .

18 July 1857:

I am much obliged by your letter of yesterday with tracings etc. If the pencil sketch by Hamlet junior is right I quite concur with you in thinking that the restoration would be more exact if the earlier capitals were substituted for the later as shewn on my sketch. But you will be so good as to understand that the drawing I sent you was not for the guidance or use of the Masons: more exact instructions would be given to them, and before doing so it was my intention that I, or Ridley, should still farther examine the work — which will be early next week. In the meantime Hamlet shall have instructions to insert stones of such scantling as shall admit of either form of capital being worked on them.

23 July 1857:

I have spent the whole day here pondering over the arches & piers & the result I have come to is stated in the accompanying paper . . . the questions are in truth so technical that I could hardly be intelligible on paper, When these archivolts etc. are roughed out in plaster on the spot, the question will simply be, does the restoration appear satisfactory or not.

A very great difficulty arises in determining on the Archivolts of the Choir Arches. In the 14th. cent. a great change was made & new work was applied and fitted on to the portion of the old work that was retained. In making the application the mouldings seem to have been *humored* in some way, but so much was cut away in Wyatt's time that it is impossible now to trace the exact original treatment otherwise than by conjecture. I *believe* I see what that treatment was but as long as there is uncertainty I feel uneasy in proceeding, because the one arch we are now engaged on will necessarily be the guide for the 7 other arches, or half the Choir, and it becomes therefore a consideration of great importance.

I propose therefore to adopt the following course: vizt. to carry on without interruption all the work of which there is no doubt or question, but to turn the archivolts and parts connected with them *in common plaster*. The effect of the whole would then be realised and a final decision safely arrived at. I shall be happy to hear that this measure of precaution meets the approval of the Dean & Chapter.

With regard to the Shafts of the Piers a great deal of which remains to be done, I do not think that the present hands are at all likely to complete them by the end of September as desired, I would beg to suggest therefore that two good masons be at once engaged.

3 August 1857:

Smirke says that he could send down two masons but at London rates of 5s. 6d. a day as against the 4s. a day of the Lichfield masons, and so suggests getting two country hands acquainted with Gothic masonry and putting Hamlet junior in charge at 5s. a day.

Hamlet Junr. is very superior to the ordinary class of working masons, he not only takes a deep interest in his work but from habit of observation he has acquired a good deal of knowledge applicable to our restorations.

Letter of Canon Hutchinson to Bishop Lonsdale, 4 August 1857:

I fear that any attempt to obtain *conjoint* drawings from the triumvirate is quite hopeless ... the best, if not the only, chance of obtaining drawings from Scott & perhaps Ferrey, is to leave to the several architects liberty of *competition*, if they choose, an opportunity of *coalition*, if they like it better. With *freedom of choice* allowed on this point, they may be pressed at once to a conclusion, which it is quite time that they should arrive at ... I think that this will be in better taste than again approaching Scott & Ferrey through Smirke.

Letter(s) of Charles Gresley to Smirke, Scott, and Ferrey, 5 August 1857:

... The Dean and Chapter now request to be favoured with sketches by Mr Ferrey & Mr Scott of such restoration. They are already in possession of a design drawn by Mr Smirke. They leave it to Messrs Ferrey and Scott to furnish joint or separate drawings as most agreeable to them ... Mr Smirke's relation to the Cathedral, except as above stated, will remain as hitherto ...

Smirke was invited to 'modify his drawings already sent in ... if he shall think fit to do so'.

Letter from Sydney Smirke to Charles Gresley, 21 September 1857:

Smirke reports Ferrey's wish to withdraw from any competition.

Letter from G. G. Scott to the Dean, 22 September 1857:

Scott sends sketches of the fittings and the arrangements with a long explanation of them despite beginning — 'I have felt some delicacy in complying with your request for fear of appearing to clash unduly with your architect Mr. Smirke'. This was evidently overridden by 'the deep interest I feel in the work you have undertaken & the pleasure it would afford me to be of any assistance in carrying it out providing only I should not be interfering with the position held by Mr. Smirke'.

Letter of Sydney Smirke to Charles Gresley, 22 September 1857:

Smirke adds a perspective view to assist the appreciation of his design of the altar screen, but does not intend to submit more designs.

The only remark that I have happened to have heard in the way of objection to the designs has been that the proposed Screen is somewhat later in style than the architecture of the Choir.

This objection has not appeared to me to be valid. The East end of the Choir itself is nearly 100 years later than parts of the West end of the Choir; — which end therefore should be the standard?

Even if the whole Choir were of one uniform date & style, there seems to me to be no impropriety in making these Choir fittings (being no integral part of the architecture of the Cathedral) of somewhat later date than the surrounding structure: a capricious departure from the date of the surrounding structure would not be justifiable, but there are in this case two reasons for adopting a style somewhat later than the Choir.

1st. because the screen work of this later date is undeniably lighter more delicate & graceful, than the early screen work.

2ndly. because the mediaeval architects, themselves who erected the Altar Screen, (subsequently removed by Wyatt) thought proper to adopt this later style, and I am content to abide by their judgement.

The design now submitted is in all its essential details similar to the Screen then put up: the central pinnacles etc. being adapted from the Screen at Durham of like date.

24 September 1857:

Smirke does not intend to attend the Chapter meeting re. the choir furnishings as 'I might be rather *in the way* than otherwise.' 'My clerk is busily looking into the old masonry of the arches etc. & reports daily to me, with sketches of what he finds.'

Letter of Charles Gresley to Sydney Smirke, 26 September 1857:

The Dean and Chapter have considered Smirke's and Scott's drawings

and they have come to the conclusion to entrust to that gentleman the work of the restoration of the Choir. Mr. Scott expresses a hope that he may be able to secure your cooperation in this work ... the terms of such an arrangement must be left entirely to yourself & him ... it will be better to suspend the works now in progress in the Choir until it be ascertained whether they are to be continued under the joint superintendence of yourself & Mr Scott or are to be left to the sole responsibility of that Gentleman.

REFERENCES

1. Research for this paper was greatly assisted by Mrs Jane Hampartumian at the LJRO, Mr F. W. Stitt at the William Salt Library, Stafford, and Dr Ben. Benediktz at the Lichfield Cathedral and the Birmingham University Libraries. Illustrations are reproduced by kind permission of these libraries, the Dean and Chapter of Lichfield Cathedral, the RIBA Drawings Collection and Christie's.

   Abbreviated references to material in the LJRO are either to *D* 30 etc. or to *CAB* (*Chapter Acts Books*) or to Cox (J. C. Cox, *Catalogue of the Muniments* ... (1892)). Material in the William Salt Library, Stafford is referenced either as *M* 1064 etc. or as *Staffs. Views*, etc.

2. *CAB*, VIII, f. 21ᵛ.
3. *Gent. Mag.*, LXXI (1801), 311 (An Architect).
4. D. Johnson and A. Kettle, *VCH Staffordshire*, III (1970), 187.
5. John M. Frew, 'Cathedral Improvements: James Wyatt at Lichfield Cathedral, 1787–92', *TSSAHS*, XIX (1977/8), 33–40.
6. E.g. LIX (1789), 401–2; LXV (1795), 924–5, 998, 1074–5, 1194–6; LXVI (1796), 193–4, 299; LXX (1800), 16–17; LXXI (1801), 309–13.
7. *The History and Antiquities of Staffordshire*, I (1798), 29–31.
8. 100–10. Griffith's original wash drawings appeared in an extra-illustrated 3 vol. copy at Christie's (18 November 1980, Lot 2).
9. Op. cit., and G. Cobb, *English Cathedrals: The Forgotten Centuries* (1980), 140–51.
10. John M. Frew, *An Aspect of the Gothic Revival in England, c. 1770–1815: The Antiquarian Influence, with special reference to the career of James Wyatt*, unpublished DPhil Thesis, Oxford University, 1976.
11. 'Joseph Potter: Cathedral Architect at Lichfield, 1794–1842', *TSSAHS*, XXI (1979–80), 34–47.
12. Browne Willis, *A Survey of the Cathedrals*, I (1727).
13. *D* 30, 7/4.
14. Cox, O.35.
15. Ibid.
16. *M* 1064, (5) and (20). Shaw, op. cit., 29.
17. Cox, O.36.
18. *Staffs. Views*, VI, ff. 87 and 98 (illus. here). Both drawings are in grey wash.
19. Cox, O.36.
20. *Gent. Mag.*, LXV (1795), 520, quoted by Shaw, op. cit., 30. This reporter attributed the original design to Benjamin West rather than to Sir Joshua Reynolds; Eginton copied work by both. Shaw is a rare source of information about Eginton's career as a painted glass maker.
21. The *Glory* below the *Resurrection* anticipates Rossi's altarpiece at Fonthill illus. as the title page to J. Rutter, *Delineations of Fonthill and its Abbey* (1823). For the juxtaposition of curtains and glass and for the colour scheme used by Wyatt for his Lichfield furnishings cf. coloured copies of the prints in J. Britton, *Graphic and Literary Illustrations of Fonthill Abbey* (1823), e.g. the illus. there of St Michael's Gallery.
22. *D* 30, 8/5. *CAB*, IX, f. 51 records Wyatt's last connection with Lichfield Cathedral (1804) when his offer to see to the installation of the Herckenrode stained glass was accepted, although apparently he did not do so. The Reynolds-Eginton window was put up in shortened form in St Chad's, Lichfield, although a John Anderson of Dublin had been negotiating with the Chapter, presumably in order to have it installed in a church in Dublin. *Staffs. Views*, VI, f. 86, wash drawing signed and dated J. Buckler, 1833.
23. As well as Shaw, op. cit., see also W. R. Aitken, 'Francis Eginton', *Birmingham & Midland Inst. Archaeol. Soc. Trans.* (1872), 27.
24. *Staffs. Views*, VI, f. 85 for C. Wild, *An Illustration of the Architecture of Lichfield Cathedral* (1813) where it is reproduced in aquatint by M. Dubourg.
25. *M* 1064, (17), pen and wash, 13½ × 20 in. Wyatt uses blue, crimson and gold for the drapes. The design differs from that executed. There are approximately 20 drawings from the Wyatt office in the Salt Library.
26. *Staff. Views*, VI, f. 105, pencil, pen and wash, 19 × 11¾ in.
27. Op. cit., 145. *M* 1064, (16), pencil and pen, 17½ × 19 in.
28. LJRO, Box 54, pen and wash, 30 × 21¾ in.
29. *M* 1064 (4): 'Litchfield Cathedral/Entrance from the Choir into the side Aisle', pen, 18½ × 12 in.
30. J. Britton, *The History and Antiquities of the See and Cathedral Church of Lichfield* (1820) — 'Choir looking West', eng. J. Cleghorn after F. Mackenzie (Pl. X). For the Potter-Woodhouse works carried out just after the publication of Wild's book, see my 'Joseph Potter...', 38/9 and n. 40.
31. Frew, 'Cathedral Improvements ...', 35.
32. *M* 1064, (12): 'Stalls from the West Entrance — Bp Throne', pen, 16 × 20 in.; (8a): 'Plan for altering the Chapel of our Lady in Lichfield Cathedral', pen, 18½ × 21½ in.
33. *M* 1064, (7): 'Plan ot Lady Choir as intended to be converted into the Grand Choir', pen and wash, 20 × 22 in.

34. *M* 1064, (2): 'Lichfield', pen and wash, 19 × 38 in.
35. *M* 1064, (9): 'Lichfield', pen and wash, 17½ × 32 in.
36. *M* 1064 (10), pen and wash. This will, no doubt, have been among the plans carried to Lichfield in 1783 at a cost of 4s. 4d. — Cox, O.40. The only other dated drawing before that dated 1787 is one for a font dated 1786. LJRO, Plans *M* 1064, (11) is an uncoloured 'Copy of the Design for altering the Chapel of our Lady', pen, 9 × 14 in.
37. Rickman defined the Decorated Lichfield Lady Chapel as 'late in the style' — *An Attempt to discriminate the Styles of Architecture in England*, 3rd edn (1825), 66.
38. *Staffs. Views*, VI, f. 104, pencil, pen and white, 17¾ × 22 in.
39. *M* 1064 (15), pen, 11 × 18 in.
40. *D* 30, 8/1 and 8/5.
41. Most of Potter's and Smirke's Reports are in *D* 30, 8/1 and fabric expenditure is recorded ibid., 8/5. Some of Smirke's earlier Reports are in *CAB*, XI.
42. *CAB*, XI, f. 84.
43. *Report of Ewan Christian Esq., Architect to the Ecclesiastical Commissioners for England, on the State of the Fabric of the Cathedral Church of Lichfield, March 28th, 1872* (Lichfield 1880).
44. 'Sydney Smirke, George Gilbert Scott and "The Rearrangement of Lichfield Cathedral for Divine Worship": 1854–1861', *Inst. for the Study of Worship and Religious Architecture*, University of Birmingham, *Research Bulletin* (1980).
45. 67.
46. Dean Savage, in a paper published in 1914 occasioned by the completion of the new sedilia on the north side of the altar, drew attention to some heraldic evidence that suggested that the medieval reredos should be dated to the reign of Edward IV.
47. See N. Pevsner and P. Metcalf, *The Cathedrals of England*, II (1985), 181–96 for the high altar reredos and the furnishings generally. Correspondence for 1863–6 shows that Philip found it necessary to make some alterations to Scott's original design.
48. LJRO, Box 94, pen, 21¾ × 17¾ in. *c*.1867/70. This is signed: 'Geo. Gilbert Scott, R.A.' but is ins. rev. 'a drawing made by Mr. J. D. Wyatt'.
49. *A Sketch of the Restorations completed and in progress in Lichfield Cathedral from the designs of G. G. Scott, Esq., R.A.* (Lichfield 1861), 6.
50. *D* 30, 5/4.
51. LJRO, Plans, signed: 'G. G. Scott, Architect'.
52. LJRO, Box 44, pen on tracing paper, 17½ × 24½ in. signed: 'Sir G. Gilbert Scott R.A.' and inscribed 'To the Dean of Lichfield, 1877'. J. O. Scott's name is on another variation on the same theme.
53. Kempe also took over the furnishing of St Chad's Chapel following J. O. Scott's structural restoration.
54. RIBA, Drawings Collection, Ran 23/1. Elevation of the east and north faces of the north-west tower, signed: 'Sir G. Gilbert Scott, R.A.'
55. *D* 30, 2/i. Scott recommended the restoration of the west front at least as early as May 1864.
56. MSS II/VI/I Nott. The drawings, which measure approximately 10½ × 9½ in. (Kings) or 18 × 12 in. (Statues), were bound up in 1883 in an album ins.: 'Album containing 36 Wash Drawings of Statues in Niches in Lichfield Cathedral'. The album also contains a letter from G. F. Nott to Dean Woodhouse of 26 October 1820; Nott had apparently been asked to advise about the antiquarian evidence for crowns. This information was probably relevant to the north transept glass rather than to the restoration with Roman Cement of the west front Gallery of Kings.
57. *Staffs. Views*, VI, f. 21, watercolour, 14¾ × 10½ in. signed: 'A. E. Everitt Aug 27 1842'.
58. Op. cit., 11/12.
59. Revd J. G. Lonsdale, *Recollections of Work done in and upon Lichfield Cathedral from 1856 to 1894* (Lichfield 1895), 35.
60. *D* 30, 2/1.
61. Letter dated 11 August 1892 published by the Chapter to accompany an appeal for funds.
62. Op. cit., 12.
63. *CAB*, XV, 305.
64. *D* 30, 8/1.
65. *D* 30, 2/1.
66. Op. cit., 34.
67. 28 December 1900, 409.
68. *D* 30, 2/1.
69. RIBA, Drawings Collection, Ran. 23/H/3.
70. *CAB*, XV, 227.

THE PLATES

I. Lichfield Cathedral from the south-east. An engraving by J. Le Keux after a drawing by F. Mackenzie from John Britton's *History and Antiquities of the See and Cathedral Church of Lichfield*, 1820.

IIA

IIB

II

IIIA.   Croxden Abbey: west front
Photo: author

IIIB.   Croxden Abbey: south transept from the
north-east
Photo: author

.   Lichfield Cathedral: interior of the Consistory Court (now sacristy) in the former St Peter's Chapel; view rth-west, *c.* 1888. The remains of a Transitional arcade can be seen in the choir wall, partly obscured by the apel vault of *c.* 1220–30
oto: *Lichfield Cathedral Library Collection*

.   Lichfield Cathedral: late 12th-century walls and pier bases associated with the earlier phases of the sacristy-apel on the south side of the choir, seen here in a Victorian heating duct beneath the floor of the Consistory urt; view east
oto: *Warwick Rodwell*

.   Lichfield Cathedral: sacristy-chapel complex attached to the south choir aisle, *c.* 1220–40. St Chad's Head apel is on the upper floor, and below it is the Consistory Court (formerly St Peter's Chapel). There is a bterranean barrel-vaulted crypt beneath the latter
oto: *Warwick Rodwell*

IVA. Croxden Abbey: south transept west wall interior

IVB. Croxden Abbey: respond between north choir aisle wall and north-west ambulatory chapel

IVc. Croxden Abbey: south transept. Junction of east and south walls

IVd. Croxden Abbey: west respond of south nave arcade

Photos: author

VA.   Croxden Abbey: south wall of south transept with outlined masonry breaks and numbered sequence of construction
Photo: author

VB.   (below, left) Croxden Abbey: south transept east arcade south respond
Photo: author

VC.   (below) Croxden Abbey: exterior of south transept south wall above door to sacristy
Photo: author

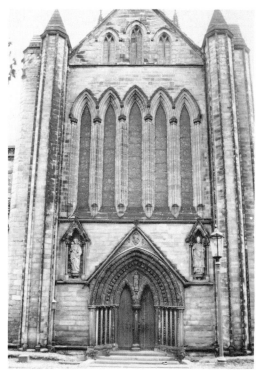

VIᴀ.   Lichfield Cathedral: south transept façade

VIʙ.   Lichfield Cathedral: north transept façade

VIᴄ.   Lichfield Cathedral: south transept interior to south-east

VIᴅ.   Lichfield Cathedral: south transept interior to south-west

VIIA.   Lichfield Cathedral: north transept
interior to north-east

VIIB.   Lichfield Cathedral, north transept
interior to north-west

VIIc.   Lichfield Cathedral: south transept
clerestory bays S1E and S2E

VIID.   Lichfield Cathedral: south transept
clerestory bay S1E exterior

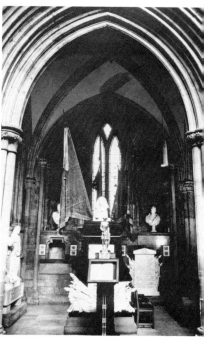

VIIIA.　Lichfield Cathedral: St Chad's Head Chapel,
interior to south

VIIIB.　Lichfield Cathedral: south
transept chapel 1 to east

VIIIC.　Lichfield Cathedral: south transept by
S1E inside roof space

VIIID.　Lichfield Cathedral: south transept, east
clerestory

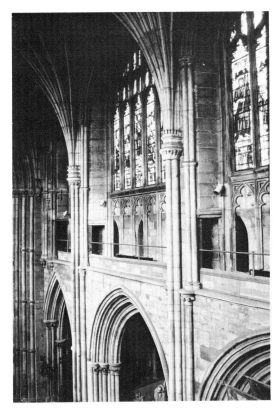

IXA.   (above, left) Lichfield Cathedral: south transept interior from south-west

IXB.   (above) Lichfield Cathedral: north transept clerestory bay N2E

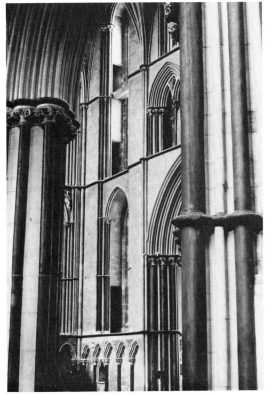

IXC.   (left) Worcester Cathedral: Lady Chapel, interior to south-east

XA. Lichfield Cathedral: south transept
pier SII

XB. Lichfield Cathedral: south transept
piers SIII and SIV

XC. Lichfield Cathedral: north transept,
pier NII

XD. Lichfield Cathedral: north transept,
piers NIII and NIV

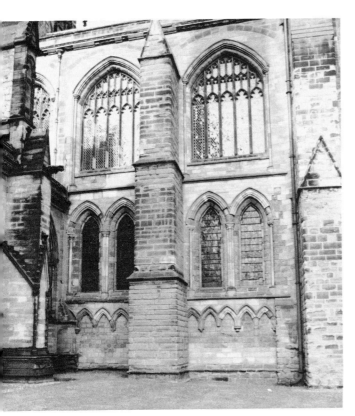

XIA. Lichfield Cathedral: south transept exterior from west

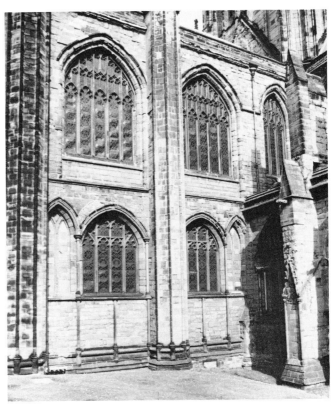

XIB. Lichfield Cathedral: north transept exterior from west

XIIA.   Nuneaton, St Mary, north-east
crossing pier

XIIB.   Nuneaton, St Mary: north-west crossing pier
from south

XIIC.   Nuneaton, St Mary: choir and north
transept exterior from north-east

XIID.   Chester, St Werburgh's chapter house:
exterior from north-east

XIIIA.   Chester, St Werburgh's chapter
house

XIIIB.   Ashbourne: north transept interior,
south window

XIIIC.   Croxden Abbey: chapter house
façade, north jamb of north arch

XIIID.   Croxden Abbey: south transept
chapel interior, detail south-east capital

XIVA.   Lichfield: north-east tower of Close

XIVB.   Lichfield: north-east tower of Close, vault

XVA. Eccleshall Castle, Staffordshire: north-east tower

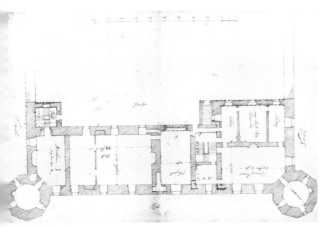

XVB. Eccleshall Castle, Staffordshire: plan of east front *c.* 1687 (Bodleian MS Tanner 217)
Photo: courtesy of Bodleian Library

XVC. Eccleshall Castle, Staffordshire: elevation of east front *c.* 1687 (Bodleian MS Tanner 217)
Photo: courtesy of Bodleian Library

XVIA. Lichfield Cathedral: Lady Chapel from south

XVIB. Lichfield Cathedral: Lady Chapel interior

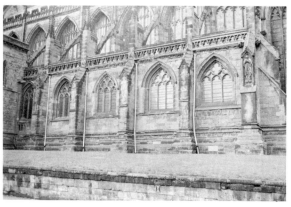

XVIC. Lichfield Cathedral: Lady Chapel from south. Watercolour by J. C. Buckler *c.* 1845

XVID. Lichfield Cathedral: south choir aisle exterior

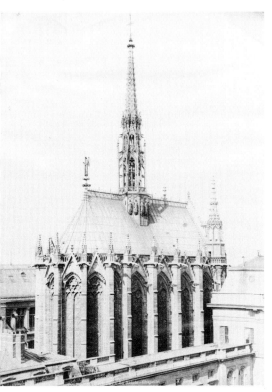

XVIIA.   Paris, the Ste Chapelle

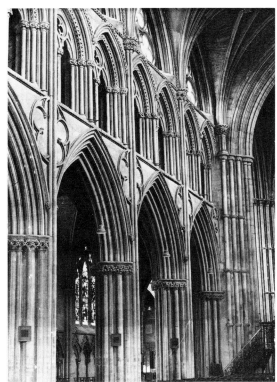

XVIIB.   Lichfield Cathedral: the nave, north side

XVIIc.   Lichfield Cathedral: base of choir
wall arcade shaft

XVIID.   Bristol Cathedral: base of choir
pier, detail

XVIIIA. (left) Lichfield Cathedral: the crossing tower

XVIIIB. (below, left) Ashbourne Church, Derbyshire: the crossing tower

XVIIIC. (below) Caernarvon Castle: the King's Gate

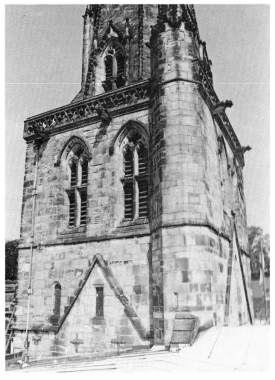

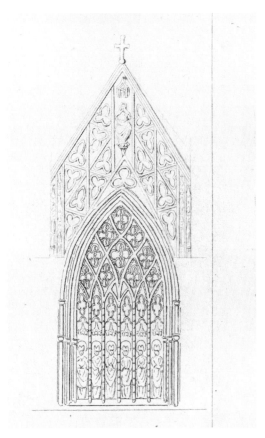

XIXA. (above, left) Lichfield
Cathedral: the medieval west
window, from a drawing by Hollar,
1655

XIXB. (above) Ledbury,
Herefordshire:
St Katherine's Chapel

XIXC. (left) Audley, Staffordshire:
chancel from south

A

B

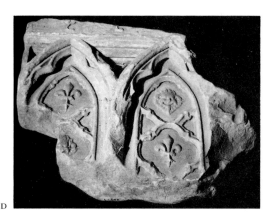

D

F

XXA.   Romanesque capital LC 125 (ht 240mm);   B.   Romanesque corbel LC 26
(ht 330mm);   C.   Gothic crucifixion group LC 104 (ht 420mm);   D.   Decorated panel LC 66A
(ht 390mm);   E.   Tomb-chest panel LC 66B (ht 320mm);   F.   Reredos angel with shield LC 128B
(ht 320mm);   G.   Reredos canopy vault LC 57F (width 480mm)
Copyright History of Art, Warwick University

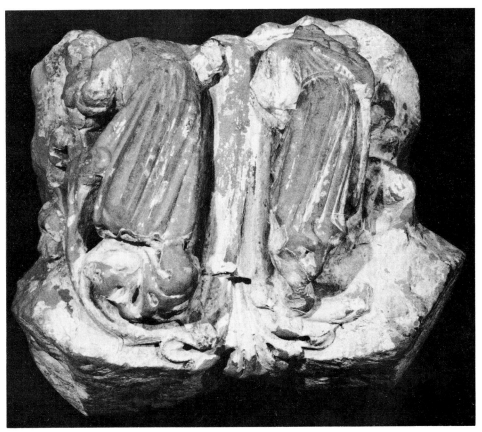

XXIA.   Gothic roof boss LC 55 (width 510mm)

XXIB.   Virgin and Child from centre portal LC 95A, detail (ht of main figure 1052mm)

XXIIA. Lichfield Cathedral from the
north-west, September 1860

XXIIB. Lichfield Cathedral: statue of
Charles II

XXIIc. Lichfield Cathedral: tomb of Bishop Hacket

SOUTHERN PART OF LICHFIELD
CATHEDRAL

XXIII.   Moses Griffith: south transept façade, *c.* 1780

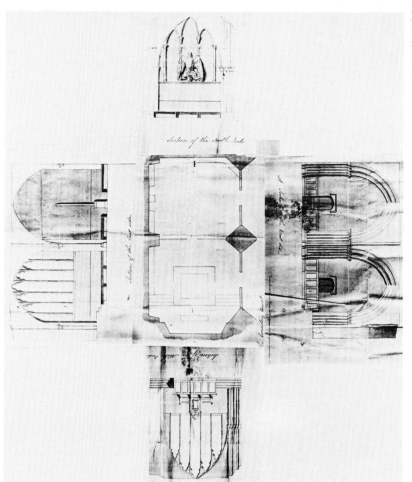

XXIVA.   James Wyatt
Office: plans and elevations
for bishop's Consistory
Court in the north transept,
*c.*1787

XXIVB.   J. C. Buckler:
interior view of the
Consistory Court, 1833

XXVA.　James Wyatt Office: design for east
windows of Lady Chapel, 1792–5

XXVB.　J. C. Buckler: interior view of the
choir and Lady Chapel, 1833

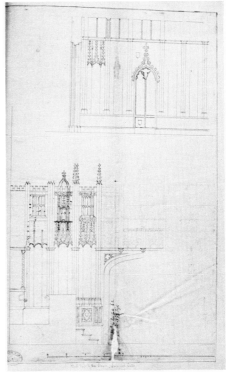

XXVC.　James Wyatt Office: design for
pulpit, c. 1787

XXVD.　James Wyatt Office: elevations
for organ screen, c. 1787

XXVIA.   James Wyatt Office: plan and elevation of choir, south side, *c.* 1787

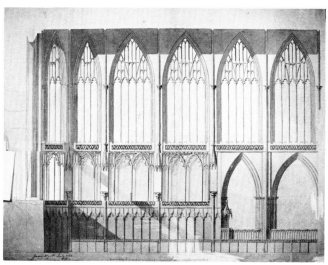

XXVIB.   James Wyatt Office: alternative elevation for Lady Chapel, 1783

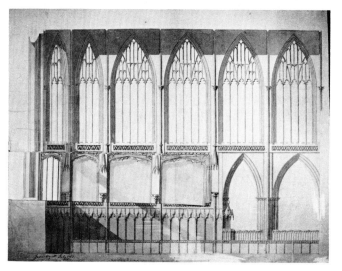

XXVIC.   James Wyatt Office: alternative elevation for Lady Chapel, 1783

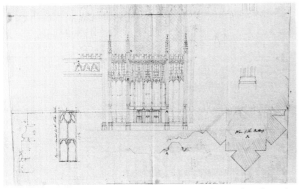

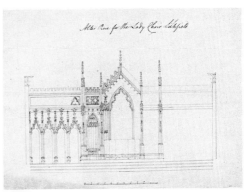

XXVIIA.   James Wyatt Office: design for Lady Chapel reredos

XXVIIB.   James Wyatt Office: design for Lady Chapel reredos

XXVIIc.   Geo. Gilbert Scott Office: design for Bishop Lonsdale monument, c. 1867/70

XXVIID.   Geo. Gilbert Scott Office: design for the west window, c. 1866

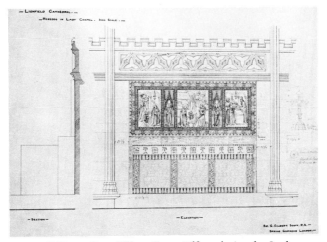

XXVIIE.   Geo. Gilbert Scott Office: design for Lady Chapel reredos, c. 1877

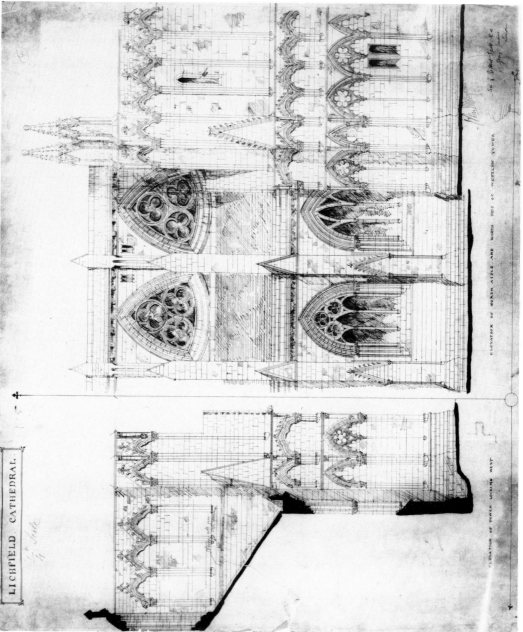

XXVIII. Geo. Gilbert Scott Office: elevations of north-west tower, *c.* 1875

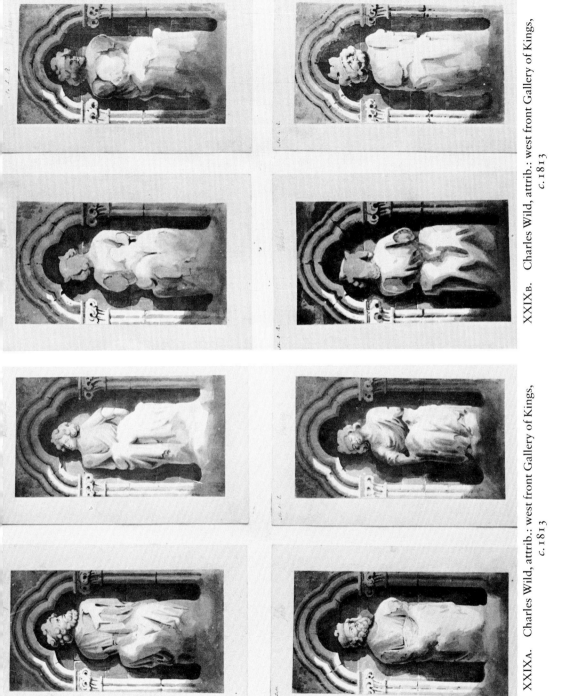

XXIXA.   Charles Wild, attrib.: west front Gallery of Kings,
*c.*1813

XXIXB.   Charles Wild, attrib.: west front Gallery of Kings,
*c.*1813

XXXB.   Charles Wild, attrib.: figure from west front centre
portal, *c.* 1813 (south side, St Peter)

XXXA.   Charles Wild, attrib.: figure from west front centre
portal, *c.* 1813 (south side)

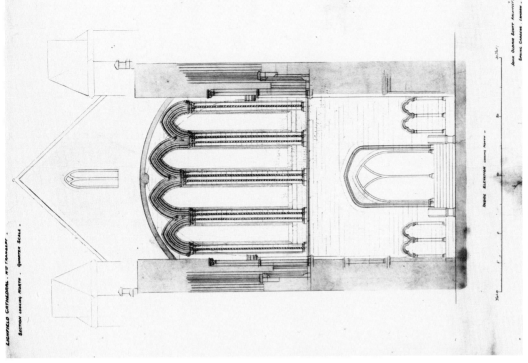

XXXIB. J. O. Scott Office: inside elevation of north wall of transept, c. 1883

XXXIA. A. E. Everitt: north transept and chapter house, 1842